NEGOTIATING DOMESTIC

CLARENDON STUDIES IN CRIMINOLOGY

Published under the auspices of the Institute of Criminology, University of Cambridge, the Mannheim Centre, London School of Economics, and the Centre for Criminological Research, University of Oxford.

Recent titles in this series:

Prisons and the Problem of Order
Sparks, Bottoms, and Hay

The Local Governance of Crime
Crawford

Policing the Risk Society
Ericson and Haggerty

Law in Policing: Legal Regulation and Police Practices
Dixon

Sexed Work: Gender, Race and Resistance in a Brooklyn Drug Market
Maher

Procedural Fairness at the Police Station
Choongh

Crime in Ireland 1945–95: 'Here be Dragons'
Brewer, Lockhart, and Rodgers

Private Security and Public Policing
Newburn and Jones

Violent Racism: Victimization, Policing, and Social Context
Bowling

Crime and Markets: Essays in Anti-Criminology
Ruggiero

Negotiating Domestic Violence:

Police, Criminal Justice and Victims

CAROLYN HOYLE

OXFORD
UNIVERSITY PRESS

*This book has been printed digitally and produced in a standard specification
in order to ensure its continuing availability*

OXFORD
UNIVERSITY PRESS

Great Clarendon Street, Oxford OX2 6DP

Oxford University Press is a department of the University of Oxford.
It furthers the University's objective of excellence in research, scholarship,
and education by publishing worldwide in

Oxford New York

Auckland Bangkok Buenos Aires Cape Town Chennai
Dar es Salaam Delhi Hong Kong Istanbul Karachi Kolkata
Kuala Lumpur Madrid Melbourne Mexico City Mumbai Nairobi
São Paulo Shanghai Taipei Tokyo Toronto

Oxford is a registered trade mark of Oxford University Press
in the UK and in certain other countries

Published in the United States
by Oxford University Press Inc., New York

© Carolyn Hoyle 1998

ISBN 0-19-829930-3

Dedication

This book is dedicated to the memory of my grandmothers, Gertrude and Margaret, who, by their example, taught me compassion and tenacity.

General Editors' Introduction

The *Clarendon Studies in Criminology* series was inaugurated in 1994 under the auspices of centres of criminology at the Universities of Cambridge and Oxford and the London School of Economics. There was a view that criminology in Britain and elsewhere was flowing with interesting work and that there was scope for a new dedicated series of scholarly books. The intention, declared Roger Hood, its first general editor, was to 'provide a forum for outstanding work in all aspects of criminology, criminal justice, penology, and the wider field of deviant behaviour.' We trust that that intention has been fulfilled. Some twenty titles have already been published, covering policing; prisons and prison administration; gender and crime; victims and victims' movements; the media reporting of crime news, and much else, and other will follow.

Negotiating Domestic Violence describes the policing of violence against women in the Thames Valley area, and it marks the convergence of three important intellectual movements in contemporary criminology: the established and successful tradition of ethnographic field studies of the police; the desire to appreciate the impact of the criminal justice process on women; and the emerging analysis of victims and victimization. Carolyn Hoyle is meticulous in her deployment of a variety of research methods, sources and intellectual stances to construct a detailed portrait of a complex, nuanced and embedded process. Policing is depicted as a special kind of pragmatic activity that employs 'cop culture' to mediate the demands of law and organizational management, on the one hand, and the contradictory and shifting exigencies of everyday life, on the other. Hoyle makes it evident how very difficult it is to make universal statements about the motives and meanings of such a process. She shows repeatedly that big generalizations cannot withstand the scrutiny supplied by thick description.

Some of the facile dichotomies which litter criminology are consequently revealed to be quite misleading. Hoyle contends, for example, that the police are neither engaged wholly in law enforcement nor in social service work, but that law enforcement is often a social service and social service law enforcement. Again, she shows that many standard feminist accounts do not appear fully to appreciate the victims' own understanding of their history, situation and demands. What emerges particularly clearly is that the majority of victims visited by the police principally seek an authoritative intervention rather than punishment or an end to their relationship. They want a police presence because, in Bittner's words, officers are uniquely defined by their capacity to act when people are beset by *'something-that-ought-not-to-happening-and-about-which-some-one-had-better-do-something-now!'*

David Downes and Paul Rock

Preface and Acknowledgements

This book reports the findings of empirical work, conducted for my doctoral thesis, on policing domestic violence. This study, conducted in the Thames Valley, sought to understand the factors which shape the police and Crown Prosecution Service responses to domestic violence in the light of policy changes which recommended arrest in such cases. It responded to a gap in the literature on domestic violence between studies of the police response on the one hand, and studies based on victims' experiences on the other. This book places the victim firmly within an understanding of the response of the criminal justice system, in that it examines, amongst other things, the impact of victims' needs, desires and expectations on decisions made by police and prosecutors.

Whilst it draws on feminist theoretical and empirical work, the approach of this book could not be described as feminist. Rather, it takes as its theoretical perspective social interactionism but, unlike many works of interpretive sociology, it does not exclude the influence of structure. In looking at the response of the criminal justice system, it questions the assumption that this system, as it presently operates, is capable of responding effectively to the needs of victims of domestic violence.

All research projects rely on numerous people for advice and support. This was no exception. First I would like to thank the Economic and Social Research Council which funded my D.Phil., having already funded my M.Sc. I am indebted to Chief Constable Charles Pollard for his permission to conduct the research in two busy areas of the Thames Valley Police and, more generally, for his support of the work of the Centre for Criminological Research. Chief Superintendents David Lindley, Ralph Perry, and Caroline Nichol were particularly generous with their time and access to their staff and other resources.

Many other people, including control room operators, administrative support staff, shift inspectors, and station duty officers assisted the fieldwork and ensured that the time I spent in the stations was both productive and enjoyable. A great debt is owed to the 219 police officers interviewed, in particular WPC Dean and PC Hunter who, despite the science of random sampling, were each interviewed nine times and still managed to show enthusiasm! The co-operation and, more importantly, the honesty of all officers meant that this central part of the fieldwork was productive and enjoyable. Special thanks must go to the two 'shifts' who tolerated my observing them on patrol duty with good humour. My understanding of operational policing and 'cop culture' in particular would not have been complete without the many hours spent in patrol cars and the canteen. More recently, continued communication with WPC Chris Bovingdon-Cox and WPC Karen Lorenzo, officers of exceptional quality, and with the ever helpful and enthusiastic Chief Inspector John Carr, has kept me informed of developments in the policing of domestic violence.

Constables Purnell, Goodings, and Barefield, and Inspectors Pratt and Wooloff, facilitated what I originally anticipated would be the most problematic stage of the fieldwork: the interviews with victims of domestic violence. This part of the research was made all the more rewarding by the professionalism of these officers, and their sympathetic and tactful behaviour towards both the victims and their families.

Two branches of the Crown Prosecution Service, covering the Thames Valley Police areas, kindly agreed to my examining case files and interviewing prosecutors. I would like to thank all prosecutors, in particular Tessa Lister, who shared information, interesting stories and biscuits with me. Staff at Women's Aid and Victim Support also co-operated with the research. Joanna Fenstermacher, Irene Manasseh, Deborah Schofield, and Dot Garratt were especially valuable sources of information. I owe a particular debt of gratitude to the residents and workers of the refuges who welcomed me into their homes and trusted me with their experiences.

Of course, this book would not have been possible without the victims of domestic violence who talked openly about their most private and traumatic experiences. Their courage and honesty was not only a source of inspiration, but was fundamental to my understanding of the role of police and prosecutors.

During the last six years I have been fortunate in being able to draw on the experience and support of my colleagues and friends at the Centre for Criminological Research. Statistical and secretarial support has been provided by Graca Cordovil, Anja Spindler, Silvia

Littlejohns, Sarah Frost, Margit Kail, and Hannah Bichard. Ros Burnett has been a constant source of advice and support since I first arrived at the Centre. Her friendship and encouragement have given me confidence. Other friends and colleagues whose support helped me to keep things in perspective are Kimmett Edgar, Ian O'Donnell, Sophia Bird, Leanne Weber, David Faulkner, Kate Joyce, Heather Hamill, and Stephanie Chester. Over the last year or so, when I have been trying to finish this manuscript whilst working on two other projects, three friends in particular have kept me sane and happy: Jane Creaton, David Rose, and Hannah McConkey. Special thanks must go to my friend and colleague, Richard Young, who provided thoughtful and helpful comments on the manuscript and who can always cheer me up when I need it. I look forward to spending the next three years working with him.

I would like to thank Professor Robert Reiner and Dr Anthony Heath, my D.Phil. examiners, for their enthusiasm and recommendations for publication. Dr. Heath also provided invaluable advice on statistical techniques. Thanks also to the anonymous readers who commented on the first draft of the manuscript.

Whilst conducting fieldwork can be, and certainly was for me, a stimulating experience, writing a book can be an intellectually lonely endeavour. That I managed to enjoy this stage is a tribute to the unfailing support of my supervisor, Professor Roger Hood. The fieldwork might not have been possible without his influence and the good reputation of the Centre to recommend me. The analysis would have been less rigorous without his meticulous attention to detail. And the quality of the writing would certainly have been poorer if not for his patience in reading and commenting on the tortuous early drafts. Operating an 'open-door policy', he was available for consultation and advice at all times and I am extremely grateful to him for his attention. His faith in my abilities throughout the process of this book, both as his student and then his colleague, gave me strength when the task seemed daunting. I look forward to the next few years as his colleague and friend.

My greatest debt of gratitude goes to my colleague and very good friend, Andrew Sanders. He has commented on numerous drafts of both the thesis and the book and our endless conversations about the subject matter have helped me to refine my ideas and improve my writing. His contribution to this endeavour has been beyond what anyone would expect—even from the best of friends. His academic work, his contributions to our joint research projects and, most of all, his companionship have been a constant source of support and inspiration.

Finally, I would like to thank my family, in particular my mother, for their support and encouragement. I must apologize to Stevan Hoyle for the many Friday and Saturday nights I spent in the back of a police car whilst he sat at home worrying about my safety. I am also grateful for his good-humoured tolerance of my unsociability during the numerous weekends and evenings I have sat at my computer, not to mention his large salary when my only income was a meagre student grant!

CH
Oxford
March 1998

Contents

List of Figures   xv

List of Tables   xvii

1. Legal Rules, Policies, and Police Practices   1

2. Conceptual and Methodological Issues   26

3. The Control Room: the First Stage in the Decision-Making Process?   49

4. The Cultural and Structural Determinants of Police Decision-Making   65

5. The Situational Determinants of Police Decision-Making   102

6. Understanding Prosecution Decisions   146

7. In the Victim's Interest?   182

8. Interrogating the Role of the Victim   209

Bibliography   231

Index   245

List of Figures

2.1a.   Incidence and progress of domestic violence calls
        reported during a seven month period—police
        action   30
2.1b.   Incidence and progress of domestic violence calls
        reported during a seven month period—CPS and
        court action   31
4.1   The negative concept of 'cop culture' and its impact
        on the police response to domestic violence   70
4.2   A reconceptualization of cop culture: its creation
        and its influences   101
5.1   The influence of situational factors and working
        assumptions on officers' decisions   130
5.2   An explanatory model of the police decision-
        making process   131
5.3   Reasons for Non-arrest in Cases where there
        was Evidence of a Criminal Offence   132
5.4   Arrest Decisions in Cases where there was no
        Evidence   137

List of Tables

4.1	WPC present at scene: number and percentage arrested	72
4.2	Disputants cohabiting: number and percentage arrested	72
4.3	Officer made a negative comment: number and percentage arrested	72
4.4	Officer suggested that the victim had provoked the dispute: number and percentage arrested	73
4.5	Officers knew that there was a history of disputes: number and percentage arrested	90
5.1	Evidence of an offence: number and percentage arrested	108
5.2	Victims' injuries: number and percentage arrested	111
5.3	Suspects' demeanour: number and percentage arrested	115
5.4	Victims' preferences regarding police action: number and percentage arrested	123
5.5	Victims' state of mind (calm): number and percentage arrested	128
5.6	Victims' state of mind (hysterical): number and percentage arrested	128
6.1	Victim withdrawal: number and percentage of suspects charged	148
7.1	Sentences for domestic violence offenders	191

1

Legal Rules, Policies, and Police Practices

Prior to the early 1970s, violence against women in the home was generally thought of as a private matter. Couples were left alone to solve their conflicts except in cases of very serious injury. The law was considered to be the last resort in the management of domestic violence, and arrest was only used occasionally as a temporary means of maintaining order. Today it is recognized that the divide between public and private violence is less distinct, and violence between intimates has become a more salient public policy issue than ever before. Increased public intervention within the private sphere has been legitimated by new legislation, new police powers, and changing attitudes towards state intervention. Domestic violence is now, in theory, recognized as 'real' crime, and the fact that it typically occurs in the home does not deflect from its status as a criminal offence.

This book will examine the way in which incidents of domestic violence are responded to in the 1990s by the criminal justice system. It is based on research which aimed to understand the factors which shaped the decisions made by the police and the Crown Prosecution Service in the light of policies which recommended increased intervention in such cases. It examines the extent to which the choices made by police and prosecutors can be understood in terms of evidential criteria and offence seriousness, and the extent to which they are shaped by the informal 'rules' of the organizational culture. The roles of police officers, prosecutors, victims, and suspects in respect of these considerations are explored.

This chapter will provide the context within which this research was carried out. That context comprises changing government policies on domestic violence; a large body of prior research on the policing of domestic violence; and the political and theoretical background against which that research, and my own, were done.

Changing government policies on domestic violence

The first developments in public policy concerning domestic violence began in 1975 with the Parliamentary Select Committee hearings on *Violence in Marriage*. Prior to this, police officers had been advised against arresting men who were violent to their partners. Giving evidence to the 1975 Committee, the Association of Chief Police Officers denied the need for any change in their service: 'Whilst such problems take up considerable police time...in the majority of cases the role of the police is a negative one. We are, after all, dealing with persons *bound in marriage*, and it is important, for a host of reasons, to maintain the unity of the spouses' (original emphasis) (Parliamentary Select Committee 1975: 366).

Despite sympathy for police reluctance to intervene because of victims withdrawing charges and traditional ideas about domestic privacy (para. 43), the Report recommended that the police keep statistics and that Chief Constables should review their policies for dealing with domestic violence. It argued that the police should treat assaults in the home as seriously as they do assaults in other places and should be ready to arrest the assailant on the spot where there is evidence of an injury (para. 44). However, whilst there were resultant changes in the civil law, the police response stayed the same, reinforcing the idea that domestic violence was predominantly a matter for the civil courts. Nevertheless, it was a major achievement for the women's movement that the government had reacted to pressure and made the decision to establish a Committee to take evidence and make recommendations for action.[1] It was the first time that the police had been questioned about their role, and hence it established the foundation for future enquiry and criticism.

Following the Report, Parliament passed legislation aimed at helping women who are abused by partners and helping the police to improve their service to these victims. This legislation comprised:

[1] For a thorough discussion of the role of the women's movement in the changing government response to physical and sexual violence against women see Dobash and Dobash (1992); Hall, James, and Kertesz (1981) and Haste (1992).

The Domestic Violence and Matrimonial Court Act 1976; the Housing (Homeless Persons) Act 1977; the Domestic Violence and Magistrates Act 1978; and the Matrimonial Homes Act 1983. It provided for the eviction of violent men, their arrest for a breach of an injunction and the rehousing of victims of domestic violence.

During the 1970s and 1980s, in both the United Kingdom and the United States, the feminist movement had put the issue of men's violence against women in the home on the public agenda (Stanko 1995). In doing so, it created the environment for government change and for empirical studies of the character, prevalence, and incidence of domestic violence as well as assessments of the response of the criminal justice system. Hence, a plethora of studies on domestic violence emerged.[2] Indeed, the growth of literature in this area has been such that a decade ago Kelly alleged that there had been a 'knowledge explosion' (1988: 43). Early research was directed towards assessing the effectiveness of the spate of legislation enacted during the 1970s and early 1980s, with researchers attempting to establish why statutory agencies were failing to give an adequate service to victims.

A vast literature emerged on all aspects of domestic violence, but the police and other criminal justice agencies attracted disproportionate attention. Feminist writers in particular discovered, through empirical work, that the police were reluctant to intervene in most cases of domestic violence. They examined the role of the dispatcher or radio controller (Faragher 1985); the influence of operational police officers who first attend the scene and who must decide whether or not to arrest a suspect (Dobash and Dobash 1980); and the role of the custody officer who must decide whether or not to charge the suspect (Edwards 1989). Some studies have analysed police records and/or carried out observations of police behaviour (Faragher 1985; Oppenlander 1982; Edwards 1986), whilst others have gathered data from interviews with, and questionnaires completed by, female victims of domestic violence (Binney, Harkell, and Nixon 1981; Bowker 1983; Brown 1984; Pahl 1982, 1985).

This body of research showed that few perpetrators of domestic violence were prosecuted, or even arrested, for an offence of violence against the person (Pagelow 1981; Bowker 1982; and Binney,

---

[2] With these studies came the development of a specifically feminist research methodology (Stanley and Wise 1983).

Harkell, and Nixon 1981). For example, more than half of the 350 victims of domestic violence Pagelow interviewed who had asked the police to arrest their partners reported that the police had failed to make an arrest. It seemed that even when all the conditions were met for the police to make an arrest, including the co-operation of the victim, this was rarely done (Edwards 1986; Dobash and Dobash 1980). Most of these studies suggested that victims were dissatisfied with the police (Binney, Harkell, and Nixon 1981).

Research also indicated that when suspects were charged it was often with a crime of lesser seriousness than would appear to be justified by the facts. For example, offences of 'assault occasioning actual bodily harm',[3] a crime which typically requires police action and public prosecution, were regularly downgraded to 'common assault',[4] which was, until recently, usually dealt with through a private summons (Edwards 1986). Similarly, Chatterton (1981) observed that station incident book entries which stated that a domestic dispute had arisen and the parties had been advised to seek a civil remedy often hid quite serious assaults on wives.

The anger expressed by these writers, at the apparent refusal of criminal justice practitioners to take seriously violence against wives, was channelled into campaigns to 'educate' policy-makers. These campaigns were fairly successful, with the past decade witnessing some radical changes in the societal approach to all forms of violence against women as well as to the role of the state as a regulator of behaviour within the family. The feminist-inspired research (most notably the work of Susan Edwards, Elizabeth Stanko, and Rebecca and Russell Dobash) along with the pressure from women's advocates in general, and organisations such as the Women's Aid Federation in particular, encouraged the government towards a reconsideration of its stance on all forms of violence against women in the home.

In the mid-1980s the Women's National Commission was instrumental in encouraging the government to consider the response of the various criminal justice agencies to crimes of sexual violence against women (Smith 1989). Deliberations over this issue culminated in the Home Office Circular of 1986 (No. 69) which,

---

[3] Assault occasioning actual bodily harm is an offence against s.47 of the Offences Against the Person Act 1861 and is defined as interfering with the health or comfort of the victim (Smith and Hogan 1992: 423).
[4] An offence contrary to s. 42 of the Offences Against the Person Act 1861.

whilst primarily concerned with the police handling of rape, recommended that procedures used to help victims of sexual assault should also apply to domestic violence victims. It reminded officers of the new powers provided by the Police and Criminal Evidence Act 1984 (PACE) and recommended that they advise victims on how to contact support organizations and local authority agencies.[5] It was suggested that such advice should be offered in private and might helpfully be contained in a leaflet which could be given to the victim (Home Office 1986: 3). However, this Circular did not direct Chief Constables to develop new policies. It was, as Freeman (1987) has argued, a somewhat tame response. Some police services, however, did respond positively. A number of forces issued orders concerning domestic violence. For example, the Metropolitan Police issued a force order in 1987 encouraging the use of arrest, and recommending, amongst other things, that officers involve other agencies in seeking solutions and initiatives to this form of violence.

The later Home Office Circular of 1990 9 (No. 60) (hereafter referred to as the 1990/60 circular) showed a strong commitment to an effective response to all aspects of physical, sexual, and emotional abuse in the home. It stated that complaints of domestic violence should be recorded and investigated in the same way as crimes committed by strangers; advised forces to keep accurate statistical records of all reports of domestic violence to enable officers quickly to retrieve relevant information; and recommended that there should be some sort of positive action to investigate all such calls (Home Office 1990a, paras. 12 and 13). Research, again in particular that carried out in London by Edwards, had exposed the problems of 'no-criming', misguided attempts at conciliation which exposed the victim to further danger, and interviewing victims in front of their assailants (para. 14).[6] The Circular warned officers against such practices, recommending that they should take a more

---

[5] These new powers relate to officers' powers of entry to premises for the purpose of arrest (s. 17 (1) (b)); for the purpose of saving life or limb or preventing serious damage to property (s. 17 (1) (e)); to officers' powers of arrest regarding persons suspected of committing, or being about to commit, an arrestable offence (s. 24), and to prevent physical injury to another or to protect a child or other vulnerable person (s. 25).

[6] Even a brief perusal of the 1990/60 Circular indicates that the Home Office was influenced by Edwards' research. Also, smaller localized empirical studies have had an impact on specific police areas (see, for example, Hanmer, and Saunders 1984, 1987, 1991; Hanmer 1990). Indeed, research appears to be a necessary antecedent to changes in policy with many different police forces now undertaking their own monitoring as well.

interventionist approach and consider arrest and detention in all cases (para. 16). In addition it advised them to adopt a more sympathetic and understanding attitude towards victims, providing them with information about help in the community [para. 8]. Forces were also encouraged to set up dedicated units of appointed officers to deal specifically with domestic violence cases and to liaise with other agencies working in the field (para. 10).

There appears to be widespread agreement that the Circular provided the encouragement and advice necessary for the police to develop sensitive and effective responses to domestic violence (Home Affairs Committee 1993a, para. 14). Indeed by July 1991, all forces in England and Wales had formulated policy statements on domestic violence (Home Affairs Committee (Home Office Memorandum) 1993b: 2). The Thames Valley Police put in place local policies which recommended that:

...a fresh look is required to deal with domestic violence...[if there is evidence of an injury]...the perpetrator *should be arrested*. [Officers should also reduce]...the current high instances of offenders being released 'Refused Charge' [and offenders arrested for a breach of the peace]...should be kept in custody until the next available court. (Original emphasis.) (Thames Valley Police, May 1992, paras. 4a–f.)

The extent to which these policies changed police practice 'on the ground' is, however, an empirical question.

A recent Home Office study has found that the translation of these policies into practice has been varied and sometimes very limited (Grace 1995). The methods employed by Grace meant that reliable data were not available on the extent to which officers were arresting suspects in cases of domestic violence where there was evidence of a criminal offence—as was advised by the Circular. It is this 'pro-arrest' message of the Circular with which this book is most concerned, rather than the extent to which the other recommendations of the Circular were taken on board (although these issues are discussed in passing). The book focuses on the factors which shape police decision-making in cases of domestic violence and in doing so criticizes legalist conceptions of policing which assume that a new policy will lead to a change in police behaviour regarding arrest.

Implicit in the feminists' demands for policy changes was a belief that such reforms would bring about substantial improvements for victims of domestic violence through changes in operational policing. As Edwards, prior to the 1990/60 Circular, had argued:

A policy directive on marital violence would certainly create the appropriate climate for the desperately needed changes in policing on the front line.... Policing in the absence of policy... facilitates the making of individual judgements, often based on erroneous stereotypes. (1989: 86–87.)

This comment raises the question about police discretionary powers and the extent to which they can be guided by laws, and policies. The rest of this chapter will introduce the intellectual concerns of the book, notably the factors which influence police decisions at the scene of domestic disputes in the light of their wide discretionary powers.

Analysing police discretion

In explaining what they considered to be the differential treatment of domestic and non-domestic violence, feminist critics have recognized that policing is not determined by the law but that it operates within a gap created by discretionary powers. Exploring cultural theories of police behaviour, some have focused on concepts such as police misogyny, sexist attitudes, and the 'deserving' or 'undeserving' victim (Edwards 1996; Faragher 1985; Hatty 1989; Pahl 1985; Dobash and Dobash 1980; Stanko 1989; Hanmer, Radford, and Stanko 1989). The argument, about police 'inadequacies' being due to their lack of sympathy for such victims, has been so persuasive that it has achieved the status of a 'fact'. Some of these studies which have taken a 'gendered' perspective have ignored other cultural or structural explanations of police inaction at the scene of domestic disputes, dismissing, as mere excuses, officers' legal or organizational reasons for failing to arrest suspects (these issues are discussed and evaluated in Chapter 4). On the other hand, studies of policing which have incorporated an element of structuralism (for example, McConville, Sanders, and Leng 1991; Kemp, Norris, and Fielding 1992) have included only a small number of cases of domestic violence within a larger sample of other offences. This may be because domestic violence has been somewhat marginalized from 'mainstream' research on the police and regarded as a feminist issue: an issue which it is only 'correct' to approach from a 'gendered' perspective.

Moving away from simple 'police blaming', this research aimed to understand the context within which police have to make difficult decisions. It looked at those structural and organizational factors which constrain the choice of decisions open to police officers. Such constraints include: the availability of alternative solutions, powers of arrest and perceptions of the likelihood that an arrest would lead to the establishment of evidence which the Crown Prosecution Service would regard as sufficiently strong to justify prosecution. Most importantly, the research examined the influence of informal social and organizational precepts as well as the interaction between the various actors at the scene which shape police decision-making.

Hence this study draws on the two seemingly different perspectives of interactionism and structuralism—an approach which might be referred to as 'theoretical triangulation'. This approach is based on the recognition that whilst the social structure influences how people act, this power is not total: people are active—they think and can, to a greater or lesser extent, manipulate and attach meaning to their environment. It focuses more closely on the influence of interactions between significant actors in the decision-making process than have most previous studies of policing domestic violence. In other words, it draws more on interpretive sociology. Interpretive sociologists attempt to understand the social processes which actors go through in order to arrive at an understanding of action or behaviour.[7] These theorists argue that, to understand how the criminal justice system operates, it is necessary to try to understand the viewpoint of the significant 'actors'. In the example of the criminal justice response to domestic violence the main 'actors' are the police, crown prosecutors, the suspects, and the victims.

Interpretive sociology is concerned with the way in which social meanings and definitions are generated within social situations and social processes: in how people create, sustain, and change their view of social reality. It also attempts to understand the ways in which individuals and members of certain groups act on the basis of such meanings and interpretations. These theorists argue that in any social context a negotiated social reality will soon emerge as participants reach some consensus about what is going on and how each actor fits into the situation.[8]

---

[7] This micro-sociological approach has its roots in the Weberian social action approach and it was popularized in the 1960s, in the field of the sociology of deviance, by the theories of symbolic interactionism offered by Becker (1963) and Lemert (1967).

[8] This type of symbolic interactionism has its roots in the social philosophy of George Herbert Mead (1934) whose work led to the development of certain concepts which remain central to interactionist theory today.

In explaining how elements of different theoretical approaches will inform this book, three main questions will be considered. First, to what extent can changes in policy impact on the response of operational patrol officers? Secondly, what is the role of the police? And, finally, what factors shape the police response?

The impact of policy

During the 1980s much feminist-inspired research was, not surprisingly, critical of formal police policies which advised officers to attempt to reconcile disputants before considering criminal action against perpetrators. There were many studies of domestic violence published prior to the 1990/60 Circular. These reported that the police assigned low priority to domestic violence calls: that the police rarely responded to these disputes and that they seldom made arrests or used other criminal sanctions even when the violence used would have justified such action. Indeed, this literature showed that women who made contact with the police were invariably left dissatisfied or, worse, further traumatized by inappropriate or uninformed responses.

Many of these critics argued that one of the most efficient means of addressing the 'problem' of low arrest rates was to introduce policies and training which challenge stereotypes and prejudices, reduce police discretion, and provide a formal structure for promoting good practice. This structure, it was assumed, would override the pervasive influence of 'cop culture'. The sorts of actions recommended in the 1990/60 Circular clearly constituted a major change in the policing of domestic violence from that described by the literature of the 1980s (see, for example, Edwards 1989; Hanmer and Saunders 1987). What is not clear, however, is whether changes in policy have led to changes in practice.

Prior to the fieldwork conducted for this study, the most recent thorough research was carried out by Edwards (1989), between 1984 and 1985, in two Metropolitan police stations. After a replication study of recording practices conducted in 1988, she conducted further interviews with Metropolitan officers in 1990 (Edwards and Buchan 1991, cited in Edwards 1996). This was three years after the 1987 Metropolitan force order which delivered a similar message to the later 1990/60 Circular. Edwards and Buchan were able to detect some changes in the attitudes of officers after the introduction of this force order, as well as an increase in the arrest rate.[9] The negative attitudes to domestic violence and the stereotypical approaches to victims were not so apparent. However, Edwards has recently argued that, in the main, '... traditional attitudes to domestic violence are intransigent'. And, furthermore, that: 'The law has served to institutionalise domestic violence symbolically by elevating the principle of non-interference in family life and patriarchal authority as paramount, above the principle of protection of the wife' (1996: 191).

Beginning from the normative stance that the police response to domestic violence was not punitive enough, some feminist critics have argued that it could be explained by the very wide discretion that police officers have when responding to calls from citizens (McLeod 1983; Ferraro 1989a; Hanmer 1989; Edwards 1989). These critics have tended to assume that changes in operational rules, brought about by policy reform, would result in less discretion and, hence, in more arrests. In other words, they believed that police actions could be directed, and even controlled, by procedural rules aimed to encourage enforcement of the criminal law (Edwards 1996).[10]

The policy-makers and senior police personnel who responded to the demands for 'improvements' also believed that new directives could dramatically alter the response of operational police officers.[11] They assumed that the police would respond to the seriousness of an offence and the evidence available if only they were directed to do so and given the necessary powers (the 1990/60 Circular reminded officers of their powers under PACE).

On the other hand, cultural theorists have argued that legal rules and police policies do not impact on discretion when they conflict with the occupational sub-culture of patrol officers (Bittner 1970). Jefferson and Grimshaw (1984) asserted that whilst discretion leaves a vacuum, the police culture fills the gap and structures the

---

[9] They did not find a proportionate increase in the prosecution rate.

[10] Carol Smart (1995) has been a vehement critic of this reformist approach to feminism and the law. More recently Buzawa and Buzawa (1996a) and Stanko (1995) have also questioned the role of the law in responding to domestic violence. Indeed, Stanko is very sceptical of the role of policies in changing police behaviour because rank and file officers are creative about manoeuvring around policy directives (1995: 36).

[11] With regard to domestic violence the belief that police discretion could be structured through criminal procedure has had greater impact in America than in England and Wales. Following the research by Sherman (1992), many states have now adopted mandatory arrest policies for domestic violence (see chap. 8).

choices made, leaving little room for the influence of policies. McConville, Sanders, and Leng (1991) similarly argue that legal reform cannot alter significantly the police culture, which they see as determining police actions. Taking the best of interactionist and structuralist theories, they assessed the impact of PACE, and argued that 'where legal rules cut across well-established cultural norms of actors to whom they are addressed, they are unlikely to have instrumental effect' (1991: 200). They see the notions of evidential strength and seriousness as malleable and therefore as having rather less effect on police decision-making than was often assumed. Police discretion, they argue, is structured according to a set of informal 'working rules'.[12]

Much of the empirical research and theoretical debate over the last two decades has focused on trying to understand the divide between legal rules and police practice and the effectiveness of laws and policies aimed at bridging this divide. Discussing the impact of PACE, Dixon (1992, 1997) has characterized writers from the above two different perspectives on the role of the law in policing as 'sea-change' theorists and 'new left pessimists'.[13] Looking particularly at the work of McKenzie, he argues that 'sea-change' theorists believe that PACE has fundamentally changed criminal investigation, shifting towards a supposedly American model of due process (Dixon 1997: 152). Dixon is critical of much of this work, which has, in the main, been produced by police officers and is methodologically flawed. He contrasts this position with the 'pessimistic' stance taken by Bridges, Leng, McConville, and Sanders, and, more recently included in this category, Young, to whom he refers collectively as the 'Warwick School'.[14] The Warwick School argues that PACE has had little impact on operational policing because police priorities, culture, and crime control commitments were not sympathetic to changes in police practice. Indeed these authors have argued that rather than regulating policing,

---

[12] Working rules are informal rules developed by operational police officers in response to everyday encounters which structure the way the police exercise their discretion. This term was first adopted by Smith and Gray (1983), although Ericson (1981) had previously referred to 'recipe rules'. McConville, Sanders and Leng (1991) developed the concept further.
[13] Dixon originally used this ironic term in 1992. It is absent from his most recent publication (1997).
[14] The core texts which add to the 'pessimistic' perspective are: McConville, Sanders, and Leng (1991); Sanders et al. (1989); Sanders and Young (1994).

PACE has served to facilitate and legitimate powers and practices adopted by the police in their culturally-driven commitment to crime control (Dixon 1997: 155). Dixon places himself between these two extremes. He believes that laws can affect policing but the relationship between law and policing is contingent upon the nature of the law, the type of policing, and the social and political contexts within which attempts are made to change policing through law (1997: 318; see also Chan 1996).

McBarnet (1983), in a challenge to culturalist accounts of the relationship between law and policing, argues that rank and file police practices were not only permitted by law, but were indeed created by it. The law, she maintains, provides a flexible and permissive structure within which the police can work. The law can facilitate police officers pursuing their own goals. Although, as baldly stated here, McBarnet's reproach might over-state the role of law, she was right to switch critical attention on to the law, which permits the behaviour of the police. However, implicit in her work is the idea that changes to the 'law in books' can reform police practice, the 'law in action'. This has, of course, been hotly debated.

Whilst this debate has centred on legal rules (on PACE in particular), it could inform our understanding of the influence of policies on practical policing. Indeed Dixon seems to suggest that the impact of policies can be understood in the same way as the impact of laws: '. . . a crucial assumption of policy—and law—making has been that, once rules have been clearly formulated, the police will act in accordance with them' (1997: 5).

There are various reasons why laws and policies do not translate directly into action. First, laws are permissive. They leave gaps in which discretion may operate. As Wilson explained: '. . . the law provides one resource, the possibility of arrest, and a set of constraints, but it does not supply to the patrolman a set of legal rules to be applied' (1968: 31). Hence the law cannot always be relied on to direct practical policing. There are, of course, organizations between operational police officers and the criminal law: the Home Office and the police organization. They produce policies and directives to shape the discretion left by the gaps in the law. Policies are introduced to direct operational police officers in a particular way. They remind officers of their powers and try to provide non-binding rules to apply in specific situations. As Lacey has explained, the gaps or ambiguities in the rules call for clearer interpretation or further legislative or quasi-legislative action (1992: 362).

In the case of the policies following the 1990/60 Home Office Circular on domestic violence, officers were directed towards, amongst other things, using their powers of arrest more often. Therefore, policies and guidelines, like laws (and to some extent more precisely than laws) are attempts by those higher up the organizational ladder to control the practices of the rank and file. So, policies try further to limit officers' discretion but they rarely mandate officers' actions—they still allow for discretion. The 1990/ 60 Circular did not mandate arrest. It recommended that officers consider arrest and detention in all cases, but this recommendation still left a gap within which officers could exercise discretion. As we shall see in Chapters 5 and 6, the police did not in fact arrest in a significant minority of cases where there was sufficient evidence to do so. In other words, both the law and the policy contained in the 1990/60 Circular permitted the police to arrest but did not mandate them to do so in all cases. Consequently, they did not do so in all cases.

Secondly, laws and policies can be manipulated. This means that laws and policies set out for one purpose can be used by law enforcement agents for other purposes. A good example is the use of the 1986 Public Order Act. This was ostensibly designed to protect the public. However, it has been found that, at least in relation to the more minor offences covered by this legislation, the police frequently arrest in order to protect themselves and to assert their own authority where there is no discernible threat to the public at all (Brown and Ellis 1994).

Thirdly, laws and policies can be followed by the letter but not the spirit. For example, under PACE custody officers are obliged to offer suspects legal advice and to read them their other rights. It has been found that the police do usually do this, but frequently in such a way that many suspects are unlikely to, and are possibly not intended to, understand what they are being told. Whether this amounts to deliberate ploys to cheat suspects of their rights (Sanders *et al.* 1989; Sanders and Young 1994) or simply a brisk indifference to the plight of the suspect (Dixon 1997) is irrelevant (see Brown 1997 for a review of the literature on PACE). What this shows is that this kind of law will often be technically complied with without securing the result for which the law was ostensibly designed.

Finally, laws and policies can be ignored or broken. More than thirty years ago sociologists started from the premiss that police violate rules and regulations (see, for example, Skolnick 1966). As Hawkins has argued, discretionary powers allow, or even encourage the police sometimes to ignore or to distort the word or spirit of the law. It also allows them to assume a legal authority they do not in fact possess, or deny an authority which they do (Hawkins 1992: 12) (see Chapter 5).

What all these examples show is that the issue is not the importance of *either* the law *or* the police, but the two in combination. McBarnet's criticisms of the literature which blamed front line officers for the apparent discrepancy between the 'law in books' and the 'law in action' created a false dichotomy—do we blame law enforcement officers or the law itself? It is necessary to look at the interaction between the two.

This book will question the assumption that policy reform significantly changes police practice. Whilst it does not claim that the criminal law and official policies have *no* impact on police behaviour or decisions, it argues that social and organizational precepts are more important to an understanding of police behaviour than are evidential criteria or official rules or policies.

Most criminologists recognize that the nature and the form of criminal law and policies affect operational policing. They could be positioned along a spectrum somewhere between the two extremes as described by Dixon. Hence, most disagreements are over the *extent* to which, and *under what circumstances*, policies bring about change. Analysis of the Thames Valley data sought to understand where upon this spectrum police and prosecutors' decisions regarding domestic disputes could be positioned. But it also sought to answer the more interesting question raised by Evans in relation to guidelines on cautioning. Evans recognized that police forces often ignore guidelines: 'At the moment the Home Office guidance is merely *guidance* which police forces . . . may choose to ignore. An assessment of the impact of previous guidance suggests that this is precisely what many forces did to a greater or lesser extent.' He then goes on to identify the more interesting question: '. . . whether forces ignore guidance when they disagree with it but comply when they agree' (1994: 574–5). He later examined the impact of the 1994 Circular on cautioning and found empirical support for this hypothesis (Evans and Ellis 1997). Soothill, Francis, and Sanderson have argued that: '. . . cautioning guidelines are subject to variable inter-pretation contingent upon police perceptions of "real world" issues' (1997: 488). They conclude from this that '. . . we need to recognize when guidelines may work and when they are likely to fail' (1997: 488–9).

Drawing on the work of Baldwin and Kinsey (1982) and Brog-den, Jefferson, and Walklate (1988) it will be suggested that policies and laws cannot fundamentally alter the way in which rank and file police carry out their duties. It will be shown that whilst policies can influence the police culture and this, in turn, influences police work-ing assumptions, they cannot fundamentally change other working assumptions or working rules which contradict the recommenda-tions of policies.

The role of the police

Police policies on domestic violence are premissed upon the belief that laws, and an efficient use of police resources, can protect women from future violence (Stanko 1995). They emerged from feminist criticism of the police failure to protect women. Hence, the assumption is that the police can, if directed and helped to do so, protect the public from crime. Not only is this naïve, but it is based on a false assumption of what policing is about (Stanko 1995).

The belief that policing can be controlled by laws and policies is based on an underlying assumption that policing is mainly about crime fighting and that this is achieved by the enforcement of the law (Reiner 1992). Edwards argued that there is a 'public/private divide' in both the law in theory and the law in practice 'which organizes and ratifies a different level of response to similar conduct in the two terrains, including a different level of police response and priorities' (1989: 4). In practice, she argued, domestic violence was the lowest priority. Hence, officers are eager to make arrests in public disputes, whilst seldom arresting men who are violent to their partners in private. This implies that the police spend most of their time enforcing the law rigorously, except at domestic dis-putes where they rarely intervene and when they do they attempt only to keep the peace (1989: 49). However, not only do most academics, especially cultural theorists, start from the axiom that policing is highly discretionary, they also assert that most of it is *not* about law enforcement:

... the policeman on patrol is primarily a 'peace officer' rather than a 'law officer'. Relatively little of his time is spent enforcing the law in the sense of arresting offenders; far more is spent 'keeping the peace' by supervising the beat and responding to requests for assistance ... the most striking thing about patrol work is the high proportion of cases in which policemen do *not* enforce the law. (Original emphasis.) (Banton 1964: 127.).

The police role, they argue, is about service provision and order maintenance not usually achieved by law enforcement (Ericson 1982; Bittner 1970). Whilst the police role includes crime control and law enforcement, there is a wide variety of other service and administration functions including environmental and traffic functions, assistance in times of emergency, crime prevention and conciliation, and conflict resolution (Morgan and Newburn 1997). Indeed, as Morgan and Newburn argue: '... the police handle everything from unexpected childbirths, skid row alcoholics, drug addicts, emergency psychiatric cases, family fights, landlord-tenant disputes, and traffic violations, to occasional incidents of crime' (1997: 79). Since the observations of Banton and Bittner, various British and North American empirical studies have shown that relatively little police time is spent on actual criminal cases (Morgan and Newburn 1997).[15]

In discussing the public/private dichotomy, certain feminists, such as Edwards, may have focused on the studies which show the resentment of a large proportion of 'rank and file' officers concerning the amount of time spent on their service role. This resentment derives from the belief that 'social service' work detracts officers from 'real' police work (Skolnick 1966; Holdaway 1977; Smith and Gray 1983). Reiss, for example, through interviewing patrol officers, came up with an oft-cited quotation which some feminist critics have taken on board as summing up the attitude of police called to domestic disputes: 'Every time you begin to do some real police work you get stuck with this stuff. I guess 90 per cent of all police work is bullshit' (1971: 42).[16] Such academics see the police role as divided into two categories: law enforcement and keeping the peace. It has been argued that when police intervene in domestic situations they are often performing peace-keeping

[15] Home Office research conducted in the 1980s concluded that 'criminal incidents' constituted only one-third of all of the incidents attended by patrol officers and some of these were false alarms (Hough 1985) (see also Ekblom and Heal 1982).

[16] See also Smith and Gray (1983) and Southgate (1986).

functions, a role inclined towards reconciliation rather than prosecution (Johnson 1985). Oppenlander (1982) believes that victims
do not want the police to act as 'counsellors', but to enforce the
criminal law.

By arguing that the police see the family as a private domain and
do not think that they should become involved in 'social work' or
'counselling', writers such as Edwards have separated social service
from law enforcement roles. Reiner (1992) has argued that most
work is neither law enforcement nor social service, but is 'order
maintenance'—the settlement of conflicts by means other than formal law enforcement. In such situations the law is not ignored, it is
used as a resource. The decision about whether or not to enforce the
law is rarely preordained by the initial call to the police or the type
of dispute. It is, rather, arrived at through a process of negotiation
between the significant actors. An effective police officer may not
need to exercise his legitimate use of force to achieve the desired
resolution. His authority is typically secured because civilians know
he can use coercion if he considers it necessary (Chatterton 1983).
Thus, law enforcement is a *means* to achieving social order and the
furtherance of officers' own 'cultural' interests, not usually an end
in itself (Ericson 1982). This book will show, as Reiner has argued,
that the law enforcement/service debate rests on a false dichotomy.
This book will show that the police use the law as a resource when
they want to achieve goals established by their own social and
organizational precepts and by other significant actors, most typically the victim.

What shapes the police response?

Most empirical work has been motivated by the recognition that
police practice often deviates from legal standards and from a desire
to close the gap between the 'law in books' and the 'law in action'.
The literature has shown that the police typically under-enforce the
law by exercising their discretion not to arrest (see, for example,
Chatterton 1983; Holdaway 1977, 1979; Manning 1977; Reiner
1978). This exercise of discretion has largely been explained by
reference to informal police culture and the police working personality (see Skolnick 1966; Reiner 1992). Feminist academics seized
on the findings of general policing research relating to the discretion
exercised by rank and file officers to explain the low arrest rates in
cases of domestic violence. Hence, whilst feminist academics aimed

to set new agenda and challenge the consensus of mainstream sociology and criminology, they learnt much from both the empirical methods and sociological theories adopted in the general policing literature.

Feminist commentators were right to focus critical attention on officers' powers and opportunities for exercising discretion at incidents of domestic violence. The criminal law rarely dictates action. Instead, it allows its agents to make decisions based on a range of other social and organizational factors. As Hawkins has argued, discretion is inevitable '...because the translation of rule into action ...involves people in interpretation and choice....[It] is the means by which law...is translated into action' (1992: 11). However, some critics have underplayed the constraints that the criminal law and organizational factors can impose, and have ignored the role of the victim in the negotiation of a resolution to a dispute. Furthermore, they have tended to suggest that discretion is exercised capriciously, pointing only to gender and prejudices about certain types of victim (Stanko 1989; Ferraro 1993). This book will argue that having discretionary powers does not mean that individual constables have the absolute freedom to act as they want. They are sometimes constrained by the criminal law or by organizational factors. What is more important is that officers do not exercise discretion in a random or patternless way, nor do they, in the main, make decisions based solely on gender stereotypes and prejudices. Rather, the exercise of discretion is structured according to broader cultural and situational precepts.

Within the interactionist framework there are different and competing social constructions of any specific social phenomenon. These are not static constructions but are constantly evolving and are open to other social forces and dynamics. Police officers who find themselves as actors in complex domestic situations must try to decipher what has happened and what response the various actors expect, or indeed will accept, from them. In order to do this they do not blindly follow the criminal law or force policy, but, rather, interpret the information provided for them and try to make sense of it.[17] To understand this process of information-gathering

---

[17] Herbert Blumer (1969) has shown that the meanings of actions are not necessarily given, but have to be interpreted by those who either witness them or are told about them.

and decision-making the author has drawn on the work of McConville, Sanders, and Leng (1991) and Kemp, Norris, and Fielding (1992).

McConville, Sanders, and Leng put forward the most convincing argument about 'the process by which a case is constructed, from the moment the subject becomes an object of police suspicion' (1991: 12). Criminal justice purports to deal with facts and truths. But these critics talk about a *process* in which knowledge 'has to be worked out, constructed, rationalised, negotiated' from the arrival at an incident through the process of police investigation to trial and judgment (McConville, Sanders, and Leng 1991; Sanders *et al.* 1989: 139). Kemp, Norris, and Fielding (1992) explore the idea of the police response to domestic disputes as a process of negotiation. They examine the process whereby police officers handle incidents subject to the wider constraints on policing, in particular the interplay between legal rules, organizational rules, policy, and occupational culture.

Drawing upon these two approaches, the study on which this book is based aimed to discover how officers attending domestic disputes defined the situations and the disputants' actions. It looked at how these definitions, in turn, shaped officers' actions at the scene; and how officers negotiated solutions by interaction with the suspect and, in particular, the alleged victim within the constraints and parameters of the criminal law and organizational factors. It was found that cultural, structural, and interaction effects all influence police decision-making.

This study, like the work of McConville, Sanders, and Leng and Kemp, Norris, and Fielding, was theoretically rooted in interactionism (see Chapter 2). However, it is not argued that each time an officer arrived at the scene of a domestic dispute he was a blank page awaiting a solution to be reached through negotiation with the various actors involved. Even pure interactionist accounts (of which this is not one) do not suggest that human behaviour is infinitely variable across similar situations depending upon who the actors are. Any one police officer, for example, will behave similarly in response to many different incidents of domestic violence, and different officers will respond to similar situations in similar ways. Whilst there is a process of negotiation with the disputants and a response to the particular dynamics of the situation, there are certain routines and scripts which ensure some continuity.[18] These routines, which, to some extent, structure officers' discretion, have been explained by reference to 'working rules' developed by policing on the ground. By analysing officers' own accounts of their actions and decisions the research attempted to discover the 'working rules' which routinely inform their decisions; their links with legal rules and official guidelines; and the extent to which 'working rules' prevail over legal rules.

However, in this attempt to understand the dynamic processes involved in negotiating resolutions at the scene I have attempted to problematize and develop the concept of 'working rules'. This term has been criticized for suggesting rigidity and determinism, especially when used in the context of socio-legal work on the role of legal (formal) rules and policies.[19] One reply to this is that not even legal rules are entirely formulaic. Rules are not rigid but always incorporate fluid elements in that they nearly always allow for discretion. Hart (1961) has identified two elements in legal rules: a 'core' of settled meaning and a 'penumbra' of uncertainty. He has argued that all legal rules have both but some have more extensive penumbras than others. Dworkin (1977) has argued against this legal positivist position. He asserts that it is not the rules which are fluid but the principles which underlie and fill the gaps between rules. It is these principles which require continual interpretation and reinterpretation.[20] Either way the message is clear: interpreting disputes and deciding upon a course of action cannot be dictated by legal rules, and so using the concept of rules should not connote rigid formalization. The greater problem with the concept of 'working rules' is that it ignores or takes for granted a crucial stage of the negotiation process between suspects, victims, and police officers. It refers only to the 'obvious' choice of action once the negotiation process is over and the officer has decided what has gone on and what is likely to happen in the near future. It does not explain the process of deciding what has happened or what might happen, which also does not take place within a vacuum but is informed and structured by various legal, social, and organizational factors. During the negotiation stage the various actors try to 'tell their

[18] Erving Goffman's (1959) research into self-presentation has informed this understanding of some continuity between different situations.

[19] Personal communication with Richard Young.

[20] For an illustrative example of these applications to the law regulating policing and a fuller discussion of the 'realist' and 'positivist' schools of legal theory see Sanders and Young 1994, chap. 2.

story' and the police try to make sense of often competing and conflicting descriptions of what has happened, as well as what is likely to occur in the near future. Their understanding of these social interactions, and the context within which they are taking place, enable them to arrive at certain 'working assumptions' about what has occurred, what is occurring, and what is likely to occur. During this interpretive stage, judgements are made based on how the police officers routinely make sense of information. It is only when these judgements, that is, these 'working assumptions', are made that the police know which 'working rule' to apply. The negotiation process as well as their own cultural capital allows them to decide on the appropriate rule for the assumption. The rule cannot be chosen without having first made the assumption.

This distinction between 'working assumptions' and 'working rules' is grounded in a social science rather than a legalistic approach to understanding discretion. Legal philosophers have sought to understand the relationship between discretion and rules, in particular the extent to which rules authorize discretionary behaviour (see, for example, McBarnet 1983). Social scientists, on the other hand, have tried to understand the law in action,[21] that is, how the words of the law may, or may not, be translated into legal action (see Hawkins 1992). This position on discretionary powers is similar to that of Galligan, who argued that '... within a defined area of power the official must reflect upon its purposes, and then settle the policies and strategies for achieving them. There may be discretion in identifying and interpreting purposes; there may also be discretion as to the policies, strategies, and procedures to be followed in achieving these purposes' (1986: 22).

This is, of course, a dynamic interactive process. Hence, there is room for limited negotiation between all of the actors. There are two types of evolving interaction. First, there are 'feedback loops'. This is where the 'working rules', or, rather, knowledge of the 'working rules', affects the 'working assumptions' reached. For example, one 'working rule', identified by this and other studies, is that confrontational and belligerent suspects are usually arrested (see Chapter 5). However, arrest at that moment may not be desirable if a previous incident has left the police van full of prisoners.

---

[21] This term is more helpfully reconceptualized by Kemp, Norris, and Fielding as the 'police in action' (1992: 87).

This could bring another working rule (workload) into play (see McConville, Sanders, and Leng 1991). The officer might mentally renegotiate the assumption. Hence he might decide that the suspect is not being 'too' confrontational and the officer would not 'lose face' by walking away. In such a case the competing 'working rule' would feedback into the 'working assumption'.

The second type of evolving interaction concerns the use of a 'working rule' as a resource (this is developed further in Chapter 5). This is where the suspect is threatened with the rule, rather than the law, and the suspect consequently changes his behaviour. This means that the officer can change his assumption and by doing so apply a different 'working rule'. To use the same example of a confrontational suspect, the officer might threaten the suspect that if he does not calm down and shut up he will have to arrest him. Taking this 'advice', the suspect may become quieter and more deferential. Consequently, the officer changes his assumption about the suspect which means that a different working rule, one which does not see the necessity of arrest if the suspect is quiet and calm and not likely to cause any further trouble, comes into effect. It can be seen that the notion 'working assumptions' is not an alternative but a necessary precursor to the notion 'working rules' (this is shown in Chapters 5 and 6).

Negotiating domestic violence: a study of processes and decisions

Working assumptions are reached according to information provided and gathered at the scene and occasionally information provided in advance. This is not only information about the suspect and the victim and any other parties involved, it is also information about what has occurred. Hence, knowledge of, or evidence about, legal infractions also shapes police decision-making. These assumptions derive from a process of interaction. The working rules derive from these assumptions and the stock of knowledge which officers take with them to any incident, domestic or otherwise, about how things generally are and about what is expected of members of the public and of the officers themselves. Hence, decisions are shaped by a process of interaction and by the organizational culture which creates and sustains such working rules. Just as working assumptions are informed by laws and policies, the culture is influenced by structural forces, such as the criminal law and operational policies. As Hawkins (1992: 34) acknowledges, people usually negotiate within a broad framework of rules, or with a mandate conferred on them by law. Hence, this understanding of decision-making is neither purely interactionist nor purely structuralist.

By concentrating on small-scale interactions, classic interactionist accounts of policing have placed too much emphasis on the sub-culture of policing to the neglect of wider social forces and the role of power (Cain 1973; Rubenstein 1973; Punch 1979; Holdaway 1983). They have paid little attention to the role of organizational rules (typically in the form of directives or policies) and they have, in particular, underplayed the significance of legal rules in shaping police work. McBarnet (1981) was influential in reintroducing the role of the law into discussions of policing. McBarnet's (1981) structuralist approach to police decision-making (which pointed out that the 'law in books' was ambiguous and permissive and therefore condoned deviation from due process legality) encouraged greater understanding of the interplay of the 'law in books' and the 'law in action'.[22] She argued that the actions of police officers (and, by extension, prosecutors and courts) were generally consistent with the law rather than contrary to it. Therefore it is at least arguable that the law helps to shape actual behaviour and, because it allows for discretion, that it can be used as a resource. The following chapters will show that the criminal law is both a constraint on police behaviour and a resource used by the police to maintain order and solve problems. It will be argued that neither the substantive law nor the occupational sub-culture of constables alone can account for the outcome of a given policing incident (Jefferson and Grimshaw 1984).

The main aim of this book is to examine the factors which shape the disposal of 'domestic violence' cases. It seeks to understand decision-making processes. The role of the law in relation to other social and organizational factors is examined. Police and prosecutors' behaviour is explored to see what role legal rules play in choices, how they both shape and constrain their actions. In particular, it shows how the police construct 'cases' for prosecution from some incidents whilst deciding to take no further action in others. In other words, it examines the processes by which some acts are

---

[22] See Reiner (1994) for a thorough discussion of the development of sociological research in this area.

defined as criminal (as violence, property or public order offences) whilst others are not assigned such labels. In examining the process of reporting, police communication with complainants and suspects, and the response of Crown prosecutors, it was hoped to discover why so many cases do not result in an arrest or prosecution. From an understanding of the police role at present, and of victims' perceptions of the benefits or otherwise to be gained from supporting a criminal prosecution, the book aims to consider the role of the victim in the response of the police and the Crown Prosecution Service.

In order to achieve these aims a local study of policing 'domestic violence' in the Thames Valley Police was carried out. The research had four main objectives: to understand the patterns of arrest, charge, and prosecution in relation to incidents of domestic violence; to understand the needs, desires, and expectations of victims of domestic violence; to evaluate feminist explanations of the police response to domestic violence and to formulate alternative explanations; and, to consider the normative question of what the role of the police should be in relation to domestic violence. In achieving these aims, the book will address the question of how far a legalistic approach to individual incidents (which is the traditional response of the police to crime) is capable of effectively responding to an ongoing social phenomenon.

Chapter 2 describes the methodological approach of the research. The following four chapters chart the progress (from initial reporting through to the conviction of offenders) of 1318 domestic violence incidents reported in two areas of the Thames Valley Police during a seven month period in 1993. Chapter 3 looks at the first stage of this process—the reporting of incidents to the police control rooms. Interviews with control room personnel are drawn on, as are recorded details of all calls reporting domestic violence, in an attempt to measure the extent to which policy changes affect the management of these calls. It is also aimed to assess the impact of choices made by control room operators on the decision-making practices of patrol officers.

Chapters 4 and 5 discuss the response of patrol officers to 387 incidents (a random sample of the 1318 reported incidents) drawing on data from interviews with officers and victims and a patrol observation diary. The complex issue of police discretion is explored in the light of officers' decisions about their role vis-à-vis the disputants and the negotiation of a peaceful and effective solution. The role of evidential versus 'working' rules is examined in relation to the decision to arrest and, in Chapter 6, the decision to prosecute (using data from interviews with police officers and crown prosecutors).

Interviews with victims are drawn on in Chapter 7 in order to explore what women wanted from the police when they called them into their homes. Finally, Chapter 8 looks at the changes in the police response since the fieldwork was conducted. It examines critically the present trend towards responding in victims' interests rather than according to their wishes.

2
Conceptual and Methodological Issues

Chapter 1 described the intention of the Thames Valley study to unite different theoretical approaches to satisfy a range of aims. An eclectic approach to methods was deemed to be necessary in order to achieve theoretical triangulation. Hence, I chose not to restrict myself to using *either* positivist *or* interpretative methods, but to adopt a pragmatic approach to data collection. It was decided to use any appropriate method in as accurate a way as possible: to unite holistic analysis, which is characteristic of the positivists, and atomistic analysis, characteristic of the interpretive sociologies. This pragmatic approach resulted in the use of triangulation techniques; both 'methodological triangulation' and 'data triangulation'.

There are two forms of 'methodological triangulation'; 'within-method' and 'cross-method'. The former involves the use of differing strategies within a broad research method. In this study the use of semi-structured interviews with officers which generated quantitative data and qualitative descriptions fits the 'within-method' type. 'Cross-method' triangulation refers to the procedure of using different types of methods to study the same phenomenon. Interviews with police officers and victims, observation of officers on duty, and the examination of official records were all used to understand (amongst other things) the police response to incidents of domestic violence.

The use of different types or sources of data within one study is known as 'data triangulation' (see Denzin 1970). This study generated data sets on police officers, prosecutors, and victims in order to consider what the role of the criminal justice system is, and should be, in relation to victims of domestic violence. Triangulation not only allows for examination of the various facets of a given social situation, but also improves methodological validity. Each discrete data set provides a unique perspective and therefore can be considered in isolation from the others. However, when they are considered together, as complementary parts of a whole, with interconnected elements or features, the overall perspective can be appreciated fully, and a broader, more complex, theoretical framework can be developed.

This chapter will describe how this integrated approach, which balanced the strengths and weaknesses of various methods, facilitated the realization of the multifarious areas of enquiry detailed in the previous chapter. First, however, it will cover the conceptual issues raised by any study of domestic violence and explain how these difficult issues were resolved.

Defining the subject of empirical enquiry

For the purpose of this research, it was necessary to establish a clear definition of the forms of behaviour which would be the subject of enquiry. The terms 'domestic violence', 'family violence', 'interpersonal violence', 'wife abuse', 'spousal abuse', 'violence between intimates', and 'wife battering' are but some of the labels scattered about the literature on violence between partners or ex-partners, and they are invariably used synonymously. Most labels have attracted some criticism. The name 'battered wives', for example, has been rejected by some critics for excluding violence between couples who are cohabiting but not legally married and for excluding violence between separated or divorced couples. It has also been suggested that it focuses on women as victims, rather than on men as perpetrators. The term 'domestic violence' has been criticized on the ground that it does not specify that it is mainly women who are victims. Nevertheless, it is used in this book because it is the term adopted by the police, and, as the study upon which this book is based was interested in the police response, a shared understanding of concepts was considered to be vital in order to avoid misunderstanding.

The most contentious label used in this book is 'victim'. Many feminists in the early 1980s started to erase the term 'victim' from their vocabulary and to replace it with 'survivors' (Kelly 1988). They preferred to emphasize women's strategies for coping, resisting, and surviving violence and rejected the passivity implicit in the word 'victim'. I considered using the more neutral label of 'complainant' when discussing the response of police and prosecutors. However, one of the main focuses of the chapters dealing with the police and the Crown Prosecution Service is the reluctance of many victims to make a complaint, or to proceed with a complaint, and so the term 'complainant' could also be misleading. I decided on 'victims' rather than 'survivors' as the latter word is somewhat of a euphemism. The word 'victim' captures women's predicament soon after the abuse—the very stage at which the police intervention took place which is discussed in this book. Taking this temporal perspective into consideration, the word 'survivor' seems rather presumptuous. Furthermore, women differ in the time for, and extent of, recovery. The word 'survivors' might accurately describe some but not all women, and certainly does not accurately portray the feelings of many at the earlier stages after victimization. There were also, in my sample, four women who, as victims of murder, literally did not survive the assaults against them.

There are various forms of 'abuse' that women define as violence and, more pertinently, from which they seek police protection. These range from various types of 'controlling behaviours' (including: limiting a woman's contact with her family and friends; scrutiny of, and restriction of her actions; threats to hurt her, her children and/or her pets; and financial control) to physical violence, rape, and murder (Edwards 1986; Dobash *et al.* 1996; Dutton 1995; Hilton 1993; Mullender 1996). Violence is not only restricted to those women who remain with violent partners. It can continue, and indeed sometimes become more severe, after separation or divorce.[1] Any working definition of domestic violence needs to take these factors into account. Hence the working definition of domestic violence decided upon for this research was: 'the physical, sexual and emotional abuse of women by male partners or ex-partners'. It might be thought that as the main concern of this study is with police decisions to arrest, controlling behaviours, referred to in this definition as 'emotional abuse', are irrelevant. Such behaviours are not irrelevant as the study examines the various reasons why women call the police—one of which is, of course, emotional abuse. Furthermore, whilst the police rarely

[1] Figures for England and Wales in 1986 and 1987 show that in approximately 30 per cent of incidents where men killed women spouses, the couple were separated (cited in Edwards 1989: 200).

charge violent men with psychological violence,[2] they do sometimes arrest suspects without evidence of physical violence where the victim is being subjected to emotional violence (see Chapter 5).

The working definition is gender specific as the research was concerned only with violence against women by men and not vice versa, as all studies point to this as the most prevalent form of reported interpersonal violence. It is also specific to heterosexual relationships and excludes violence between other family members. It is not intended to deny the existence of these other forms of inter-relationship violence but to have attempted to cover them all would have been unrealistic. Furthermore, to include other types of rela-tionship would have detracted from the issue of violence rooted in specific power imbalances between male and female intimates (see Chapter 7).

In order to understand the dynamics of these intimate relation-ships as well as the dynamics of the various interactions between police, prosecutors, victims, and suspects, a number of different, yet complementary, data sets were created. To guide the reader through the creation of each data set, the rest of this chapter is structured according to the progress of all calls relating to domestic violence which were recorded by the police during a seven month period in 1993 (as shown in figure 1).

Stage one charts the incidents reported and the control room response; *stage two*, the decisions regarding arrest; and, *stage three*, the decisions regarding prosecution.

Stage one: reported incidents and the control room response

It is quite unusual for officers on patrol to encounter a crime, let alone a domestic incident, while it is occurring (Ackroyd *et al.* 1992). Police information about the majority of incidents comes from members of the public calling the police control room. Some callers want to pass on messages, or enquire about local services, and some need only advice which can be given over the telephone. When the police are contacted in relation to a crime (whether it has

---

[2] Since this study was completed there have been two cases of domestic violence which resulted in the Thames Valley Police charging the suspects with 'psychological assault'.

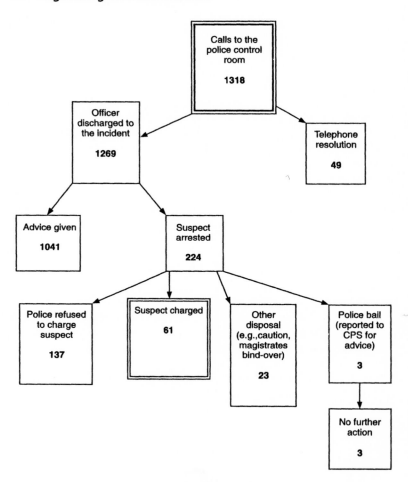

FIG. 2.1a.   Incidence and progress of domestic violence calls reported during a seven month period—police action

occurred, is occurring, or is anticipated) the telephone operator in the control room records brief details about the incident. He then passes this information to a radio operator (sometimes called the dispatcher) also located in the control room (police officers or civilians). The radio operator interprets information received and decides whether police action is required, and, if so, whether the response should be immediate or routine (in due

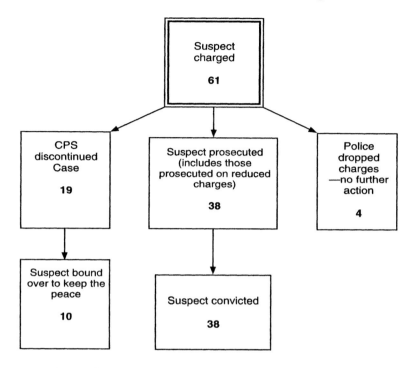

Fig. 2.1b. Incidence and progress of domestic violence calls reported during a seven month period—CPS and court action[a]

[a] This chart does not include information on sentencing decisions. These data are presented in Chapter 7.

course). He[3] is responsible for assigning a 'unit' (dispatching a patrol car or an area beat officer) to each incident. Communicating with officers through either car or personal radios, the radio operator will give the officers as much information about the location of the incident, the parties involved, and the caller as is possible.[4]

---

[3] Throughout the book the male pronoun is employed when references are made to police personnel (including control room operators, patrol officers, and administrative staff) as well as to prosecutors, although, of course, some of the interviewees were female. This allows for a clear distinction between the 'service providers' and the 'service users', that is, the victims of domestic violence.

[4] In emergencies, when urgent 'resourcing' is necessary, the telephone operator transfers brief details, as 'partial incidents'. so that the radio operator can dispatch a patrol car, and then continues to interrogate the caller.

Before the advent of information technology, details were recorded on paper and passed manually between operators. The responding officer, on return to the station, would then complete the information on the message pad, providing details of how the case was dealt with. Thames Valley Police now stores information on computers using programs devised for the management of calls into the control room and transfers this information via the computer network. This computerized command and control system (known as 'CoCo') is an electronic means of creating, storing, and providing information. An 'incident log' (a computer record), detailing all communications in the control room, is created for every call requiring a police response and for some of the calls which are resolved on the telephone. When a caller is connected to an operator an information 'page' is created on the operator's computer screen. This 'page' requires him to interpret the information gleaned from the caller and to document relevant details about the caller and the incident.

When the incident has been dealt with by a patrol officer, even if it is referred to a specialist police department, the 'live' incident log is closed. The radio operators type a concluding comment, such as 'advice given—NFA [no further action]' or 'person arrested'. A closing classification will also be recorded: for example, 'crime—violence against the person' or 'disorder—domestic dispute'. These incident logs are held on CoCo for approximately a month and then retained on magnetic tapes for a further year, after which only paper records are kept.

This computerized information management system facilitated the easy retrieval of data on all reports of domestic violence.[5] The computerized system also enabled me to peruse (from terminals in a number of different locations) reports on all incidents within the Thames Valley. The data recorded on the computer were examined every twenty-four or forty-eight hours. All disputes were considered in order to select those involving domestic violence. However, it was found that some incidents of domestic violence, where the caller had not known that the incident involved partners or ex-partners, were subsumed within other classifications such as 'burglary in progress', 'crime: violence against the person', and 'criminal damage'. Thus,

---

[5] Previous studies had relied on message pad entries which were fallible. For example, Edwards (1989) suggested that officers recorded information only about incidents where some sort of positive action, usually an arrest, had taken place.

these other classifications were also searched in order to identify as many of the reported disputes as possible. It is believed that by conducting such a thorough inspection all of the domestic disputes were identified which fell within the working definition adopted by this study.[6]

During the seven month period, from 1 February to 31 August 1993, there were 1318 calls relating to domestic violence recorded on the command and control system in the two areas under study. As figure 2.1a. shows, patrol officers responded to 96 per cent (1269) of these requests for assistance. Essential details for all of these incidents, such as the unique reference number, the grade of response (routine or immediate), the opening and closing classifications,[7] the date of the incident, and the result, were taken from the incident log and recorded on a statistical database.

At any one time there are a number of calls which do not result in an officer being dispatched to the scene, but are resolved on the telephone. In a proportion of these cases (this cannot accurately be estimated) the operator chooses to create an incident log.[8] Forty-nine (4 per cent) of all calls during the fieldwork period were recorded as 'telephone resolutions', but, of course, there was no way of knowing how many incidents were resolved on the telephone without being recorded. To discover the real rate of unrecorded telephone resolutions would have necessitated a long time spent observing operators' practice with the knowledge that my presence might have encouraged an increase in the dispatch of officers and the creation of incident logs for calls which would not normally be recorded. Hence, it was resolved to ask operators how often, and why, they chose not to dispatch officers, and why they sometimes failed to record such calls.[9] Other areas of interest regarding the categorizing of incidents and the provision of relevant

[6] Of the 1318 incidents, 104 had no reference to domestic disorder or dispute in either the opening or closing classification and so would not have been identified without this more thorough searching.

[7] The category assigned to each incident when the dispute is initially reported and that assigned after the patrol officers have attended and reported back to the radio operator.

[8] Operators are supposed to record *all* calls on the computer (see chap. 3).

[9] Whilst it is recognized that this approach provides information only on the operators' perceptions of their behaviour and not on their actual behaviour, it was felt that the data would be fairly accurate. Operators, like all other interviewees, were promised anonymity and they seemed keen to 'tell it like it is', believing they had valid reasons for their occasional deviations from the 'rule book'.

information to both patrol officers and callers were also investigated through these interviews.

Interviews were sought with control room staff from all four shifts in the two areas under study.[10] Fifty-five of the sixty-five operators were interviewed.[11] Semi-structured interviews were considered appropriate for a number of reasons: first, the research issues were not clear cut; secondly, there had been little previous research in this area and hence this was largely an exploratory study; and thirdly, it was thought that the replies to the questions might be complex and discursive.

Stage two: decisions regarding arrest

Officers' decisions regarding arrest were examined from three different perspectives: that of the officers; the victims; and my own, as an observer.

Interviewing patrol officers

It was decided to interview patrol officers about their response to *specific* incidents of domestic violence because it was thought that the approach previously used by other researchers (of interviewing officers about their *general* response) can yield limited information and a sometimes distorted picture.[12] Thus, officers were interviewed about a sample of the 1269 incidents identified on the command and control computer. The cases identified from each computer search (conducted approximately every other day) were categorized into two groups (those incidents where the suspect had been arrested and those where there had been no arrest). A stratified random sample of three of every four 'arrest incidents' and one of every five 'non-arrest' incidents was selected after each

---

[10] Staff were asked to participate if they were working on the first day of interviews with each shift. Any of those who could not be interviewed on that day, due to time pressures, were interviewed on another day. Members of each shift who were not at work on the first day of interviews with their shift (whether due to sickness, rest days, or annual leave) were not pursued.

[11] Only one operator refused to be interviewed.

[12] This was found to be true. In chap. 4 this methodological approach is compared with that adopted by Edwards (1989), showing that interviews about general attitudes can result in a fairly superficial understanding of 'cop-culture', without revealing the factors which influence decision-making at the scene of incidents.

computer search and the responding officer interviewed as soon after the incident as possible. Hence, officers were interviewed about 168 incidents where there had been an arrest and 219 incidents where no one had been arrested. Whilst it was not possible to ensure that the sample included an equal proportion of incidents from each of the two territorial areas under study, it was found that the distribution of all of the incidents across the two areas was almost identical to the distribution of the interview incidents. The majority of officers were keen to co-operate with the research and were generous with their time. A few, on first being approached, seemed nervous and stated that they did not have the time to be interviewed, but when approached again, a short time later, all agreed to take part. Hence, the study boasts a 100 per cent success rate.[13]

The main aim of these interviews was to compare the features of those cases which resulted in arrest and prosecution with those in which a decision was taken not to proceed. Both open-ended and pre-coded questions were used in order to gather quantitative and qualitative data. Pre-coded directive questions can lead to a loss of accuracy because the answers might reflect the biases and world view of the researcher rather than that of the interviewee. This problem was minimized because the coding scheme grew out of the responses to open questions in the pilot study. Similarly, accuracy and reliability can be lost if an interviewee becomes annoyed at not being able to give, or expand on, his or her views. This frustration was avoided by allowing all interviewees to answer any question as fully as they considered appropriate. Most of what the interviewees said was recorded even when it was not relevant to the study and would later be discarded. In this sense, each interviewee was given the freedom to tell his 'story' as he believed it had happened. Of course, it is not possible to be free of the effects of interviewer–interviewee interaction. As in all social interactions, in interviews parties have certain expectations about each other's attitudes which can affect their responses. However, methodological triangulation can go some way towards improving the reliability of the data.

Occasionally other attempts were made to assess the reliability of the information gathered from officers. In most cases only the

[13] Occasionally an officer was called away to respond to an incident during an interview, but in all cases any outstanding questions were completed at a later date.

officer who had reported back to the control room was interviewed, but on some occasions, when his story was not clear, his partner was questioned (officers normally attended disputes in pairs). When this happened, their stories proved to be highly consistent.

Police records (crime complaint forms, witnesses' statements and, where applicable, suspect statements) were perused in those incidents which had resulted in an arrest, and for those cases which had been prosecuted *all* recorded information was examined. Of course, the printed information pertaining to each case, including witnesses' statements, had been 'constructed' by the officers in charge of the case and so it could be argued that these were not independent checks on the reliability of the interview data.[14] And it was certainly the case that there was no totally reliable way to test the accuracy or truthfulness of any officer's version of an incident where he had decided not to arrest anyone. As police failure to arrest in these cases has attracted the most adverse criticism from feminist commentators it was decided that the officers' 'stories', whether verbal or written accounts, required some substantiation. Towards this end I attempted to interview a sample of victims, whilst further validation was provided by patrol observation.

Interviewing victims

Most researchers who have wanted to appreciate the perspective of victims of domestic violence have taken their samples from Women's Aid refuges, which, it could be argued, do not contain a representative population of such victims. Refuges are politicized environments which tend to be run according to feminist philosophies and, therefore, might encourage scepticism about the criminal justice system in general and a low regard for the police in particular.[15] Also, there are some women, those with relatively high independent incomes for example, who might not choose to move into a refuge. Whilst women in refuges were spoken to (see below), a sample of the victims from incidents attended by the police was also interviewed.[16]

[14] See McConville, Sanders, and Leng (1991) for a discussion of case construction relating to suspect statements, and Maguire and Norris (1992) regarding witness statements.
[15] There is some anecdotal evidence that this has begun to change as the police have made efforts to improve their response to victims of domestic violence.
[16] Of course, this is also, to some extent, a biased sample as there are some women who choose not to report to the police. However, as this study was concerned

This sample of victims comprised all with whom the police had dealt during one month of the fieldwork period where the officer had been interviewed. It was decided not to contact victims by telephone or letter to ask if they would be willing to be interviewed, as it was thought that this would result in a poor response rate. Instead, a 'cold call' method, unannounced visits to their home, was adopted with the intention of securing the highest response rate. In order to improve the chance of gaining access into victims' homes, and for reasons of personal safety, it was agreed that I would be accompanied by a police officer. The officers were not in uniform and 'unmarked' cars were used so as to cause as little anxiety to victims as possible. This method secured a satisfactory response rate: thirty-nine of the forty-nine victims who were dealt with in the chosen month, and about whom officers were interviewed, were spoken to.[17]

It might be thought that using a police officer in order to secure access to research subjects could lead those subjects to believe that they had no choice but to agree to be interviewed. In accordance with the statement of ethical practice which informed the empirical work, I was careful to ensure that victims, as other participants, were aware of their right to refuse participation whenever and for whatever reason they wished. Furthermore, in order that the consent was freely given and informed, victims were told, in terms which were meaningful to them, what the research was about, who was undertaking it and financing it, why it was being undertaken, and how the data were to be disseminated. They were told that their 'stories' would be anonymized in order to protect their privacy.[18]

The accompanying officers were asked not to become involved in the interviews and to be as discreet as possible. This was to avoid influencing the victims and preventing them from making adverse criticisms against the police. It was thought that if the male partner was at home he might be antagonistic, or dissuade the victim from being truthful. Hence, a separate interview schedule was devised for

with the criminal justice response to domestic violence this method of sampling was considered to be most appropriate.

[17] Some victims were not at home despite repeat visits being made, some had temporarily or permanently changed address and two declined to be interviewed. One of these two women was afraid of provoking another dispute with her husband and the other was feeling unwell and did not wish to be visited on another day.

[18] The Socio-Legal Studies Association, *Statement of Ethical Practice* (1993), informed the planning and execution of the empirical work.

these occasions. Men were told that the research was intended to examine public perceptions of the police handling of disputes. This ploy enabled me to speak to the victim alone, whilst the officer took the man into another room and conducted an interview with him. Whilst originally intended as distractions, these interviews provided some valuable data. There could, of course, be an ethical objection to misleading participants as to the purpose of an interview. As stated above, freely given and informed consent to be interviewed implies a responsibility on the researcher to explain as fully as possible what the research is about and why it is being undertaken. However, it was thought that minimizing the risk of provoking further violence towards the victims outweighed this obligation to be completely truthful with their male partners. When the partners were not at home the officers were helpful in entertaining inquisitive or demanding children or pets, leaving the victim free to concentrate on the interview.

It might be assumed that women would not want to speak about something as painful or as personal as domestic violence. This did not seem to be the case. The majority of the women were keen to co-operate once the purpose of the interview had been explained. They were informed that the research was independent and, whilst having the full support of the police, was not *for* the police. They were asked to be totally honest in giving their opinions about the police and there is no reason to believe that they were not.

The purpose of the interviews with victims, apart from validating the officers' accounts, was to assess how they felt the police had responded to their calls for assistance. An attempt was made to measure the victims' expectations of the police response as well as satisfaction levels in order to provide a measure of what police 'success' or 'failure' means to each victim. In addition, victims were asked about their reasons for wanting or not wanting their partners to be arrested and prosecuted.

A less formal interviewing style was adopted for talking to victims than that used for officers or prosecutors. I was careful to choose the right time to ask another question, to know when to listen and to know when an encouraging or sympathetic response was appropriate.[19] Oakley (1981) took the view that formal,

---

[19] The interview schedules contained predominantly open-ended questions. When victims did not provide sufficient detail in their replies the flow of their monologue

survey-type interviewing was unsuited to the production of good sociological work on women. Whilst I agree with this in respect of interviewing women about the police response to their experiences of domestic violence, I would not argue along gender lines. Rather, it is about avoiding the abuse of power that an 'outsider' necessarily has over an interviewee from whom she wants to gather intimate, personal, and sometimes painful, information. Therefore, the preference should be in favour of less-structured research that avoids creating a hierarchical relationship between interviewer and interviewee. The quest for objectivity, which characterized the other interviews, was purposely abandoned here. I aimed to ask all the questions covered by the interview schedule, and indeed this was always accomplished, but victims were given the space to talk as fully as they wished, even if the details were not necessary for the research. These interviews were extremely hard work, being both emotionally demanding and time consuming. Many hours were spent drinking cups of tea, trying to ignore over-enthusiastic children or pets, and listening to distressed, but courageous women tell their stories.

As well as interviewing victims in their homes, a day was spent in the Women's Aid refuges which serve the two areas under study talking, at length, to the staff and residents. It was not considered appropriate, or even necessary for the research, to conduct structured interviews with any of these women. Conversations were used only to support the individual victim data. In one refuge I was introduced to a group of residents. I explained the nature of the research and invited the women to talk, either privately or in a group setting, about their experiences of the police. A few women left the room, making excuses that related to work or family commitments, but nine remained and a very lively group conversation ensued. We spoke for over two hours and the stories told, many of which it was decided would not be reported, brought forth a gamut of emotional responses from the women, ranging from anger to tears to laughter. In the other refuge there were fewer residents present during my visit but there was still the opportunity to speak with some of the women and a long conversation with a member of staff was very informative. The data from these

was not interrupted but, instead, 'reflecting back' questions were used later in the interview to allow for further probing of an area of interest.

conversations are necessarily extremely raw and the opinions prejudiced by the women's own experiences and their present environment. It is for these reasons that no attempt is made to generalize about abused women from this particular data set, but their comments provide some support for other aspects of the study.

Some researchers have reported that interviewees wanted to 'place' them as women with whom they could share experiences (Oakley 1981). This seemed to be the case in this research. One victim refused to let the police officer and me into her home, explaining that she was too busy to talk. Her style of communication was such that I was encouraged to return alone the following day. The woman, who then agreed to be interviewed, explained that she had not wanted to talk about the dispute in front of a man. It was not his occupation which she objected to, but his gender: 'I don't trust men, I don't want to talk to them'. It was not only being a woman, but, being a married woman ('single women just don't understand'), that made me seem sympathetic. Some of the victims asked me if I was married before discussing their relationships and seemed to believe that I would understand, in particular their reluctance to leave violent relationships, when I replied in the affirmative.

Interviewees sometimes ask questions of the researcher. Traditional ideas about interviewing, which emphasize objectivity, suggest that researchers should not offer advice or information if it might jeopardize the reliability of the data being sought. In interviews with police officers, and during patrol observation, I was sometimes asked what I thought something meant or what I thought the officers should have done. I tried to avoid giving direct answers if I thought that they might impact on the information being provided by the officer. However, in interviewing women about their experiences, such distancing is not possible or desirable. Women sometimes asked about the research or for information pertaining to their victimization. I willingly supplied them with such details. However, at other times, they asked personal questions about what they should do. In such instances I said that I felt unqualified to give such advice and gave details of the agencies that could offer help.

I was concerned that interviewing victims about painful experiences might have further harmed those participants. The ethics of social research on women's lives is a thorny issue, deserving more attention than can be paid to it in one chapter covering various different methods. All social science researchers '... have a responsibility to ensure that the physical, social and psychological well-being of research participants is not adversely affected by their research' (Socio-Legal Studies Association, *Statement of Ethical Practice*, 1993 (see footnote 20)). This is particularly important when the interviewees are relatively powerless and when they might be vulnerable to further abuse. However, the nature of domestic violence means that any 'intervention' from outside the family might be considered by the perpetrator to be provocative. Hence, research on this issue—in particular interviews conducted within the victims' homes—is more likely to result in further harm to the participants than research in most other areas of social science. This cannot mean that such studies are not contemplated, as good research can benefit the general victim population, if not these specific victims. It does mean, though, that interviewers need to be sensitive to the dangers to which victims might be exposed as a direct result of the interviewer's presence.

On two occasions the perpetrators returned home whilst the victim was being interviewed and were angered by the presence of what they assumed were two police officers. One of these men calmed down after being told that we were interested in interviewing both him and his partner on the police response to requests for help and he agreed to be interviewed by the police officer. However, the other man refused to be interviewed, became verbally abusive, and told his wife not to talk to us. Seeing that we were provoking his anger, which could have made her vulnerable to further abuse, we should perhaps have left immediately. However, she asked us to stay and once he went out into the garden she continued to talk and answer our questions. She wanted to 'have her say', as she put it and, furthermore, when the interview was over she wanted advice and information from the officer about the possible civil and criminal avenues she could pursue. According to strict ethical standards I should have aborted this interview. However, I decided at the time that, on balance, it was in her best interests to continue. This is, of course, debatable.

Another interview almost certainly breached ethical standards. The incident about which I wanted to interview the victim was unusual in that the victim's son had called the police and the victim had told the police, in no uncertain tones, to leave. When the officers insisted on talking to the son the woman attacked one of them. When I visited her she told me on the doorstep that she did not wish to be interviewed by another 'nosy bloody cow'. She added that she hated the police and thought that they should not interfere with 'rows' between couples. She considered me to be another 'interfering busybody'. However, she proceeded, still on the doorstep, to tell me why 'people should not have the right to interfere between husbands and wives who choose to batter each other'. With this 'encouragement', I continued to ask her the questions on the interview schedule without looking at the schedule and without recording her responses. We 'chatted' for about fifteen minutes after which she realized that I had 'got my bloody interview' and told me that I was a 'cheeky cow'. At this stage she smiled at me and told me to 'piss off'. I thanked her profusely and asked her if I could use her comments for my research, to which she replied 'I don't care what you do with them', laughed and shut the door.

In no way could it be said that I had secured her consent before the 'interview' and her 'consent' after the event was not informed and yet I have used her interview to inform the research analysis. Gaining consent to interview someone is not a discrete event. It is an on-going process where consent has to be agreed on and then may need renegotiating and may be denied during the interview. Hence, her consent was not forthcoming and yet she answered my questions. I continued asking questions because I believed that she might have been reconsidering her decision. Conducting interviews is a process. It is not always clear when the interview has started and when it has ended. For example, occasionally interviewees say things which they wish to be 'off the record', that is not recorded as part of the 'formal interview'. This 'doorstep' interview was a fluid situation whereby the woman formally declined to be interviewed but then stayed on her doorstep describing the police response to the recent incident. At any time she could have shut her door or refused to speak but, despite her initial decision, she continued to talk. Hence, I continued to listen and to ask further questions. My justification for breaching ethical standards by analysing and discussing the interview is founded in the atypical nature of her opinions. However, whilst accurate and truthful reporting of findings serves the integrity of social science as a discipline, my decision to use these data did not meet the ethical standards which I intended to follow in *all* cases.[20]

[20] There needs to be an *honest* debate within the social sciences about researchers' behaviour when faced with such predicaments.

The other interviewees were all happy to co-operate and the majority admitted to enjoying the opportunity to talk. Only one interview, lasting over two hours, seemed to cause the interviewee much distress. However, at the end of the interview the woman thanked me for giving her the opportunity to discuss things about which she had never before talked to anyone, saying that she felt 'better' for having confided in someone. As with all other interviewees, she was informed about the available sources of information and assistance.

Patrol observation

Observation of police officers whilst attending domestic disputes was considered necessary because it was thought that certain types of behaviour or ways of interacting might be so taken for granted by the police that they would be unaware of them and, therefore, not mention them. Observation field notes provided supplementary data that qualified and helped to interpret the findings obtained through interviews which were, necessarily, retrospective reports of the interviewees' own behaviour. By enabling me to record behaviour as it occurred, it filled the gap that detachment or distortions in recall may have created, and allowed for comparisons to be made between what officers said they did and what they actually did.

Securing permission to 'shadow' patrol officers on duty was easy. Officers of all ranks were enthusiastic and co-operated readily. They knew what I wanted to observe, and the disputants, and any other members of the public whose homes were entered, were told briefly of my identity and purpose in being there. Hence, professional ethics were not compromised. Patrol observation was carried out over 106 hours. Most of this work was carried out during the late 'shifts', and in particular on Fridays, Saturdays, or Sundays.

The work involved going out in a patrol car with one or two officers, for the duration of a shift, and 'shadowing' them whilst they responded to any incidents, and conducting informal interviews (asking questions of the officers in order to make sense of what was happening). Field notes were not taken whilst on patrol, as this would have created a distance between the officers and myself. Short visits back to the station (meal-breaks, for example) provided valuable time to make brief notes, but detailed notes were written after the shift was over.

Ethnography, with its roots in social anthropology, derives from a desire to understand the everyday meanings and definitions of group members and from a reluctance to impose on the 'actors' the concepts and meanings of the academics carrying out the research. Information on the culture, values, and belief systems of members of specific organizations are thus revealed.[21] From observing patrol officers, I was able to interpret their organizational culture. It was aimed to observe how disputants reacted to the presence of the police; what goals, other than the 'official' goals, the participants seemed to be pursuing; whether the goals of the various participants were compatible or antagonistic; what were the different behaviours; and what were the qualities and the effects of the behaviour.

Observational work, as well as interviews, necessitates a balance between professional objectivity and the establishment of rapport which will result in co-operation. It was decided that it would be appropriate to remain with one group of officers in each of the two areas, rather than attempting to observe all of the different teams, in order to minimize the 'observer effect' whilst maximizing affinity. I soon became familiar with the officers working for these 'teams' and they accepted me as 'part of the team', frequently joking and sharing gossip about other officers.[22] Seeing me temporarily as a member of the group, none of the officers expressed any resentment at my presence. Having completed a substantial number of interviews prior to commencing patrol observation work, I was fairly familiar with the organization, the legal as well as the working rules and, probably most importantly, the argot. This knowledge expedited acceptance.

Participant observers, who progress by a 'discovery-based approach', become, necessarily, immersed in the 'field' (Burgess 1984). That is, the observer attempts to empathize with the actors in the social situation and to understand how they are interpreting the actions and behaviours of significant others. Aware of the knowledge to be acquired by becoming immersed in the field, I was, nonetheless, keen to maintain some distance from the interac-

---

[21] Holdaway's (1983) study of British police and Punch's (1979) study of officers in Amsterdam are good examples of participant observation.

[22] Occasionally they told jokes or made sexist or racist comments. However, these occasions were few and far between. As someone trying to blend into the environment and not alienate myself from the officers, I had consciously to resist the temptation to challenge prejudice.

tion between police officers and disputants so as to have minimal effect on the dynamics of the situation. Sometimes this was difficult because, as a woman within a still male-dominated environment, female disputants invariably tried to include me in dialogue. They maintained eye contact with me whilst 'telling their story' or directed their questions towards me. This was, not surprisingly, most conspicuous when the officers were both male. In addition, away from the scene, I would often be asked by officers to assess their response. Whilst careful not to be judgemental, which might have affected their behaviour for the rest of that shift, I did, at least casually, discuss the incidents, the disputants, and the officers' responses.

Irving, in a report for the Royal Commission on Criminal Procedure, claimed that he became so accepted by a group of CID officers that his presence had no effect on their behaviour (cited in Smith and Gray 1983). This claim requires some qualifications. The first time that a researcher joins a subject group she or he is bound to have some impact on the dynamics of that group, or, if observing just one actor, there will almost certainly be some 'observer effect' on the behaviour of that individual. However, once the observer has spent even a short amount of time with the observed that effect appears to be minimal. As Smith and Gray note: 'The longer the observer is with [the police officers], the more the officers tend to settle back into their usual pattern of activity' (1983: 302).

Hence, 106 hours of patrol observation was considered sufficient to establish rapport and to better understand the interactions between police and disputants whilst minimizing the personal consequences of observation work. This type of fieldwork invariably means working unsociable hours, as well as exposing oneself to unusual and, at times, intimidating situations. There is also the problem of over-involvement in the group being studied, of becoming more of a participant and less of an observer. Several researchers have discussed this problem. James Patrick (1973), who carried out a participant observation study of a Glasgow gang of youths, found that he got too close to the gang. This resulted in him missing things about the gang that an outside observer might have seen. He was also concerned that his presence might have altered the behaviour of the gang. Similarly, William Foote Whyte (1943) found that whilst he had begun as a non-participant observer, as he became accepted into the community he almost became a 'non-observant participant'.

Punch also experienced the problem of over-identifying too readily with the police officers he was observing. He explained that '...the patrol group is a cohesive social unit and the policeman's world is full of seductive interest so that it is all too easy to "go native"' (1979: 16). Thus, observation work should be stopped when the researcher becomes too closely aligned with the subjects under study, reducing his or her ability to look beyond their immediate explanations for behaviour or actions. I realised that I had spent sufficient time observing officers when I looked forward to speeding and weaving through traffic with the police car 'blues and twos' going; felt disappointed when arriving at yet another activated burglar alarm which had been set off by a cat or an electrical fault; and empathized too readily with officers who missed the excitement of a violent pub brawl because they were held up at a neighbourhood dispute over dustbins.

Stage three: decisions regarding prosecution

Having examined the officers' decisions regarding arrest, I intended to try to understand the factors which best predicted the next stage: a criminal charge being laid. Of the 224 men arrested for various offences connected with domestic violence, sixty-one (27 per cent) were charged (although not necessarily with the offence for which they were arrested). It was originally decided that, in those cases where a suspect was charged with a different offence to the one for which he was arrested or where the charge was subsequently changed, the custody officer would be interviewed to establish the reasons for any changes. This was the only aim not achieved because, during the pilot study, it was found that the responses offered by custody officers did not warrant the time spent trying to interview them.[23] Thus, it was aimed to understand the decisions made by custody officers through qualitative and quantitative analysis of the officer and victim interview data as well as the patrol observation notes. In addition to this, official police records were examined.

In order to inspect custody records for those cases where a suspect was arrested, the co-operation of the custody officers was necessary. Both custody areas were nearly always busy, with patrol officers, suspects, and solicitors demanding their attention. This invariably

[23] For an explanation of why the interviews with custody officers proved to be unproductive see chap. 6.

meant spending a great deal of time waiting for a quiet moment when custody officers could trace the relevant forms or locate details of a suspect on the custody computer.[24] This provided opportunities to observe interactions between different officers and between officers and suspects.

Sixty-two per cent (thirty-eight) of the sixty-one charged suspects were prosecuted (although not necessarily with the offence for which they were originally charged) and in all of these cases the suspect was convicted. Information about prosecutions and court results was provided by the Administration Support Unit, the department responsible for communication with the courts. Again, various databases (interviews and official records) were drawn on in order to distinguish the characteristics of charged incidents which were successfully prosecuted from those that did not result in a prosecution. However, the main source of information was the Crown Prosecution Service.

Interviews with Crown Prosecutors

Semi-structured interviews were carried out with prosecutors in relation to twenty-five cases which were dropped or where different charges from the ones initially preferred were pressed at the prosecution stage.[25] Prosecutors were asked to explain decisions not to proceed or to agree to a reduced charge; to evaluate the response of the officer in charge; and to comment on police handling of, and the criminal justice system's response to, domestic violence cases in general. Prosecutors, like police officers, were enthusiastic about the research and keen to take part, appearing to talk frankly and fully, and giving me access to relevant files.

The role of various actors in the decision-making processes

The fieldwork described above uncovered the decisions made by the various actors in the negotiation of domestic disputes. The progress

---

[24] These computers were introduced into the custody suites in April 1993, over two months into the fieldwork. As there were some teething problems in the early months, paper records were usually referred to for accurate information.

[25] There were twenty-seven such cases in total but administration staff at the Crown Prosecution Service could not locate the files for the remaining two. There was no reason to believe that these were 'lost' in anticipation of critical academic scrutiny.

of each case examined was followed from the initial call made by victims to the first response of the patrol officer and the choices made by prosecutors and those responsible for sentencing offenders. At each stage the role of the victim was examined. The study sought to understand her influence on police and prosecutors' decisions and, in doing so, explored her own personal aims and motivations. The following chapter begins with her initial call for help.

3

The Control Room: the First Stage in the Decision-Making Process?

The control room is the critical point at which public demands can be met by available police resources. Control room operators deal with all incidents, emergency or otherwise, reported over the telephone. Hence, it has been argued that this is the first stage in the police decision-making process and that operators, like patrol officers, have the opportunity to exercise discretion in the disposal of cases (Goldstein 1960). This book is primarily concerned with identifying the factors which impact on the decisions regarding the arrest and prosecution of domestic violence perpetrators. Thus, it is important to examine the responses of control room operators to see if they influence the decisions taken by officers at the scene of domestic disputes.

Commentators who have argued that the control room does play a significant role in the response of patrol officers have tended to advocate one of three explanations. The first explanation focuses on operators' ability to exercise discretion by 'filtering' out reported incidents (most notably incidents of domestic violence), and choosing not to dispatch patrol officers. This discretion is said to be structured by cultural prejudices about offences and/or offenders and/or callers (see Ekblom and Heal 1985; Faragher 1985, in the United Kingdom, and Sumrall, Roberts, and Farmer 1981 (cited in Edwards 1989); La Fave 1969; Parnas 1971, in the United States). The second explanation emphasizes the ability of control room operators to define situations for patrol officers in advance of their arrival at the scene. Hence, operators are considered to play an integral role in the 'case construction' process. Whilst McConville, Sanders, and Leng recognize that patrol officers at the scene seek, elicit, and construct facts (by questions and observation), as part of the initial construction process, they argue that they do so from a perspective already partly 'constructed' by the information received from the control room (1991: 34). The third explanation is provided by Pepinski who explains how operators, aided by technology, exert powerful control over the actions of patrol officers (1975, 1976, cited in Ericson 1982). The patrol officer is seen as an automaton who is routinely responsive to, and made responsible through, the dispatcher who closely follows the rule book and force policies.

These writers all agree that operators' decisions are consequential for the patrol officer, and, therefore, for the individuals who make the calls (or about whom the calls are made). However, their explanations were put forward prior to the establishment of a computer-aided dispatch system[1] (aimed at assisting the police in managerial control over the allocation of resources) and new force policies on domestic violence (introduced after the 1990/60 Home Office Circular[2]). Also many of these writers had conducted their empirical work in North America. It is now appropriate to reconsider the role of the control room in the United Kingdom in the light of these recent national changes.

Examining the various stages at which choices are made in the control room, and looking, in particular, at the 'mediation' between callers and patrol officers, this chapter will assess whether operators influence the decisions made by patrol officers at the scene. Hence, the choices regarding the dispatch of patrol officers, the categorization of disputes, and the provision of information to patrol officers will be examined. In order to achieve these aims, three sources of information will be drawn on: first, data gathered from computer records of all domestic disputes over the seven month period of the fieldwork (including incidents resolved on the telephone); secondly, data from interviews with operators; and, thirdly, data from interviews with patrol officers.[3]

Choosing to dispatch an officer

Most writers agree that domestic violence is massively under-reported.[4] Many have also maintained that there is a further high attrition rate within the control room once the decision to report

---

[1] Discussed in chap. 2.   [2] Discussed in chap. 1.
[3] See chap. 2 for a discussion of these methods.
[4] See Morley and Mullender (1994) for a recent review of the extent of under-reporting.

has been made. It has been argued that dispatchers screen or divert domestic assault cases (a practice that has been referred to as 'cuffing') or otherwise accord them a lower priority than other non-domestic assault incidents. Research carried out in Canada, for example, estimated that for victims of domestic violence there was only about a 50 per cent chance of getting help other than advice from the dispatcher (Dutton 1977). Manning has claimed that historically, family violence calls have been categorized as low-priority misdemeanours deserving little police interest, and that call-screening is still common, even with computer-aided dispatch systems. He argued that twenty-five years of improvement in information technology had done little to alter the quality of police response to reported incidents (Manning 1992). However, Edwards (1986) found that 'cuffing' was rare, although not unknown.

Since the majority of these studies were published, the Home Office (Circular 1990/60) has advised that all 'domestic' calls should result in the dispatch of a police officer at some stage:

The first priority for police officers answering such calls is to find out whether immediate police help is required, or whether there is no imminent danger of an assault. Even if immediate help is not sought, the call must be recorded and *there should always be some sort of positive action* to investigate the case—for instance, an interview with the victim to establish in more detail what prompted her call and whether it was part of a history of violence. (Para. 12.) (My emphasis.)

Thames Valley Police incorporated this recommendation to control room operators in its force policy on domestic violence. Hence, evidence of 'cuffing' in the Thames Valley Police could be considered to be contrary to force policy. It would also, more importantly, be a clear manifestation of control room operators using their discretionary powers. However, little evidence of this practice was found. Records of reported incidents suggest that there were very few calls which did not result in a visit by a patrol officer. As mentioned in the previous chapter, there were only forty-nine reports of domestic violence which were resolved on the telephone during the seven month fieldwork period—a mere 4 per cent of all calls—and in the majority of these cases a visit from a patrol officer was clearly unnecessary.

Almost half of these forty-nine calls reported incidents which were over before the caller contacted the police (none were particularly serious). Other calls reported threats made over the telephone by ex-partners and disputes which had ended whilst the caller was talking to the operator (often the perpetrator had left because the police had been called). Most of the callers did not request police attendance but were keen for their complaint to be recorded in case of further disputes, and some requested information on other sources of help. The majority of these calls were from the alleged victim (in all of the incidents reported where the caller was a relative or friend of the alleged victim the dispute was over). When asked why, in general, they would choose not to dispatch an officer to a domestic dispute, the operators gave the same reasons as had clearly been applied in these cases.

Whilst the computer records suggested that operators rarely chose not to dispatch a patrol officer to domestic disputes, it was necessary to establish whether they resolved some incidents on the telephone for which they did not make records. Hence, operators were asked how frequently they chose not to dispatch an officer. Two-thirds said that they rarely, or never, did this, whilst a third said that they sometimes did, but that in such cases they would ask the local area beat officer to follow up the incident. Only two of the fifty-five operators admitted to frequently 'cuffing' complaints of domestic violence. Over half of the civilian operators said that they did not feel qualified to judge the necessity of a response and so were particularly cautious. They dispatched officers even when they thought that it probably was not necessary. As one said: 'I'd always dispatch an officer because there's a fine line between arguments going into violence and people losing control.' Ekblom and Heal (1982) call this the unofficial 'just in case' rule: the need for all police personnel to 'cover their back' against any likely complaint.

The majority of operators claimed that if they considered that it was unnecessary to dispatch an officer they would make sure that the caller had sufficient advice and understood that they would not be seeing an officer, and, furthermore, that they agreed with this decision, before terminating the call. They explained that they would rarely make a unilateral decision not to dispatch an officer: 'Providing the caller is satisfied with the advice given—it's an informal contract with the caller. We send an officer if they're insistent.' The consensus seemed to be that 'If they (the callers) want attendance, they'll get attendance'.

The demands of the callers and the fear of repercussions meant that operators rarely chose not to dispatch an officer. Additionally, the computer system and the high demands on operators' time seemed to encourage dispatch. With each call a 'page' appears on the operator's terminal requesting information, the purpose of which is to facilitate the process of dispatching an officer. With constant demands on limited resources[5] the operators did not appear to have the time to make decisions about the allocation of resources, and, consequently, they seemed to be almost automatically electing to dispatch. Therefore, as far as the choice to dispatch an officer was concerned, it appeared that operators rarely exercised discretion.

The grade of dispatch

The command and control system was originally established, in the 1970s, to ensure that calls from the public were being met with as quick a response as was possible. There were two main reasons for the assumed need for rapid response. First, it was thought necessary to satisfy the public's increasing demand for swift police action and, secondly, it was believed that it would improve the arrest and conviction rates by ensuring that officers arrived at incidents quickly enough to apprehend offenders. The police laid down a minimum response time for all calls, irrespective of the nature of the call, leaving control room staff without discretion (Waddington 1993).

This way of allocating resources soon proved to be unpopular with the public[6] who, whilst appreciating the rapid response to their calls, wanted more officers visible in their community, to provide an illusion of safety and order (Waddington 1993). The police were similarly disappointed with the rapid response system. Command and control was creating 'fire brigade' policing without securing a substantially higher number of arrests (Holdaway 1977). It was decided that, whilst the police still needed an immediate response to emergencies, they could defer many calls without any adverse effect. Hence, the need to set priorities was recognized. It has been argued that the changeover to the graded response system[7] returned

---

[5] Periods of time spent retrieving information in the control rooms served as opportunities for occasional observation work, and confirmed the operators' opinions that the control room is usually very busy.

[6] Research conducted in Kansas City, America, showed that citizens were willing to accept longer response times if they were given realistic expectations of when the officers would arrive at the scene (Kelling *et al.* 1974).

[7] This system is now in place in all police forces in England and Wales, with calls being assigned an immediate or a routine response according to specific criteria.

the powers of discretion to control room staff, by allowing operators to decide which incident 'deserved' an urgent response and
which could be deferred or dealt with routinely (Waddington
1993). Whilst this is undoubtedly so, the Thames Valley Police
study found that operators did not exercise their discretion in an
arbitrary way, but followed a consistent pattern, as, indeed, one
would expect when we consider the literature on police discretion
(see, for example, Hawkins 1992). When asked to identify the
features of calls reporting domestic disputes which would persuade
them to assign an immediate, rather than a routine, response, most
mentioned objective criteria such as actual, or a threat of, violence,
background noise, children present or the aggressor being present.
They all responded to the same types of information in the same
way. Hence, there was very little differentiation in operators' interpretations of the 'facts' elicited from callers. It became apparent that
'default decisions' were made whereby certain types of information
necessarily resulted in certain decisions, regardless of which operator had taken the call.

Of the 1269 Thames Valley incidents attended by patrol officers,
48 per cent were assigned a routine response and 52 per cent an
immediate response.[8] If the grade of dispatch impacts on the patrol
officer's response we might expect that it would have some effect on
the decision to arrest. Hence, if all things were equal, calls
responded to immediately would be more likely to result in an
arrest. A rapid response is what many victims of domestic violence
expect from the police,[9] and yet it was not correlated with the
decision to arrest: 18 per cent of those incidents which were
assigned an immediate response resulted in an arrest, which is
identical to the overall rate of arrest.[10] There are two possible
explanations for this. First, the factors which most influenced patrol
officers were to be found at the scene of the incident (see Chapters 4
and 5). They were typically strong enough to outweigh any preconceptions (whether formed by the grade of response assigned or
by information provided) which the officer might have brought with

[8] These findings match exactly those of Waddington's research on the graded
response of *all* calls over a three week period in a control room in another area of the
Thames Valley Police.
[9] See the discussion of victims' expectations of the police in chap. 7.
[10] The correlation between response time and its police decisions has been fairly
well undermined by various other studies (see, for example, Manning 1988).

him to the incident. Secondly, the patrol officer might take little notice of the grade assigned.

Ericson has argued that patrol officers have techniques and devices to circumvent the control of the dispatcher (1982). They alter the dispatcher's priorities and instructions by delaying their responses, not responding at all, or responding even when not called to do so and not informing the dispatcher about their actions (Ericson 1982; Manning 1977).[11] Manning (1979, 1980) believes that this is because patrol officers base immediacy more on the context of the call than on the official priority system. Ericson similarly contends that: '. . . variable responses mirror the *contextual* nature of patrol officers' judgements, as well as their level of desire for an exciting drive and for the work that awaits them at the encounter' (1982: 95).

Oppenlander, who compared response times to domestic violence incidents with those for non-domestic violence, holding constant other variables, found that police officers took longer to reach the scene of domestic assaults. Interviews with these officers revealed that they delayed their response in the hope that the 'problems' would be sorted out before they arrived on the scene (1982). Similarly, 54 per cent of the officers Edwards interviewed believed that a 'cooling off' period was helpful when dealing with domestic disputes (1986). In neither of these studies was it the decision of the dispatcher to delay the response, indeed the response was delayed in spite of the dispatcher.

It seems that, contrary to Pepinski's theory, the actions of patrol officers were not dictated by control room operators and, furthermore, when patrol officers responded to incidents as instructed by operators this cannot be shown to have had any impact on the outcome of the police-citizen encounter.

The categorization of disputes

Research has suggested that the information given by a caller, which is coded within organizational categories and passed on to patrol officers, is crucial for understanding their response. For example, Parnas (1967) found that the information given to the dispatcher,

---

[11] During the empirical study a patrol officer was observed responding to two calls to which he had not been dispatched.

interacting with his or her attitudes, determined the categorization assigned to domestic incidents. This, he argued, determines both the speed of the officer's response and the officer's attitudes towards the parties involved before he even reaches the incident. However, there was no correlation between the categories assigned to incidents of domestic violence in the Thames Valley and the outcome of the police response.

As with the grade of dispatch, the officers made decisions according to criteria discovered at the incident, and not according to information provided prior to their arrival at the incident. Also, officers soon learnt not to be too influenced by information provided by the control room as it was sometimes highly unreliable. Officers often mentioned that the categories assigned to incidents did not accurately describe the incident which they had attended. Indeed, sometimes they complained that the classification bore no resemblance to the incident they arrived at. This complaint was supported by the recorded data. Some domestic disputes had, for example, been initially classified as burglaries. This may have been as a result of confusion—an estranged partner seen entering a home through a window or by forcing a door could, understandably, be considered, by a neighbour, to be a burglar. Alternatively, it may have been as a result of a deliberate attempt to mislead the telephone operator—some victims admitted that they had told the telephone operator that a stranger was trying to break into their home in the hope of securing an immediate response.

As it was not always clear why a specific incident had been assigned a particular label, operators were asked how they would classify a call from a woman who alleged that she had been assaulted by her partner. Less than half of the operators agreed on a classification. The labels assigned were variable,[12] and the range of responses suggested confusion and a lack of an understood and applied policy.[13] For example, some said that they would classify it as a 'violent domestic', some as a 'disorder', some as a 'crime', etc. The responses were also inconsistent with what the operators do in practice. Use of some of the categories seemed to be random and interchangeable. The data suggested that two apparently very similar reports might result in the assignation of any of two or three

---

[12] Ericson (1982) found this to be the case with most offences.
[13] The Thames Valley policy did not cover the categorization of incidents.

categories. Indeed, when operators were asked to explain how different categories should be assigned, their replies demonstrated a great deal of confusion. However, the majority were not concerned by inconsistencies. As one explained: 'It doesn't matter what we categorize them as—the main concern is to brief the officer attending—the categories are not important.' However, the descriptions of the incidents were, more often than not, extremely brief. Often patrol officers were told only that 'It's a domestic', without any further information.

More often than not, at this initial stage the operator is reliant on brief, and often ambiguous or incoherent, messages from callers (Morgan and Newburn 1997). Hence, he is not able to offer the patrol officer a reliable classification. Many of the patrol officers I spoke to complained about the unreliability of the information received from operators, which led them to feel sceptical about the details given about most cases. This scepticism meant that they were usually reluctant to allow the information to influence their approach to disputes.

The provision of information

Operators have access to intelligence on suspects (information on bail, firearms, previous offences, injunctions, etc.) and are supposed to provide patrol officers with any details which might be relevant to an incident. Consequently, they are in a position to influence officers' responses by 'constructing' suspects before officers reach the scene. However, operators in the Thames Valley Police did not, on the whole, provide patrol officers with enough information to influence their decisions. This was not only the opinion of the patrol officers, but also of the operators themselves. One operator, critical of his civilian colleagues, said: 'Some just say "domestic" and unless an officer asks for more information they just pass it on.'

Many patrol officers complained that they either received insufficient information prior to arriving at the dispute or, less frequently, they received inaccurate or misleading information. For example, one officer responded to a call from a woman whose estranged husband had forced an entry into her home whilst she was out and damaged items of her property. The radio operator had told him that this was a domestic dispute, but had provided no other details. The perpetrator was no longer present when the officer arrived at the scene and so he left after advising the woman but having taken no further action. It was only later that the officer learnt that on the day before this incident the estranged husband had held his wife hostage in her home and threatened her. Officers from another shift had used shields and dogs to force an entry into the home and taken the suspect before the court for breaching an injunction. The judge had warned him that if he went back to his wife's home he would be imprisoned. Neither the victim nor the control room operator had provided the officer with this crucial information. Accurate information provided by the control room might have resulted in a very different disposal.

There are essentially two ways in which operators could provide patrol officers with accurate and thorough information on domestic incidents. First, they could attempt to obtain clear and concise details from callers and, secondly, they could check available information on the names or addresses of disputants.

Ekblom and Heal's study of control room operators' interactions with the public concluded that on many occasions much more information could have been obtained from the caller—possibly avoiding the necessity of dispatching a mobile patrol at all.[14] And because operators hung up too soon, typically with the 'we'll send someone round straight away' message, they had little information to give to patrol officers on the way to the dispute. These authors argued that if operators took greater care over eliciting more information there would be less ambiguity and a closer correlation between public needs and police deployments (1982). However, 80 per cent of Thames Valley operators said that the callers were often unable or reluctant to co-operate in the process of gathering information. Either they were incoherent, or they had little knowledge of the dispute, or some purposely gave false accounts of the dispute. As one operator explained: 'It's not always easy to get information from the caller—they just want an officer dispatched and don't want to answer questions.' A fifth of the operators referred, more specifically, to aborted calls: 'They worry if you're talking that you're not dispatching someone. They often hang up once they know (that an officer has been dispatched).'

---

[14]   On a few occasions, officers in the Thames Valley study argued that the control room sometimes dispatched them to incidents which should have been dealt with over the phone.

The author had the opportunity to listen to a sample of taped conversations between members of the public and operators.[15] The recordings highlighted the problems of getting accurate, intelligible information from callers. The poor audio quality of some telephone conversations meant that sometimes callers and operators could not hear each other. However, more importantly, excited or hysterical callers tended to talk very quickly and sometimes offered irrelevant information at the expense of necessary details. One caller whispered a rather cryptic message, in an attempt to avoid her partner discovering her communication with the police. She pretended to be talking to a friend on the telephone and said 'Come round—I really need to see you'. When the operator asked her for her address she would not reveal this but kept repeating 'it's happening again'. Eventually this caller replaced the receiver and the call was traced, enabling patrol officers to attend. When officers arrived they found the aftermath of a very violent dispute. Another caller was a neighbour who could hear the dispute but could not see anything, whilst a young child, calling the police about a dispute between his parents, was uniquely difficult to interrogate for pertinent information. As Ekblom and Heal noted: 'A straightforward and articulate exchange of messages between the police radio controller and members of the public seeking assistance is the exception rather than the rule' (1982: 15). Shapland and Vagg similarly commented that 'during the brief period of conversation on the telephone between . . . [operators and callers] confusion is rife' (1988: 39).

Manning (1992) argued that because calls made by the public are typically so complex and imprecise they need to be interpreted and rendered intelligible in order that an appropriate response be chosen. In other words, operators must exercise their discretion in a similar way to patrol officers at the scene. However, the opportunities for exercising discretion are kept in check by organizational factors, such as limited resources and the need to respond quickly in cases where there is little or uncertain information (Waddington 1993: 167). Almost three-quarters of the Thames Valley operators blamed high demand and inadequate human resources for their failure to

[15] In one of the two police areas I randomly chose magnetic tapes from three different dates and identified the recorded domestic disputes. All communications pertinent to these disputes were listened to, allowing for a better understanding of the interactions between callers, operators, and patrol officers, and providing a test for the reliability of the operators' assertions.

pass on sufficient information to patrol officers: 'If you're busy and undermanned the quality of your questioning will decrease.'

Many others talked about the pressure to answer the phones quickly in order to avoid creating a backlog. Sixty per cent of operators suggested that the technology could not cope with the demands of the patrol officers. They explained that 'air-time' was precious and could not be taken up with irrelevant or superfluous information. Some operators also expressed concern about passing detailed confidential information to officers over the air because of the illegal use of scanners by members of the public. In addition, radio 'black-spots' occasionally caused operators to lose communication with patrol officers. Clearly, as Waddington (1993) and Manning (1982) have acknowledged, information is not an unambiguous collection of facts which can be relayed unproblematically from caller to operator and then on to patrol officer.

However, even if operators cannot decipher clear, intelligible information from callers, they can check their own records if they have the name of a victim or an offender, or the address of the disputants. However, almost half of the operators interviewed admitted that they rarely did this. Approximately a quarter said that they checked the available information sometimes, but only a quarter said that they made frequent checks.[16] The 1990/60 Circular recommended that:

Records should be kept in a manner which permits easy information retrieval so that officers dispatched to an incident can readily establish whether there have been previous reports on the household, their frequency and the nature of previous threats or violence. Officers should also find out whether any court orders or injunctions are in force in respect of members of the household. (Para. 13.)

Unfortunately, control rooms are not the libraries of complete and comprehensive data that the Home Office and patrol officers would like them to be. Information technology systems used by the Thames Valley Police were not developed according to a formulated plan. Different systems were introduced, in a largely ad hoc fashion, at various stages, dependent on bursts of funding and other resources. Hence, some effective systems are hindered because of their incompatibility with the other, older and poorer systems.[17]

---

[16] Civilians were more likely than officers to check information.
[17] A recent Home Office study found that thirty-three of forty-two police forces in England and Wales felt that they had an adequate system for recording and monitor-

Many Thames Valley operators and officers pointed out that the technology was inadequate for intelligence gathering. They considered that CoCo was inefficient as an information provider, and that the domestic violence register was never up to date and hence unreliable. Similarly, copies of injunctions were either missing or out of date. However, the point of contention for many officers was the inability to access the local intelligence computer. Sixty-two per cent of the operators interviewed mentioned the need for a local intelligence computer terminal in the control room. One operator explained: 'If we had an LIO [local intelligence] terminal we'd all use it. We've been told that we can't have one because it would cost too much.'[18]

Accurate information can only be collected if operators always create records of 'telephone resolutions'. However, whilst three-quarters of the operators admitted that they *should* record details when officers are not dispatched (for the benefit of local intelligence in case the dispute re-erupted), only a third of the operators claimed that they *always* created computer records of all incidents. A further few said that they *rarely* created a record if they were not going to dispatch an officer.[19]

Of course, the provision of accurate, up-to-date information on domestic disputes is also partly reliant on patrol officers relaying relevant details to operators after they have left the scene of an incident and the operators, in turn, recording and classifying that information precisely. However, even when they do record all incidents, inconsistent classification practices can render the retrieval of data problematic. As Bottomley and Coleman (1981)

ing incidents of domestic violence (Grace 1995). However the researchers found little evidence of any systematic recording or monitoring of domestic violence cases. Only a quarter of operational officers said that they were consistently able to check police records for any previous history of assaults before attending a domestic violence incident.

[18] Neither of the control rooms examined in this study had a terminal connected to this computer. Therefore, whenever operators wanted to check this data they needed to go physically to another part of the police station (to the main terminal) or call through to headquarters (something which could only be done within office hours). The civilian operators are not trained to use the local intelligence computer and therefore do not have passwords and even some police officers are not yet trained to use this computer.

[19] As with the data on non-dispatch rates, there was little difference between the two stations studied over how frequently operators created an incident log for a 'cuffed' call, or between civilians and police operators.

have argued, the latitude allowed to the police, in deciding whether and under what category incidents are recorded, is such as to undermine the validity of statistics of recorded crime. An effect of the variable processing of primary data is the unreliable nature of any intelligence the police, whether it be operators or 'managers', gather from the tertiary data collected by CoCo. In other words, intelligence on any offence or offender may not be easy to obtain and may be distorted by inaccuracies.

After officers have attended an incident and reported the result back to the control room, the operator records a closing classification. These classifications are based on the patrol officer's 'story'. If his story is partial it might result in an inaccurate categorization. However, even when the operators are provided with very clear details about an incident they offer a range of different responses. As with the opening classifications, there were inconsistencies and much variance in the categories chosen to 'close' the same hypothetical incident provided for the operators. The incident involved an assault and yet over half of the operators said that they would 'close' the incident as a 'disorder', with only 7 per cent choosing to categorize the incident as a crime. There were two other categories chosen by the remaining operators, with almost a quarter choosing to classify the incident as 'miscellaneous'.

The Home Office tried to address the problematic nature of the official statistics on domestic violence:

All complaints of domestic violence by victims or witnesses should be properly recorded in the same way as similar incidents involving strangers. The seriousness of an incident should not be downgraded because it takes place in a domestic context and no incident should be 'no-crimed' unless the police conclude, after investigation, that the report was inaccurate or false. (1990/60 Circular, para. 13.)

This recommendation, adopted by Thames Valley Police, suggests that if a woman reports an assault by her partner it should be recorded as a crime against the person, in other words as an assault. However, this recommendation was ignored by operators, most of whom did not know which categories should be chosen for specific types of incidents.

The Home Office also recommended that: 'Where there are computerised command and control systems they should specifically log reports of domestic violence so that they can be monitored by supervisory officers and an accurate statistical record kept' (1990/ 60 Circular, para. 13).[20]

In April 1993, in response to this advice, Thames Valley Police included a closing category of 'Domestic Violence' on the command and control computer. This was an optional category to be used as a further distinction after 'Disorder: Domestic Dispute', to indicate that the dispute involved violence.[21] From April until 31 August the new category was used only once. Only 60 per cent of the operators knew about the category, and the majority of these said that they did not use it because they were too busy or they forgot. Almost a third said that no one had explained when they should use the category or who would benefit from this additional information.

Many of the operators argued that the categories are unimportant. As far as the response of the patrol officers is concerned, *most* of the information recorded on CoCo is insignificant. Message pads used to become part of the case files when an arrest was made. This is no longer the case with incident logs (except in rare circumstances) and so the way that the operators interpret and record information received has no long term implications.

Operators as administrators

The control room is clearly an integral part of communication between the public and the police. Control room staff provide an information thoroughfare between anxious or agitated callers and often similarly agitated patrol officers. However, the choices made by operators cannot really be said to mark the start of the criminal justice process.

Operators are administrators. They 'manage' calls rather than make decisions, and, as such, their response has little effect on the outcome of cases. They try to impose order on multifarious calls which can involve the interpretation of information and adherence to policies and directives. However, this only affects how quickly the police get to the incident, which does not seem to impact on

---

[20] This is not contradictory. It does not mean that the closing classification needs to be 'domestic dispute', as opposed to 'crime'. Rather it means that some sort of other category needs to be entered in order to distinguish crimes arising from an incident of domestic violence from other 'non-domestic' offences.

[21] There was no option to include this category if the incident had been 'closed' as a crime.

police decisions in domestic disputes. This is partly, as discussed above, because there is usually little or no information provided, and that which is provided is either vague or inaccurate. As Ericson argued: '... dispatch messages are usually imprecise enough to allow the officer interpretive latitude' (1982: 95). In other words, they: '... need to do their own contextual analysis beyond what they are told...' (1982: 97). One Thames Valley operator commented that this is what *should* happen, as background information on the disputants might adversely affect the operational response: 'It could be detrimental. It could stop officers responding according to criteria of that specific incident.'

Clearly the Thames Valley study provides no support for any of the three explanations of the impact of the control room discussed in the introduction to this chapter. However, this is not to say that these explanations were not appropriate in their time. Since then, the control room has become 'routinized'. Operators have, to a large extent, lost the resources (through changed working conditions) to use their discretionary powers in a creative way. This is because of four organizational factors: first, the introduction of the computer-aided dispatch system; secondly, a sharp rise in demand for police services (preventing operators spending sufficient time on each call to collect information which might influence the patrol officers); thirdly, the partial civilianization of the control room[22] (civilians in Thames Valley Police were even less inclined to exercise discretion); and finally, the introduction of a force policy on domestic violence.

The following chapter will further explore the issue of police discretion. It will be shown that patrol officers have the ability to use their discretionary powers more creatively than control room operators. The chapter will focus on the cultural, organizational, and situational variables which shape police decisions within the gap, left by the criminal law and force policies, where discretion operates.

---

[22] About half the control room staff are civilians, who do the same work as police officers, although the supervisory roles are held by police officers only.

4

The Cultural and Structural Determinants of Police Decision-Making

When the police are called to a dispute between partners or ex-partners they try to decide on the best course of action to achieve the quickest and most effective resolution to the conflict. The dispute may or may not have involved violence or damage to property, the conflict may appear to have subsided or may be occurring as the officers arrive, the victim may be 'requesting' that the officers arrest her partner, or she may be uninterested in, or opposed to, police action. Accordingly, the police can use their legal powers to arrest one of the disputants, they can attempt to mediate, or they can decide that it is not a police matter and leave. Research has shown that the typical response during the 1980s was to leave without arresting anyone. Indeed, the most rigorous study conducted during this period found only a 2 per cent arrest rate for incidents of domestic violence (Edwards 1986).

Since Edwards conducted her research the Home Office has insisted on 'the need to treat domestic violence as seriously as other forms of violence' (1990/60 Circular, para. 11), and stated that 'the arrest and detention of the alleged assailant should... always be considered' (para. 16 (d)). The Thames Valley study, conducted three years after the publication of this policy, found that 17 per cent of domestic violence perpetrators were arrested.[1] This is a significant rise in the rate of arrest but despite this it can be argued that the arrest rate still remains low when looked at in the context of the local force policy. This incorporated the Home Office recommendations of the 1990/60 Circular that advised officers to arrest perpetrators where there is evidence of an offence (see

---

[1] See Tables 2.1a. and b.

Chapter 1). This and the following chapter will critically evaluate attempts to explain the relatively low arrest rates in cases of domestic violence and develop an understanding of the impact on police decision-making of cultural and structural determinants. It will be argued that previous accounts of policing domestic violence which have focused solely on 'cop culture' without problematizing the term have failed adequately to explain decisions regarding arrest. By considering only the negative values and attitudes of police officers, they have ignored the more structural constraints to be found within both the police organization and the criminal law. More importantly, they have paid too little attention to the effect of interaction between officers and disputants—in particular the victims. This chapter will look at the wider cultural and structural influences on all police behaviour and Chapter 5 will consider the situational and contextual variables that interact with these wider influences at the scene of domestic disputes.

The purpose of this chapter is to explore the extent to which the police sub-culture can explain police behaviour—in particular the decision to arrest in cases of domestic violence. In order to explore the usefulness of the concept of police culture, it will be argued that it is necessary to problematize the term 'cop culture'. In attempting to clarify this term, I will argue that negative police attitudes and stereotypes, which have in some of the literature been referred to as 'cop culture', are better understood as 'canteen culture'. Furthermore, I will argue that canteen culture is just part of a wider 'cop culture' and is not, in itself, helpful conceptually or empirically in understanding police decisions.

Understanding the concept of 'cop culture'

Starting from the observation that policing is not greatly shaped by criminal or procedural law, academics have sought to explain how rank and file officers exercise their wide discretionary powers (see Chapter 1). The impact of the informal culture of rank and file officers is the explanation of police working practices most commonly put forward by those who have carried out research on, or theorized about, the police (Reiner 1994). The concept of 'cop culture' was first discussed over thirty years ago by Michael Banton (1964) and Jerome Skolnick (1966). Skolnick, offering an account of the police 'working personality', argued that certain problems inherently associated with the nature of policing generated a shared sub-culture among the police rank and file which facilitated the resolution of these difficulties.[2] He identified the themes of police suspiciousness, internal solidarity, social isolation, and conservatism as being characteristic of this 'working personality'. Since then most studies, in particular ethnographic studies, of routine police work have uncovered a range of informal cultural norms, values, and beliefs at work in the translation of law and organizational rules into practical policing (Cain 1973; Holdaway 1983). Recent studies have referred to themes of racism, sexism, and homophobia (Smith and Gray 1983), with the more traditional themes of solidarity and isolation and the desire for action and excitement reoccurring in the literature (McConville and Shepherd 1992).[3]

As sociological interest in 'cop culture' emerged, along with it came an understanding of police discretion. During the 1960s the writings of Goldstein (1960), Piliavin and Briar (1964), Skolnick (1966), and Packer (1968) explored how discretionary powers enabled officers to behave according to cultural attitudes rather than according to the rule book. Indeed, Reiner (1992) has argued that police culture shapes much of what happens on the streets. The law, he claims, does not determine practical policing because it leaves huge gaps to be filled by discretion and so the culture influences who will be stopped, arrested, and charged. The majority of commentators on policing (Packer in particular) focused their concern on how often, and indeed how much, rank and file officers deviated from the 'due process' model. The tendency, they argued, was to eschew 'due process' principles in favour of 'crime control' measures (see Sanders and Young 1994). In other words, they were concerned that officers too often used their discretionary powers in unfairly discriminatory ways—controlling certain marginal groups whilst paying little attention to others (for example, victims of racial attacks).

Over the last decade or so, there would appear to have been examples of police responses to certain communities which indeed owe more to the cultural prejudices of officers, both senior and junior, than to the criminal law. The use of the 'suspected persons' provision of the 1824 Vagrancy Act in the 1980s provides a good

---

[2] 'Cop culture' could be described as a response to the pressures and conflicts which officers routinely face whilst on patrol, and, to a lesser extent, within the station.

[3] This book will not discuss in any detail the core characteristics of 'cop culture'. This has been dealt with elsewhere in some depth (see, in particular, Reiner 1992).

example. This legal power was used in a discriminatory way to stop and search young, typically male, Afro-Caribbeans in the streets of Brixton and other south London areas with a high incidence of street robberies ('muggings') and illicit drug taking (Willis 1983; Smith and Gray 1983). It has been argued that police cultural beliefs—which appear to increase the likelihood of coercive police action directed against ethnic minorities—decrease the probability of perpetrators of domestic violence being arrested. This is because machismo, sexism, and an emphasis on crime-fighting are important traits of 'cop culture', with the result that crimes against women in the domestic context are not taken seriously (Young 1991; Heidensohn 1992).

The divides between policing public and private space, 'deserving' and 'undeserving' victims, 'legitimate' and 'illegitimate' targets, and social service and law enforcement policing were the focus of many theories of policing domestic violence (see, for example, Dobash and Dobash 1992; Stanko 1989; Edwards 1989). It was claimed that police attitudes and the organizational structure of policing created a set of cultural norms, beliefs, and attitudes that determined not only how police thought about domestic disputes, but, more importantly, how they responded to them. Officers see adversarial encounters, preferably resulting in an arrest, as 'real' police work (McConville and Shepherd 1992). This image of 'real policing' persists despite the fact that quantitatively very little police time is spent dealing with crimes whilst many police hours are spent on 'social service' roles (Holdaway 1983; Reiss 1971; Punch and Naylor 1973). Domestic disputes, in contrast, were seen, within traditional 'cop culture', as messy, unproductive, and as not being 'real police work' (Reiner 1978; Young 1991). In other words, 'cop culture' defined domestic disputes as trivial in general. This led the police to treat them as trivial occurrences when dealing with actual incidents. Hence, decision-making was determined by officers' whims, stereotypes, and cultural attitudes regarding 'serious' or 'proper' police work and 'rubbish' calls (see Dobash and Dobash 1980; Davies 1982; Fine 1981; Southgate 1986; McConville and Shepherd 1992). Stanko has claimed very recently that the police have still not overcome their doubts that domestic violence is real crime (1995: 33).

Cultural theorists have, in the past, argued that officers make judgements based upon their inherent assumptions regarding 'proper victim conduct' and that these judgements can lead them to disregard violence against certain women (Manning 1978; Skolnick 1966). Drawing on this work, some critics, feminist[4] and others, have claimed that officers share cultural assumptions about women in general, and wives and mothers in particular, according to which some women are negatively stereotyped. It has been argued that when this occurs such women are unlikely to benefit fully from the protection of the law (Edwards 1996). The onus was said to be on the female victims who had to demonstrate that they did not 'deserve' to be attacked (Dobash and Dobash 1980; Chatterton 1983; Smith and Gray 1983; Stanko 1985). Hence, the question of whether to arrest and prosecute only arose in domestic disputes when the investigating officer deemed the victim to be both deserving and significantly injured (Hatty 1989; Sanders 1988). Some feminist authors have argued that discretion is used in an arbitrary way, unrelated to organizational ends. Officers' attitudes, often described as 'masculinist' and guided by notions of patriarchy, are said to persuade them to value family unity at the expense of protecting women against violence in their home:

The patriarchal attitudes of both police officers and the overall police organization...inevitably influence the exercise of discretion and shape what police 'police' and how... [V]iolence in the home is accorded a low priority because it happens behind closed doors, has a low visibility, occurs within a sphere traditionally considered to be private and is perpetrated against women by male partners.' (Edwards 1989: 31.)

Some feminist commentators have suggested that the inappropriate or ineffective approach of many officers towards domestic violence derived from individual officers' experiences of familial relations or from the masculinist ethos of their particular force. Hence, it was thought that the police made fewer arrests in cases where the victims were married and living with the offenders because they deferred to the sanctity of the family (Dobash and Dobash 1980; Martin 1976; Worden and Pollitz 1984). It has also been suggested that the relationship was considered important for evidential reasons; when officers perceived a commitment to a relationship they

---

[4] Most feminist empirical work aimed at investigating how police deal with cases of domestic violence has been based on interviews with police officers (see Edwards 1986, 1989; Homant and Kennedy 1985). In addition, interviews with victims have provided another way of assessing police performance (see Pahl 1982, 1985; Binney, Harkell, and Nixon 1981).

thought that the woman would be less likely to support a prosecution (Black 1976). The influence of 'gendered' attitudes was thought to have been proven by the research finding that female officers were more likely to be understanding, sympathetic, and helpful in their provision of information about legal rights and shelter (see, for example, Homant and Kennedy 1985; Lunneborg 1989). Of course, the extent of this gender difference has been questioned by some other authors (see Radford 1989; Stanko 1989).

In writing about domestic violence, many feminist authors have started from the normative stance that the police response was inadequate. From this standpoint they have sought, through empirical research, to demonstrate and explain this inadequacy. In doing so, they have explored the influence of police attitudes and beliefs. They have put forward analyses of policing which place the victim of domestic violence as a passive recipient of police choices rather than an actor engaged in the interactive process of decision-making. Furthermore, they have assumed that the wishes of complainants and police officers are always in conflict.

The narrow negative concept of 'cop culture' advanced by some critics of the police response to domestic violence (detailed above) is crudely summarised by the model presented in figure 4.1.

NO ARREST	EXPLANATORY VARIABLE	ARREST
Cohabiting	Marital status of disputants	Not cohabiting
Male	Gender of officer	Female
Victim provocation	Victim blaming	Victim not implicated
Negative comment	Officer's opinion of victim	No negative comment

FIG. 4.1. The negative concept of 'cop culture' and its impact on the police response to domestic violence

Figure 4.1 shows that according to some explanations of the police response to domestic violence the marital status of the disputants and the gender of the officer both impact on the decision to arrest. In other words, female police officers are more likely to arrest perpetrators and all officers are more likely to arrest perpetrators who are not co habiting (whether married or not) with the victim. It also shows that when officers blame victims for provoking the violence and when they express negative opinions of the victims they are less likely to consider her deserving and therefore less likely to make an arrest. All of these factors have been located within some feminist explanations of the impact of 'cop culture' on the policing of domestic violence.

A quantitative assessment of the negative concept of 'cop culture'

In order to test the usefulness of the negative concept of 'cop culture', quantitative analysis of the 387 domestic incidents dealt with in the Thames Valley study was carried out. An attempt was made to gauge the influence of the gender of the officers attending the disputes, the marital status of the disputants, and the attitudes of the officers towards the victims (two attitudinal measures) on the decision to arrest. These were the only 'negative' cultural factors that could be measured quantitatively. As tables 4.1 to 4.4 show, none of these four variables were found to be correlated with the decision to arrest when two-way cross-tabulations were carried out (none of them reached the 0.05 level of probability).

These four variables taken independently were not significantly correlated with the decision to arrest. However, it was decided to see whether, when combined with other variables, any of these variables could partially explain the decision to arrest. Hence the variables were tested by logistic regression analysis. Logistic regression analysis is a multivariate technique used to predict whether an event will or will not occur and to identify the variables useful in making the prediction. In this case the event was the arrest of the male disputant. The independent variables are usually chosen according to their chi-square scores when cross-tabulated with the dependent variable.[5] Hence, as tables 4.1 to 4.4 show, none of the

---

[5] They are included in the analysis if they are significant at a 5 per cent level and preferably at a 1 per cent level. This means that there is a less than 5 per cent, or less

TABLE 4.1.   WPC present at scene:[a] number and percentage arrested

WPC present	No arrest	Arrest	Total
No WPC	153 (58%)	109 (42%)	262
WPC present	66 (53%)	59 (47%)	125
Total	219	168	387

$X^2 = 1.079$ (p < 0.29)[b]

[a] One or both of the responding officers was female.

[b] When there is only one degree of freedom (as is the case with all two-way cross-tabulations) the probability test should be significant at the 5 per cent level at least, and, preferably, at the 1 per cent level (which would be a chi-square figure of 6.635). The chi-square for this table would only have a 30 per cent probability.

TABLE 4.2.   Disputants cohabiting:[a] number and percentage arrested

Cohabiting	No arrest	Arrest	Total
Not cohabiting	87 (55%)	72 (45%)	159
Cohabiting	132 (58%)	96 (42%)	228
Total	219	168	387

$X^2 = 0.385$ (p < 0.53)

[a] This included both those couples who were cohabiting and those who were legally married. The couples who were separated or divorced were labelled 'not cohabiting'. Originally, categorical variables were created but these were later aggregated as some cells contained too few cases.

TABLE 4.3.   Officer made a negative comment:[a] number and percentage arrested

Negative comment	No arrest	Arrest	Total
No negative comment	205 (56%)	160 (44%)	365
Negative comment[b]	14 (64%)[c]	8 (36%)	22
Total	219	168	387

$X^2 = 0.471$ (p < 0.49)

[a] The officer made a negative, judgemental comment about the victim.

[b] The officer made no negative or judgemental comments about the complainant.

[c] As the numbers are so small these percentages are not very meaningful.

cultural variables would normally be used in a logistic regression analysis. However they were included to see if they contributed to

than 1 per cent, chance of two variables being correlated by chance. In other words, a 95 or 99 per cent probability that one variable is correlated with another.

TABLE 4.4.   Officer suggested that the victim had provoked the dispute:[a] number and percentage arrested

Provoked	No arrest	Arrest	Total
No comment re provocation[b]	205 (57%)	154 (43%)	359
Comment re provocation	14 (50%)	14 (50%)	28
Total	219	168	387

$X^2 = 0.533$ (p < 0.46)[c]

[a] The variables 'negative comment' and 'provoked' were derived from a content analysis of the interview data. This information was coded only when officers had volunteered it when asked what had happened in each incident.

[b] The officer did not blame the victim, in any way, for provoking the dispute.

[c] An American study reached similar conclusions. Waaland and Keeley (1985) found that victim antagonism and victim drinking influenced police judgements of responsibility, but judgements of responsibility did not influence police decisions to arrest. These decisions, whilst based on hypothetical scenarios and therefore to be treated with some caution, showed that the arrest choice was most strongly influenced by victim injuries, the assailant's behaviour and his assaultive history. The data reported here are derived from real situations and support Waaland and Keeley's finding that there is not necessarily a causal link between judgemental attitudes and behaviour.

the power of the model to predict arrest.[6] In the event, all of these negative cultural variables were excluded from the equation during logistic regression, as will be shown by the final model presented in Chapter 5.[7]

On the quantitative evidence it does not appear that an understanding of the negative values and attitudes of police officers is very helpful in explaining the outcome of police-citizen encounters in domestic disputes. However, it is necessary to look more closely at these attitudes before dismissing them as unrelated to police behaviour.

Figure 4.1 raises two different, but related, questions: first, do these negative cultural attitudes comprise what we refer to as 'cop culture'; and, secondly, do they adequately explain police decisions regarding arrest, or indeed any other police behaviour. The rest of this chapter will argue that these attitudes do not comprise what we

[6] Backward stepwise regression using the Wald statistic.

[7] 'Cohabiting' was excluded with a score of 0.3851 (0.53 significance); 'WPC present' was excluded at 1.0791 (0.29 significance); 'negative comment' was excluded at 0.4716 (0.49 significance), and 'provoked' was excluded at 0.5335 (0.46 significance). The significance tests are based on the Wald statistic.

refer to as 'cop culture', but are just a part of that culture; and they do not adequately explain police behaviour although they are not entirely divorced from decision-making processes. As Chan has explained, 'police culture has become a convenient label for a range of negative values, attitudes, and practice norms among police officers' (1996: 110). These negative attitudes and values do not, however, comprise 'cop culture'. Nor can they alone explain police decision-making. What they represent is cultural expressions of attitudes held by some police officers. The critics cited above have focused on what officers say about domestic disputes but this does not necessarily mean that talk translates into action. What officers say and what they do can be two different things (see also Fielding 1994). It is necessary therefore to explore the conceptual distinction between descriptions of 'cop culture' which focus solely on attitudes and those that focus on behaviour. The Thames Valley data were examined both qualitatively and quantitatively in order to show just how inadequate is a focus on police negative attitudes towards domestic violence in explaining the police decision-making process at the scene of disputes.

A qualitative assessment of the negative concept of 'cop culture'

Clearly there seems to be some confusion in the literature on 'cop culture' as to just what is being described. In order to understand the extent of the influence of sub-cultural norms and values on operational policing, it is helpful to consider the terminology. The term 'cop culture' is used by academics, whilst journalists and senior police officers prefer the name 'canteen culture', a term generally accepted to refer to the same set of norms and values. These terms should not, however, be used synonymously, as 'canteen culture' is but one element of 'cop culture'.

'Canteen culture' refers to the ways in which officers communicate with each other, interactions which are characterized by expressions of solidarity and cohesiveness. It is directed internally to meet the demands of operational policing and thus reflects divisions between the police and the public, in particular, suspects, and divisions between the various ranks within the service. Its name is appropriate because expressions of sub-cultural biases and prejudices are more likely to be heard in the police canteen than on the streets. Officers, when surrounded by their colleagues in the station, use cultural themes to communicate with each other and establish a shared identity (Smith and Gray 1983). They discuss incidents they have dealt with using language entrenched in cultural myths, prejudices, and stereotypes. Thames Valley officers, for example, often talked about the dangerousness of attending domestic disputes. In particular, the 'problem' of trying to help women involved in domestic disputes who 'turn on' them, 'ganging up' on them with their partners and threatening or assaulting them. Many officers insisted that this happened frequently and yet few had personal experience of it. In this study there was only one example in 387 incidents of a 'hostile' woman and in this case neither of the officers had sustained any injuries (although the uniform of one of them was covered in gravy!). Some writers have described this 'canteen culture' but, rather than seeing it as a small part of a wider 'cop culture', have assumed that it *is* 'cop culture' and that, as such, it translates directly into action. 'Canteen culture' allows officers to articulate their fears, and vent their frustrations and anger. But neither *causes* them to behave in a certain way when dealing with members of the public, nor corresponds with their actual practices.

As discussed in Chapter 2, interviews with patrol officers were based on a semi-structured questionnaire. However each interview was preceded by a general opening comment which informed the interviewee that he would be asked about domestic disputes.[8] This statement was followed by a pause to give the interviewee time to offer an initial reaction, which was frequently quite negative. Many officers looked slightly exasperated at the mention of domestic disputes, commenting that 'domestics are so much trouble', or that they hate going to them because they are so 'griefy', or that they did not have the time or the inclination to deal effectively with them. They gave the impression that the police role simply was to enter the homes of disputants and arrest suspects if they were provided with indisputable evidence of a criminal offence having taken place, and leave if they were not, without either listening to or advising the disputants. They occasionally made negative comments about victims as described by some critics (see above). But when asked a general open-ended question about the dispute—'So, tell me what happened here?'—their replies seemed to contradict their

---

[8] Some officers were interviewed more than once over the fieldwork period. This introductory question was only used for the first interviews.

initial response. Despite a negative initial comment being made in ninety-eight of the 387 interviews (forty-three of the 168 arrest incidents, and fifty-four of the 219 non-arrest incidents), their actual response was usually quite different. In the majority of cases they proved that they *had* listened carefully to the disputants' 'story' (they could often recall, in some detail, the situation which had immediately precipitated the dispute, as well as how the disputants had behaved whilst they were at the scene). The initial comments were indicators of how domestic disputes are still, to some extent, trivialized by officers within canteen culture discourse, whilst the response to the questions about what officers actually did in practice indicate the divide between certain negative cultural attitudes and behaviour. The following interview extracts illustrate this.

Initial comment:

I don't enjoy being a social worker when I'm out there doing a busy shift. We haven't time to try and find out what's gone wrong in these people's lives. We just have to go in and nick sonny or leave them to it. These people expect you to listen while they slag each other off and then you're supposed to be able to sort out their lives. I don't see why I should try and understand their marital problems when I've got enough of my own.

The reference to dissatisfaction with social service type of work is typical of the language of the canteen. However this officer *did* spend time listening to a woman's story and was fairly sympathetic. He continued:

Response to first question:

We have made previous visits to this address regarding domestic disputes. Her husband had been arrested on a previous occasion for ABH but she had withdrawn at a later date. The neighbours were at the house. She complained that he had pushed her round the kitchen, and had thrown a milk bottle at her. They had only been married for a year. She's at the end of her tether. He drinks, doesn't have a job or help round the house. He just slobs around. He's very possessive. He drinks a lot and spends her money. He's been intimidating towards her and her two children.

Another officer implied that he usually spent very little time trying to help disputants.

Initial comment:

Domestics! Most of the time I go in, split them up and tell them to just calm down. They're always blaming each other these couples. Most of the time there's no offence so we can't bring anyone in. I guess most of the time we just tell them to shut it, nicely of course, and get out.

He then went on to discuss the following incident at which he had spent considerable time.

Response to first question:

A child had called us to say that his father had cut his mother with a knife. The man was still in the house when we arrived. We were waiting for support to bring knife vests when the man came out calm. I spoke to him and [the officer he was with] spoke to the wife. The family basically had lots of problems. He had a drink problem. He had seen doctors in the past and attended an alcohol clinic. He had managed to give it up until recently when he lost his job and started drinking again. The boy is not his own child and they often argue and the mother always takes the boy's side. That afternoon he had argued with the boy about the choice of television programmes and the mother had said that the boy can always choose what he wants as a priority. The man started behaving aggressively to the boy and the mother stepped in to defend him. She said that there was no knife involved and that the child had got mixed up. They were still angry with each other and I spent quite a bit of time mediating between them.

The following extract highlights officers' concerns about their ineptitude in dealing with domestic disputes.

Initial comment:

We shouldn't have to go to domestics. We're not the right people. We're not properly trained to help these people. Okay, we should be there if sonny's kicking off and she's in any real danger, but most of the time it's just squabbling, and I, for one, don't have the time to listen to people old enough to be my parents bickering all night.

He then illustrated that he had, in fact, tried to deal properly with the dispute in question.

Response to first question:

I spent a long time listening to both of the parties and offering advice. She is a Filipino, aged about forty. He is English, he's white, aged about fifty. She was bought by him—she's a Filipino bride. They have been married and in this country for about eleven years. There are real cultural differences between them. Their marriage is falling apart. We have attended disputes between them before. She talks about 'serving' him and says he does not respect her. Both work together and she has accused him of having an affair with a woman at work. He denies this. They have money problems and problems with their sexual relationship. She's got a bad back and feels that that is why he is having an affair. They keep their money separate and argue over what each are spending money on. She has been to marriage guidance a few times and he is considering going with her. On this occasion they had argued and each had thrown things at each other. Neither had been hit—but a few possessions had been smashed. There were no injuries. She had phoned us because she wanted someone to talk to, someone to act as a mediator. I spent almost an hour discussing their relationship with them.

There were, of course, many interviewees who spoke initially in a very sympathetic way. Some officers even admitted to enjoying the challenge of a domestic incident, seeing it as a chance for them to employ their communicative skills and try to help the women and prevent further suffering. On the other hand, there were a few officers who did spend little time with the disputants and who offered no advice and showed no sympathy or compassion. However, they were a small minority.

Some studies have not attempted to ascertain the police reasons for action, talking only to victims in refuges, for example (see Binney, Harkell, and Nixon 1981). Other researchers who did conduct interviews with officers adopted the methodological tactic of discounting the reasons given by officers for their actions. They did this in order to 'discover' the 'real' reasons for their behaviour. These 'real' reasons were based on their own interpretations and victims' accounts of police responses.[9] Edwards, whilst arguably providing one of the most sophisticated feminist accounts of the police response to domestic violence, was perhaps too ready to dismiss officers' legal and prima facie reasons for exercising discretion, insisting instead on the stronger influence of moral judgements regarding blame and family ideology (Edwards 1989: 102). Such critics have chosen to marginalize or disregard police explanations for action, seeing them as unreliable whilst, at the same time, insisting that so-called 'malestream academics' should listen to the voices of the victims who have been neglected, or rendered invisible, by the criminal justice system. Just as it is not acceptable to ignore victim perceptions, it is unacceptable to discount officers' reasons for action *a priori*.

Edwards asked officers how they felt about the expectations on their performance, how they felt they actually responded, and how they felt they should respond. From these interviews she reported negative attitudes:

---

[9] See the discussion on the 'myth' of victim unreliability in chap. 5 (for a discussion of this methodological tactic see Giddens 1979).

Most patrol or beat officers held negative attitudes towards [domestic incidents]. Some said that police officers should not be involved in what was essentially, 'a waste of time'!... Their own privately held attitudes reflected feelings of reluctance, frustration, ambiguity and disdain for 'service' work. (Edwards 1989: 101.)

However, she did not attempt to discover if officers' behaviour at domestic disputes was as unsympathetic as their attitudes suggested. The more optimistic findings of the research in the Thames Valley reflect, in part, the different research methods employed. The excerpts from the Thames Valley study suggest that the type of interview conducted by Edwards may not produce an accurate picture of how officers responded when faced with the practical task of dealing with a dispute. Indeed the officers' comments, when interviewed by Edwards, were similar to the stock responses made by officers at the beginning of the Thames Valley study interviews. The Thames Valley study suggests that canteen culture does not translate directly into police action. An American study similarly found that, whilst attitudes about appropriate male and female behaviour and their own family situations can predict significant variance in an officer's attitudes towards victims of domestic violence, they have little impact on the decision to arrest (Stith 1990).

The crucial matter is the relevance of cultural beliefs to actual behaviour (Fielding 1994). Research on policing in general has similarly uncovered discrepancies between what officers say and what they do. Smith and Gray (1983) found that police attitudes relating to race were not necessarily consistent with their behaviour towards black people (research by Black (1971) came to a similar conclusion). They reported that racist language and racial prejudice were prominent and pervasive and that many officers, whether seen individually or in groups, were preoccupied with ethnic differences. However,

...on accompanying these officers as they went about their work [they] found that their relations with black and brown people were often relaxed or friendly and that the degree of tension between them was much less than might have been expected... from their own conversation... The rhetoric of abuse of black people... did not carry through into action... (1983: 388.)

They go on to say that:

Police officers themselves often draw the distinction between words and behaviour and claim that they won't let their views about black people affect the way they treat them. (1983: 403.)

The authors argued that the norms of the police occupational group encouraged racist language and comment but this did not mean that the officers would act in a racist way when dealing with members of ethnic minority groups during their working day. They explain that this is because other factors such as 'the structure of rewards and constraints within which police officers operate...' (1983: 389) impact upon police behaviour (see also Black 1970; Holdaway 1983). The social psychology literature provides further support for the contention that attitudes do not necessarily translate into behaviour, indeed that action and attitudes are often inconsistent (Raven and Rubin 1983; Ajzen and Fishbein 1980; Eiser 1986).

McConville and Shepherd (1992) provide a challenging discussion of these issues. These authors argue that prejudicial attitudes, strongly reinforced by occupational culture, do inform the way in which the police respond to incidents involving black people. The 'race riots' across England in the early 1980s and the disturbances in Brixton in 1995 would seem to support this contention by providing evidence that there are some underlying tensions between the police service and certain sections of the ethnic community. In their defence, Smith and Gray concede that some ethnic minority groups do experience differential treatment from the police. Clearly, the relationship between what people say and what they do is not a direct, straightforward one.

It is not helpful to listen to general police discussions about their role and assume that this explains their behaviour. Nor can we deny that there is no relationship between the two. Waddington has argued just this.[10] He argues that 'cop culture' is not a causal agent, but a rhetoric that gives meaning to experience. It is the means by which officers express themselves to one another, by which they make sense of their difficult social world and hence maintain group solidarity (see also Fielding 1994). 'Cop culture' is, in other words, a cognitive construct which bears little relation to the actions and behaviour of officers going about their business. This rather throws the baby out with the bath water. It suggests that

---

[10] Waddington, P. A. J., unpublished paper delivered at the British Criminology Conference, Belfast, July 1997.

rhetoric has no relationship with reality. The way officers express themselves does not accurately describe the way they behave but it does provide a crude barometer of their attitudes, which do have *some* impact on their behaviour, although not nearly to the extent suggested by many critics. There would be no purpose to the rhetoric of the police culture if it was totally divorced from police behaviour.

There is a complex relationship between police talk and police action. Attitudes are, to some extent, expressions of police behaviour. Police officers' conversations in the canteen are ways of reconstructing what has happened, or what happens generally, in order to maintain solidarity and a common sense of purpose. As such, they are necessary for coping with police work. Even extreme attitudes and sexist, racist, or other types of 'unacceptable' stories and jokes create a shared consensus. They allow individual officers to feel that they share the same social world as their colleagues. Hence, the rhetoric of the canteen is essential for solidarity—a defining feature of 'cop culture'. However, it serves another, more direct purpose. It creates and sometimes redefines the 'acceptable' limits within which operational officers 'should' act whilst outside the station.

Shearing and Ericson (1991) have argued that it is through telling stories and hearing them that officers know how to act. Furthermore, if they feel that they have shared understandings they can rely on their colleagues to back them up in specific circumstances.[11] This reinforces an individual's confidence that his working assumptions are shared by his peers, and that therefore he will not be challenged when he is dealing with members of the public. Shearing and Ericson (1991) argue that culture is conveyed metaphorically through stories and anecdotes. These do not tell officers what to do but do instil in new recruits certain recipes for action. They hint at, through example, the more appropriate responses to certain situations. Hence they contribute to the range of 'commonsense assumptions' which police officers take with them to the scene of a domestic dispute.

[11] Of course police officers are not all the same. There are some variations in attitudes along race and gender lines. However, for the purpose of understanding the relationship between canteen talk and police action on the streets these differences will be ignored. See Fielding (1994) for a challenge to this crude way of referring to police officers as if they were an entirely homogeneous group.

One of the most powerful working rules is that officers do not challenge or undermine their colleagues in front of members of the public. Canteen talk means that officers rarely do this. By telling exaggerated stories in the canteen officers can test the boundaries of acceptability amongst their colleagues. When they know that they see things in the same way as their colleagues in general they can trust their colleagues not to challenge them in specific situations. For this reason it is wrong to argue that the rhetoric bears no relation to the reality, as to some extent the rhetoric helps to establish and maintain the working assumptions which, as Chapter 5 will show, influence the choice of action at the scene of disputes. Clearly, as Dixon (1997) has argued, attitudes and behaviour interact with each other.

How can police culture more helpfully be conceptualized?

Distinguishing between 'cop culture' and canteen culture would enable some police commentators to resist a crude negative conceptualization of culture. It would allow for a more sophisticated understanding of the interaction between what officers say and what they do. Furthermore, police culture needs to be understood in more positive and less critical terms than much of the literature on domestic violence has allowed for. It needs to be understood as a dynamic force. It is dynamic in that, to some extent, it structures choices and it is dynamic in that it is constantly evolving. It changes because it emerges from the current socio-political context. Furthermore, it cannot be properly understood as separate from factors that might be considered to be structural. So-called structural factors, such as organizational goals, policing style, and the criminal law itself, are, in part, informed by police culture and, in turn, inform the culture. There is, in other words, a dynamic interaction between structure and culture that cannot be ignored if we are fully to understand how police culture shapes police decision-making.

The evolving nature of 'cop culture'

McConville, Sanders, and Leng, in criticizing the legal reform model, have argued that '... the occupational sub-culture of the police ... appears resistant to change ...' (1991: 193). However, Reiner, upon whose explanation of the characteristics of 'cop culture'

McConville, Sanders, and Leng draw, has argued that 'cop culture' is neither '... monolithic, universal or unchanging' (1992: 109) (see also Fielding 1994, 1995). Chan (1996) criticizes understandings of police culture which do not allow some scope for cultural change. She draws on the works of Bourdieu and Sackmann in order to move away from conceptions of police culture as homogeneous and deterministic and insulated from the external environment. Feminist critics were right to argue that cultural attitudes towards domestic violence were rooted in society's almost desperate trust in the family as a functional unit (see, for example, Dobash and Dobash 1992). Hence the idea that it may be better to sacrifice individual women than break down this unit.[12] However, the historic deference to the sanctity of the family has gradually been challenged during the past decades. Consequently, societal attitudes towards violence in the home have begun to change. The nature of 'cop culture' in the 1990s needs to be reconsidered in the light of such changes.

If police culture derives in part from the society within which officers operate, the culture today must be different from the culture as described by Banton—which seems to be the basis of much feminist criticism over the last two decades. In the last decade a liberal, progressive element within the police force has developed whose existence challenges the old scriptures of 'cop culture'. Interviews with police managers (ranging from sergeants to superintendents) for a recent Home Office study revealed that the culture, regarding attitudes towards domestic violence, had changed (Grace 1995). The majority of those interviewed felt that changes in the police culture had made it easier for officers to take domestic violence seriously without fear of being ridiculed by their colleagues. They believed, in particular, that younger officers not so set in their ways might find it easier to take the new guidelines into account (Grace 1995). Of course, as argued above, what officers say does not necessarily always translate into what they do. However, changing attitudes will slowly alter the cultural currency of officers, which should mean, in theory, that working assumptions can gradually adapt to new policies.

Historically, cultural descriptions of police officers have pointed to their conservatism and authoritarianism, amongst other

---

[12] This could explain the reluctance of many practitioners to intervene at the first signs of child abuse in the notorious Cleveland abuse case (see Morgan and Zedner 1992).

characteristics. However, it has not been clear whether people who joined the police service had these personality traits, or whether these were learned attitudes, imparted through training and socialization.[13] Assuming that they were at least partly the result of socialization, it is possible to argue that, whilst new probationers are socialized into the culture by spending time 'shadowing' older, more experienced officers, they are not passive recipients of a 'stock culture'. Hence explanations of 'cop culture' which imply that police officers are passive in the acculturation process are not very helpful (see also Chan 1996: 111).

'Cop culture' is not static. Rather, it is intimately related to changes in the criminal and civil law; to evolving force policies and training; and to changes in the wider socio-political and economic climate from which officers are recruited and which permeate every aspect of an officer's working life. It is important to note that Skolnick's (1966) thesis on the 'working personality' refers to the impact of the demands of police work. As that work changes, so will the culture change. In addition, if we allow that specific types of people decide to be police officers, we can argue that 'cop culture' must be affected by the changing socio-demographic characteristics of recruits to the force (see also Fielding 1989).

The social make-up of recruits to the police force, now, significantly, known as the police 'service', has changed over the past two decades. More graduates enter the service than used to be the case, and the overall educational level of recruits has improved (Smithers, Hill, and Silvester 1989).[14] This change in the type of recruit owes much to the improved salaries awarded to officers of every rank. In 1979 a new index-linked pay award recommended by the Edmund-Davies Committee was implemented, raising the pay for probationary officers by approximately 40 per cent (Rose 1996). It was during this time, and not unrelated to the rise in remuneration, that the average age of new recruits began to rise. Older officers brought with them experience from industry, social service careers, and a range of other professions. These recruits were not impressionable blank pages upon which the prevailing culture could be imprinted.

---

[13] See Reiner (1992: 125-8) for a discussion of the research that addresses this question.
[14] In addition to this, more and more of those who did not enter the service with educational qualifications are seeking to address this by completing first degrees, Masters degrees and even Ph.D.s, mostly achieved through part-time study.

Their experience and ideologies made them more resistant to, and, in time, allowed them to influence, the old-style culture.

In the late 1980s racism, homophobia, and sexism began to be challenged within the service. Each year there is an increase in the proportion of female recruits, and women police officers are increasingly prepared to take a stand against sexism. Indeed widely-reported cases have been brought against the service, such as the allegation made by the ex-Assistant Chief Constable Alison Halford. There now exists a Gay and Lesbian Police Association and a Black Police Association, and most large forces, in particular the Metropolitan, regularly launch recruitment drives aimed at ethnic minorities (Rose 1996). Whilst such initiatives might not penetrate to the core of cultural prejudice[15] it would be foolish to believe that they have had no effect at all.

Police officers from all ranks were once widely regarded as conservative in both their attitudes and approach to the public as well as being Conservative in their political affiliation. Drawing on informal interviews with Metropolitan police officers, Rose (1996) has claimed that this is changing. These officers told him that they would no longer vote for a Tory government which they believed to be too arrogant to recognize the links between social deprivation and crime and which expected the police to tidy up the mess created by their social and economic policies. He suggests that during the 1980s, at the height of the Thatcher-Lawson 'economic miracle', senior Metropolitan Police officers were vehement in their questioning and criticism of government policies which they believed were creating a divided society and a rising tide of crime.

In summary, 'cop culture' is part of the wider political, institutional, and cultural system within which values and interests are constantly evolving. As Janet Chan argues, in her sophisticated critique of the existing formulation of police culture:

> ...a sound theory of police culture should recognize the interpretive and active role of officers in structuring their understanding of the organization and its environment. ... A satisfactory formulation of police culture should allow for the possibility of change as well as resistance to change. (1996: 112.)

---

[15] McConville and Shepherd (1992) found that a large minority of the women police officers they interviewed had experienced harassment or discrimination.

The argument that police organizations do not change despite the introduction of new rules and policies because of 'cop culture' fails to appreciate that the culture itself changes. The organizational sub-culture of the police is always in a state of evolution and, for this reason, any claims made in the 1970s or 1980s regarding the influence of 'cop culture' on the police response to domestic violence should now be treated with a degree of caution. Previous researchers might have correctly identified and described the impact of 'cop culture' prevalent at the time of their studies. However, if 'cop culture' is now different, what police do could be expected to have changed as well. Also, as argued above, it is wrong to assume that sub-cultural norms, values, and beliefs translate simply into action. Instead they interact with other organizational factors.

Understanding the impact of the organization of policing on police decision-making

In trying to understand the behaviour of rank and file officers, the organization of the police service needs to be considered. This section will consider the impact of training, the policing 'style' of the Thames Valley Police, the technologies in use, the issue of finite resources, the organizational goals and rewards, and the procedural law. These have tended to be referred to as structural factors (see, for example, McConville, Sanders, and Leng 1991). However, they are all affected by the police culture. Priorities regarding resources and goals are made on the basis of cultural imperatives.

Training

Many critics of the police response to domestic violence argued that police behaviour would change if only a policy directed them towards arrest (see Chapter 1). Successful change is, of course, not achieved simply by the adoption of a policy, but by a continuing process of implementation and assessment.[16] The success of any

---

[16] Grace (1995) found that a third of operational officers (constables and ser-geants) had not heard of the 1990/60 Circular at all and a third of those who had some knowledge of the Circular were unclear about what it had said. In addition, over half said that they had not received any new guidelines on domestic violence. This was despite their managers' confidence that the guidance had been successfully disseminated.

policy will depend on the training of those entrusted with its implementation and enforcement.

Until the early 1990s, police training on domestic violence was minimal and, insofar as it occurred, it endorsed the view that the police should be careful about intervening and should encourage civil, rather than criminal, solutions (Bourlet 1990). In light of the Home Office Circular 1990/60, the Thames Valley Police improved its training of new recruits. One new training schedule emphasized the importance of the social service, rather than the law enforcement role of the police:

> The streets are not a battlefield with the enemy on every corner, they are populated by people who are prey to an ever-increasing number of social ills. The only agency available to assist twenty-four hours a day, seven days a week, is the police. This 'social work' aspect of your role takes up the major part of your working day; it is equally as important as fighting crime and, if neglected, can result in the disaffection of whole communities.[17]

Officers were taught about effective communication; the 'social' aspects of policing; community and race relations; supporting victims; and many other social skills considered necessary for the effective handling of domestic disputes. They were taught about threats and emotional and sexual abuse as well as physical attacks and made to understand the various social and economic factors which prevent some women from leaving abusive relationships. This training, aimed at breaking down common myths and stereotypes about domestic violence, was given to all new recruits. The extent to which this knowledge stayed with them or was soon forgotten once they were shadowing more experienced officers is, of course, open to debate. McConville and Shepherd (1992) found that officers soon forgot much 'social skills' training, seeing it, just a short time later, as of little relevance to practical policing. As Fielding argues: 'As operational service increases, the influence of formal training recedes and the importance of knowing how to proceed behaviourally in public encounters becomes a central preoccupation' (1989: 83). However, it was almost certainly partly responsible for the different attitudes amongst newer recruits to the service. There was, of course, little new training for established officers. Grace (1995) similarly found that there was little on-going training

---

[17] Introduction to the domestic disputes training notes used by Thames Valley Police.

on domestic violence for experienced patrol officers, some of whom remained ignorant of the changing expectations of their senior officers and, indeed, of the general public.

Chan (1996) criticizes conceptualizations of 'cop culture' which fail to take account of internal differentiation. She argues that there are multiple cultures within a police force. Training is one variable which determines the existence of various cultures. In the Thames Valley Police the attitudes and beliefs concerning domestic violence of senior (management) officers were different from those of established, experienced patrol officers. The management culture informs police training and so new recruits might start off nearer to the attitudes and beliefs of senior managers. However, the practical training, which involves long periods of time on probation shadowing more experienced officers, changes the culture of new recruits nearer to that of the established officers. A few of the older officers spoken to in Thames Valley, who had not been through the more recent training sessions, were confused about the force policy on domestic violence: some seemed to believe that the consensus was still to avoid positive action. One officer who had taken an injured woman to hospital claimed that she did not want to make a statement, so he left his 'calling card' with her and told her to contact him the following day if she changed her mind. He then added: 'It is the *informal policy* to leave the ball in their court, and not to encourage them to make a complaint' (my emphasis).

Whilst new policies and training can gradually improve the police response to domestic violence for a number of years following their introduction, there will be some officers who remain ignorant of, or resistant to, change. Furthermore, whilst policies and training can improve many areas of the police response they do not have a direct impact on the decision to arrest as other more influential factors can override policy at the scene of disputes. Levens and Dutton (1980) found that policy and subsequent improved training on domestic violence resulted in a substantial increase in police willingness to dispatch cars to domestic disputes, a significant increase in the use of mediation and referral techniques, but had no impact on arrest rates. The Thames Valley study also found that the dispatch rate had increased dramatically since the mid-1980s (see Chapter 3). Changes in policy and training, along with the changes in wider societal attitudes which led to policy reform, seemed to have altered the attitudes and values of new recruits and, to a lesser extent, older or established officers. But they did not directly shape their decision-making processes.

Neither policy nor training translates directly into action. However, it would seem sensible to argue that officers' working assumptions are gradually influenced by policies, directives, and training. Officers actively negotiate the knowledge and experience they acquire with the existing culture. In the case of domestic violence, force orders present officers with guidelines and recommendations which promote the increasing use of arrest. However, the successful application of these recommendations depends on the inter-relationship between the culture and various other situational and organizational factors.

Policing style

Low organizational priority has traditionally been accorded to dispute settlement. There is little supervision of officers by higher ranks at the scene of domestic disputes and there is little formal, or even informal, support for officers who have had to deal with complex and often distressing interpersonal disputes. Bayley and Bittner (1984) asserted, just over a decade ago, that in America police received no instruction, no guidance and, above all, no recognition for doing this type of work (see also Bittner 1975). These criticisms have been reflected in the domestic violence literature on this side of the Atlantic.

As mentioned above, the 1990/60 Circular and improved training attempted to change this. Nevertheless, in this study Thames Valley officers still felt that domestic disputes were more difficult to deal with than most other incidents. Unlike many other types of incident there is little organizational support for patrol officers responding to domestic violence. It is very rare for CID to investigate a domestic dispute unless a murder or a very serious assault has been committed. Similarly, the Family Protection Units will only take responsibility for a domestic dispute if the woman has made a complaint of rape or sexual assault, or if a child is at risk of abuse or neglect. During the period of fieldwork for this study there were no dedicated units or officers whose sole purpose was to deal with domestic violence.

Further difficulties can arise from the organizational conception of an 'incident'. Patrol policing in the Thames Valley at this time was almost entirely incident focused.[18] This means that it was reactive and based on single session intervention—criticized within the literature as 'fire-brigade' policing.[19] Domestic disputes are hard to manage within such an organizational framework because they are rarely isolated 'incidents' but, rather, on-going complex problems within dynamic relationships. Chronic domestic violence challenges the language and classification systems of the police service. The 'incident' framework can impede the appreciation of domestic violence as an enduring condition, with 'cycles of violence',[20] and thus can discourage patrol officers from responding appropriately (see Sheptycki 1993). A large observational study across various American states found that officers were indifferent towards ascertaining whether assaults were isolated incidents or part of a continuing series of violent incidents (Smith and Klein 1984). This was not true of the officers in the Thames Valley study. They often took the time to try to understand what had precipitated the conflict, which meant that they knew about a history of conflict in 60 per cent of the incidents that they had attended. Nonetheless, as table 4.5 shows, this knowledge did not seem to impact directly on the decision to arrest.

Suspects cannot be arrested for previous disputes, even previous criminal assaults, if there is no evidence to corroborate an allegation. Thus, an approach to incidents of domestic violence which has

TABLE 4.5   Officers knew that there was a history of disputes: number and percentage arrested

History	History of disputes	No history of disputes	Total
Arrest	85 (50%)	83 (50%)	168
No arrest	109 (50%)	110 (50%)	219
Total	194	193	387

$X^2 = 0.025$ (p < 0.87)

[18] Since the completion of this project, Thames Valley Police has changed its philosophy of policing away from a reactive, incident-focused style and towards a more proactive and 'problem-solving' style of policing.

[19] McConville and Shepherd (1992) have argued that despite the rhetoric of community policing, most police officers are committed to fire-brigade policing as the central mode of delivering policing. They reject the appropriateness of community policing as a viable core activity.

[20] Leonore Walker (1979) introduced the concept of a 'cycle of violence' in critical response to Murray Straus's original attempts to measure 'family violence rates'.

as its focus the choice of whether to arrest or not eradicates histor-
ical details which are not deemed relevant to the decision-making
process (Sheptycki 1993). It negates some of the very reasons for the
complaint being made to the police in the first place. Some of the
women who had experienced abuse of varying degrees for many
years, and who had finally decided to seek help at a time when the
immediate incident could not be categorized as a criminal offence,
were disappointed with the police response. They wanted the police
to recognize their victim status and help them to eliminate the
violence from their lives. The police, however, without sufficient
criteria to justify a criminal charge, felt that there were few alternative provisions available to them to offer help.

In many cases officers heard competing versions of the same
incident. In order to make sense of the situation, they had to
interpret the stories given by the various actors and decide which
version had more credibility. To do so, they needed to reduce complex stories into categories that would suggest whether or not a
criminal law response was appropriate. Categories of the criminal
law constitute the basic conceptual equipment with which police
organize their everyday activities. The police marshalled the linguis-
tic categories at their disposal in order to create an *object* to which
to respond. They tried to decipher clear, organizational categories
from often confusing and conflicting accounts of past and present
behaviours. The police expected disputants to adopt what they
considered to be recognizable and legitimate roles, and to behave
accordingly. The types of categories which officers used, in trying to
make sense of domestic disputes, were the same as those they
applied to the majority of incidents with which they dealt. They
were essentially dichotomous: victim or offender, crime or no-
crime. If the officers were not able to make sense of the information
volunteered, or the incident defied these categories, officers felt less
sure about how to respond. For example, if the labels victim and
offender were rejected by the disputants, the presumption was
against arrest (suspects were rarely arrested when their victims
refused to make statements or in any other way co-operate with
the police investigation). Edwards and Halpern (1991) maintained
that police should impose these labels according to strict legal
definitions, regardless of the subjective perceptions of the disputants
or their willingness to comply with the police definitional process.
However, most officers argued that without a victim, or without any

evidence of a crime, there is little prospect of mounting a prosecution, and hence no incentive to record the incident as a crime. Indeed, considering the implications for the police clear-up record, there is a disincentive against starting an investigation when the officer believes it is doomed to failure.

Technology

The gradual introduction of various forms of technology over the past decade has enhanced the facility for collecting and storing valuable information (see Chapter 3). Nevertheless, technological innovation has possibly engendered as many obstacles to, as opportunities for, improving services. The technological advances within the police service (the increased use of patrol cars; the use of personal radios; and the computerization of the control rooms) all mean that officers are expected to rush from one incident to the next, trying to keep ahead of ever increasing demands on their time. Holdaway (1983), over a decade ago, noted that officers were becoming less inclined to get out of their cars to communicate effectively with members of the public, preferring to drive around responding to 'exciting' incidents, thus distancing themselves further from interaction with the public. McConville and Shepherd refer to this as the 'blue light syndrome' (1992: 149). Although there have been various 'community policing' initiatives aimed at reversing this trend, they have had limited success (see McConville and Shepherd 1992).

Today there is very little pro-active mobilization of patrol officers. In the two areas under study, officers' movements were directed by a centralized command system. This meant that they spent most of their time in vehicles patrolling specific locales waiting to be dispatched in response to citizen complaints received by telephone. This type of organization sharply contrasts with the traditional beat officers who patrolled a limited area on foot, and were consequentially territorially cognizant and familiar with at least some of the local residents. The majority of the officers who responded to domestic incidents in this study were not acquainted with the families they encountered because they were regularly assigned to a number of different areas of the city. Hence, when officers arrived at disputants' homes they usually had to spend time gathering biographical information about the parties involved in order that they could make informed choices. If time impeded the accumulation of relevant data, in particular the accumulation of evidence, officers might be less likely to arrest.

If the technology is used to its best effect, the benefits of accurate and easily accessible data which can be quickly transmitted to patrol officers would outweigh the disadvantages of the technological thrust towards more reactive policing and away from community policing. However (as was discussed in Chapter 3) inadequate computer systems and poor communications in the control room meant that constables sometimes responded to domestic disputes with little or no intelligence on the disputants. In 40 per cent of the 387 Thames Valley incidents officers did not know about any history of disputes. Of course, in some of these cases there might not have been a history of violence. However, evidence from the United Kingdom and the United States suggests that in more than 60 per cent of incidents that the police attend there will have been a history of prior disputes.[21]

Resources

The problem of finite resources (the need to 'get results' without overstretching resources) impacts on the police organization as on other organizations within the public sector. The specific allocation of financial resources rarely affected operational decisions, although in a couple of cases officers could not comply with the victims' wishes because of financial constraints.[22] Usually officers were more concerned about human resources. It was not their own personal time that they were concerned about but of wasting 'police time'.

Charging someone with assault or criminal damage, the offences most frequently committed during domestic disputes, requires a considerable commitment of time in order to secure convictions at court. Copious amounts of paperwork are required in order to prepare a case for the Crown Prosecution Service. Officers bemoaned the waste of valuable police resources when victims withdrew their statements after all the paperwork had been com-

---

[21] Attacks by the same assailant are usually repeated, and tend to escalate in frequency and severity over time (see Woyd, Farrell, and Pease 1994; Strauss, Gelles, and Steinmetz 1980 for rates of repeat victimization in the United Kingdom and America; and Morley and Mullender (1994) for a discussion of the literature on domestic violence multiple victimization.

[22] A man who had assaulted his wife fled to Ireland. Although the victim wanted to press charges, the officer's extradition request was refused for financial reasons.

pleted and the suspect had spent time in police custody. Some regretted the fact that they would have to devote even more resources in the near future to repeatedly re-visiting women who refused to end their violent relationships.[23] When suspects are prosecuted the officer in charge is often required to attend court. Court appearances by officers are not only very time consuming, but are also expensive. This is because shift patterns have to be adjusted to accommodate an officer being freed from patrol duty, which invariably necessitates overtime. Officers sometimes argued that victim unreliability and the derisory sentences meted out by the courts meant that it was often not really worth preparing files on suspects arrested for the less serious assaults, or where damage to property was minimal.

Various studies conducted during the late 1970s and 1980s found that when domestic disputes occurred at the end of an officer's shift an arrest was less likely. This was found to be because the crime was not considered worthy enough to justify the officer staying late (Berk and Loseke 1980; Stanko 1989; Worden and Pollitz 1984). The Thames Valley study found no evidence of this. However, some officers admitted to feeling pressure to resolve incidents as soon as possible in case something more urgent came up, as the following comment made by an officer illustrates:

When we arrived, the dispute had calmed down. There had been no physical violence and no one wanted to make a complaint, so we left. There was no point in hanging around. It was a busy night. We needed to be free for the next shout [request from the control room to attend an incident].

Observing patrol officers responding to various types of calls, the researcher noted that this reluctance to 'waste' time, even when there was no immediate demand on their attention, influenced other areas of their work. Calls about disturbances between youths in the streets, or about suspicious persons, rarely resulted in an officer-citizen encounter. In most of these cases the police arrived, took a quick, cursory look around and, if the disturbance was over or if they could not immediately identify the people about whom the complaint had been made, they left, often without even getting out of the car.

---

[23] In this context officers had a keen appreciation of the problems of repeat victimization.

In just over a third of the domestic incidents the male disputant had left the scene of the dispute prior to the arrival of the police. Officers sometimes argued that due to inadequate resources they could not always devote sufficient time to locating absent suspects even when they had cause to arrest them. And in cases where there had been no criminal offence, or the victim would not make a statement, the police usually decided that attempts to find these men would not be a sensible use of resources. Occasionally, when officers did make efforts to locate absent suspects, a number of days or even weeks might have passed before the alleged assailant was found. This was mainly because of shift work or excessive demands on their time. In one instance an officer took three weeks to locate the perpetrator only to find that the injunction which he had transgressed had by then expired. Hence, even though the injunction had, at the time, had a power of arrest attached, the officer was informed by the county court that the suspect could no longer be arrested for having breached it.[24]

Of course, not only police resources but also other agencies' resources impact on operational policing. Service gaps created by the diminishing resources of other agencies are left to be filled by the police. During the time of this study the government consensus was that the police should 'get back to basics' by concentrating on catching criminals (Rose 1996: 88). However, the social and economic policies at the time had left many young, old, and vulnerable people literally out on the streets.[25] Rising numbers of homeless people, and other vulnerable persons with minimal assistance from social services, had created an increase in demands for 'social service policing' (see Rose 1996 for a more detailed discussion of these issues).

Organizational goals

For a long time the organizational goals regarding domestic disputes emphasized superficial mediation and discouraged recourse to

---

[24] Non-molestation injunctions, made by the county court, order a person not to assault, molest, or harass a woman and/or her children. Powers of arrest are attached only if the judge is satisfied that violence has previously occurred and may recur. A person who breaches an injunction can be apprehended for contempt of court.

[25] The most notorious of such policies was the closing of hospital wings and mental institutions as part of a 'care in the community' policy. This resulted in the eradication of one option without the creation of a satisfactory alternative.

the criminal law. As is stated above, force policies now encourage greater intervention, and in particular they encourage arrest. Policy advisors and senior police officers can attempt to determine the goals of the rank and file through training, policies and rules, rewards and punishments, and the perpetuation of an organizational culture that is in harmony with their aims. Nevertheless, patrol officers have discretionary powers which enable them to modify goals and, thus, to control outcomes of specific circumstances. Furthermore, as stated above, they have their own unique police culture that may not encourage the same priorities as their line managers.

The Police Service measures its efficiency principally by reference to collated statistics on the extent and type of recorded crime, the proportion of that crime detected and the number of cases prepared for prosecution. Within this framework crime prevention work and duties which are referred to as the 'social service' tasks of the police are undervalued, partly because they are difficult to measure. Pressures of public accountability are even greater than the internal pressures from senior management. Central government allocates resources according to demands and, as demands can only be shown by tangible statistics, this dictates an emphasis on catching and processing offenders. Hence, the reward structure for officers is determined largely by 'good arrests' (the number of 'collars felt').[26] Officers recognize that these are not very likely in domestic disputes (only 17 per cent of arrests in this study resulted in a prosecution—see figures 2.1a. and b. Therefore the wider organizational goals are sometimes compromised and working rules emerge which reduce the emphasis on arrest in domestic violence cases.

Procedural law (police powers)

When the police attend any incident they do so with the knowledge that they alone have certain powers to intervene in private disputes and to behave in accordance with legislation such as the Police and Criminal Evidence Act 1984 (PACE) and the Public Order Act 1986.

---

[26] Research has shown that a high arrest rate is considered a good measure of an effective officer and a way to impress line managers who are considering new recruits for detective work, although it is rather crude to argue that a 'good arrest' is the only thing motivating patrol officers (Cain 1973).

Under PACE (s. 17) officers have the power to enter premises in order to arrest anyone who has committed an arrestable offence. This includes assault occasioning actual bodily harm and assault occasioning grievous bodily harm and wounding. A constable may also enter premises in order to save life or limb, or to prevent damage to property. In addition to these powers, officers may, under the common law, enter property to prevent or deal with a breach of the peace. A constable may arrest anyone who is, or is reasonably suspected of being, about to commit, or has committed an arrestable offence, or for certain other specified offences, including indecent assault on a woman.[27] Arrest can also be justified as a preventative measure: to prevent physical injury to another person; or to protect a child or other vulnerable person; or to prevent a non-arrestable offence such as common assault (s. 25, PACE). Under common law a constable may arrest to prevent a breach of the peace. Officers can also use the Public Order Act 1986 to arrest for threatening or abusive conduct within or outside premises, or for noisy or disruptive behaviour in certain circumstances.

The Home Office Circular 1990/60 reminded officers of their powers under PACE in order that they can protect women and children involved in domestic disputes (see Chapter 1). However, the Thames Valley Police needed to take positive action in some situations where there was no evidence of a criminal offence—actions which their powers under PACE would not necessarily cover. It was found that in these cases, where the law needed to be used as a resource on which to draw in achieving social service aims or summary justice, the common law powers were most likely to be used (see Chapter 5). The power to arrest for a breach of the peace constitutes a powerful legal resource for officers having to deal with recalcitrant disputants. As Kemp, Norris, and Fielding (1992) argue, officers have considerable latitude both to define what behaviour might result in an outbreak of violence and to determine what behaviour would suggest reasonable grounds for considering a renewal of the breach of the peace to be imminent. Arrests for breach of the peace are attractive options for officers dealing with domestic disputes for various reasons. They allow officers to arrest people and then to release them with no further action. Of course,

---

[27] An arrestable offence is any offence punishable by five years or more imprisonment, or for which the penalty is fixed by law (s. 24 PACE).

officers can choose not to charge suspects arrested for any offence. However, it is easier to justify a 'de-arrest' or a no further action decision in cases of breach of the peace. Also, arrest for breach of the peace allows officers to hold belligerent men in custody—away from their families—overnight with the aim of putting them before the magistrates at the next available court. Furthermore, to bring a person before a court for breach of the peace the police need no independent witnesses or complainants. Of course, a magistrate can only bind over the defendant to keep the peace because, since no criminal offence has been committed, no conviction can result.

Occasionally officers hide behind procedural law when their working rules tell them not to intervene. In other words, they present a failure to intervene as arising from insufficient powers when it has little or nothing to do with the law. In the Thames Valley study there were a few occasions when the officers professed that they were keen to arrest an alleged perpetrator but were prevented by an absence of legal powers. On a few occasions officers were called to disputes and upon arrival were told by women 'cowering' behind the front door that the dispute had been resolved and they were no longer required. Without an invitation into the home the officers tended to leave. For example, one woman had opened her door only a couple of inches so she could barely be seen and asked the officers to leave, refusing to talk to them. The officers left even though they believed she was genuinely scared and they suspected that the aggressor was behind the door threatening her and preventing her from talking. When asked if he had considered forcing an entry, the answer of one of the officers suggested he was ignorant of his powers:

No, if we had better powers I would have pushed my way in but with no breach of the peace this was a grey area and I couldn't have stepped in. In such situations we have no right of entry. It was a no win situation as it could have made matters worse for the woman if we had forced our way in. This is the most frustrating type of incident to deal with.

Of course, it may have been true that this officer, and others like him, was genuinely ignorant of his powers.[28] From his reply it is

---

[28] Various other studies have found that some operational police officers are either ignorant of, or confused about, their legal powers, in particular, powers under PACE (see, for example, Bittner 1970: 129).

difficult to ascertain whether it was the perceived limitations of procedural law (misunderstood though they were) or the police working rules which prevented this officer from 'forcing' his way in.

Officers are not always reticent when it comes to 'intruding' in the private lives of the public. Often police work necessitates intrusions into privacy. The work of the vice squad and child abuse investigations and other 'family protection' matters provide obvious examples. Whilst some officers might not like this part of their work, or might hold private reservations about the anomalies of the criminal law concerning prostitution, for example, these concerns would not prevent them carrying out their investigative duties. In the incident cited above the officer's comment regarding his belief that 'it could have made matters worse' has little to do with the criminal law. It had a lot to do with the tendency of officers to make judgements, that is, working assumptions, about appropriate responses according to their perceptions of the usefulness of the criminal law in dealing with domestic disputes.

The important thing to note is that the police have powers but not obligations—they are not obliged to act according to the criteria of PACE, or any other Act. Police officers *can* arrest members of the public who are considered to be breaching the peace or who are suspected of committing a criminal offence but, in the main, *they do not have to*. Ultimately the police have powers of discretion which allow them to decide in which circumstances and with which people they will exercise coercive powers.[29] Hence the procedural law interacts with and influences working assumptions. PACE guides officers on what they can and cannot do in the streets regarding suspects, but it has also impacted on what they do in the station. It has affected police organization. For example, the introduction of the custody officer and the recording of suspect interviews, amongst other changes, impact on training and on resources, and in particular the time needed to prepare a case for the Crown Prosecution Service.

---

[29] This is not to suggest that individual junior officers always have unlimited discretion. They are 'guided' by force orders and by their senior colleagues. However, orders and policies always operate within the context of discretion. And, furthermore, policing domestic violence is low visibility work. It would be very rare for senior officers to be involved in domestic disputes. The issue of police discretion and the procedural law is explored further in chap. 5.

The organizational context of police decision-making

This chapter has discussed the 'cultural' and 'structural' context within which police officers police domestic violence. The police sub-culture was shown to be not a fixed deterministic entity but a fluid and evolving force which creates working assumptions. The culture is constantly being re-enforced and occasionally changed. Changes to the norms, values, and beliefs of the operational officers occur, in part, because of changing social conditions and attitudes in the wider society, and, in part, because of the introduction of new force policies, which are themselves the product of changing social mores. They are also influenced by what we might refer to as 'structural' factors, although to call any factors 'structural' when they are, in part, a product of the organizational culture might seem erroneous. Police culture is crucial to the translation of goals and powers into practice, and the prioritizing of resources. To take the criminal law as an example, the law is only a structure when we consider it theoretically. If we think of the application of law, which is what most of us who are interested in policing do, it only manifests itself in a situated context (see Fielding 1989). In other words, the influence of the law on police practice is only really meaningful when we consider the extent to which it is applied, or not, in specific situations and the way in which it is applied. The context of the application of law is what gives us a sense of its meaning. Having said that, the more 'structural factors' discussed above were the training of police officers, the police style, the technologies in place, the resources available, the organizational goals, and the procedural law. All of these, it was suggested, impact on the culture of operational officers and therefore influence the working assumptions and working rules which officers rely on in operational policing.

The many factors discussed in this chapter, structural and cultural, could be called the organizational context which is a constant in all types of policing. Figure 4.2 illustrates this organizational context.

This organizational context results in the establishment of working assumptions and working rules that influence the officers' decisions at the scene of domestic disputes. The working rules shape police decision-making by telling the officers how to respond when presented with certain situational variables—information about the

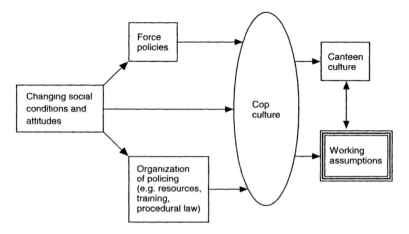

FIG. 4.2.   A reconceptualization of cop culture: its creation and its influences

type of offence and about the victim and the offender—that they interpret according to working assumptions. In other words, these situational variables provide officers with information which, when translated by their cultural assumptions, suggests appropriate courses of action in any given situation. Chapter 5 will examine these working assumptions and working rules in some detail by looking at the situational context of domestic disputes and the decision-making processes of operational officers.

5

The Situational Determinants of Police Decision-Making

In Chapter 4 it was argued that officers' responses to incidents of domestic violence are shaped by the organization of policing: the way in which they are trained; their organizational goals; technology; resources; the style of policing and procedural law. These might be referred to as 'structures', but they are inevitably influenced by, and, in turn, influence, sub-cultural norms, values, and beliefs. This chapter draws on observation of officers on patrol, and interviews with officers and (less often) victims. It shows how 'working assumptions' and 'working rules' which derive from these 'structural' and sub-cultural influences affected the choices made by Thames Valley officers attending domestic disputes (see Chapter 1 for a discussion of the concepts 'working assumptions' and 'working rules'). The question posed is: to what extent can evidential rules and force policies explain police decisions regarding arrest and to what extent are these decisions explained by working rules?

It will be argued that evidential law rarely dictates police action. Most police decisions regarding arrest are made on the basis of their working rules, which are decided upon according to their working assumptions. But it will be shown that the law is not rendered invisible by this process. Indeed, an understanding of the law is crucial to understanding officers' behaviour.

Furthermore, it will be argued that victims' preferences have a significant influence over police decisions regarding arrest and prosecution. When victims do not want their partners or ex-partners to be prosecuted this rarely happens. This does not, however, mean that violent men are not subjected to coercive police powers, but, rather, that police powers are used—by victims as well as officers—as a resource to achieve aims other than prosecution. Indeed, it will be shown that often arrest has little or nothing to do with prosecution.

The negotiation of temporary solutions

At most domestic disputes officers were faced with a series of limited choices. Contemplating the options available, they tried to decide how each of the alternative choices would impact, in the short-term, on the individuals concerned. Examining the dynamics of the interactions between officers and disputants—looking at how the parties, with their competing aims and understandings, communicated with each other—will show how decisions were made. Thus, the relatively low arrest rate (relative to the aims of the 1990/60 Circular) will be rendered comprehensible.[1] The processes by which officers made decisions will be examined as part of a wider process of negotiation between all the significant actors. As Morgan and Newburn have pointed out:

Whether or not a call involves a 'crime' depends not just on whether an offence has taken place, whether an offender is present, and so on, but also on whether the attending officer(s) decides—in negotiation with others—that he is going to record the incident as a crime. (1997: 81.)

This use of the term 'negotiation process' owes much to the work of Kemp, Norris, and Fielding (1992). Their concept of negotiation is drawn from a negotiated order approach to organizational theory (although the idea that police officers settled disputes by negotiation was used over twenty years prior to the work of Kemp, Norris, and Fielding by Albert Reiss (1971) and by Skolnick (1966)). The term 'negotiation' is used below to describe the collation and interpretation of information gathered from disputants; the decisions made which relied on this interpretation; and the attempts to implement such decisions. It also describes the mediation which occurred between disputants and officers when they attempted to reach solutions which served the interests of as many of the relevant parties as possible.

To refer to the police handling of domestic disputes as a dynamic negotiation process might suggest that each of the 'negotiators' have an equal chance of having their individual goals realized. Of course this is not the case, for they do not have equal status, authority, or power. The police interact with disputants in order to create social order. However, the men and women involved in the disputes do not always want to establish a peaceful solution. The various actors

---

[1] Part of the explanation for low arrest rates will be revisited in the following chapter in order to make sense of the even lower prosecution rate.

might have different agendas and in domestic disputes rarely does one solution satisfy the aims of everyone involved. In cases where there are conflicting stories and requirements the police have the ultimate authority to decide what 'the truth' is and the power to act accordingly, even if none of the other actors involved agree with their interpretation and their subsequent response. Having said this, as Hawkins (1992: 34) has argued, negotiation does rely on bargaining and decisions are often jointly arrived at by at least two of the relevant actors (usually the victim and police officer), and there is at least a level of mutual commitment to the decision reached. Negotiating a solution satisfactory to the majority of actors involved can mean that officers choose not to arrest when there is clear evidence of a criminal offence. Hence this dynamic process gives the lie to the 'canteen culture' myth that policing is about law enforcement. Whilst the police have the legitimate right to decide upon the outcome of a dispute, an officer may surrender power formally '. . . to enforce the law in return for an offer of compliance' (Hawkins 1992: 34).

In trying to understand the processes of negotiation, I initially considered adopting a rational choice perspective which draws on the theory of games and maintains that social life is principally capable of explanation as the outcome of the 'rational choices' of individual actors. It suggests what people ought to do in order to achieve their objectives (see Gambetta 1987 and Elster 1986). Deriving from economic theory, I found this perspective to be too formalistic for the purposes of understanding police action and, hence, I decided to explore the less deterministic work of Jarvie (1972). His understanding of situational logic informed my interpretation of the process of decision-making. I saw this process as following a logical pattern whereby actors consider rationally the range of possible outcomes at each stage. This helped to explain why different officers (some seeming to be more sympathetic or more conscientious than others) tended to arrive at similar decisions.

Drawing on the works of Hayek and Popper, Jarvie conceives man [*sic*] as pursuing certain goals or aims within a framework of natural, social, psychological, and ethical circumstances. These circumstances constitute both means of achieving his aims and constraints on that achievement. He refers to man's conscious or unconscious appraisal of how he can achieve his aims, within these circumstances, as 'sorting out the logic of the situation'. It is called logic because the actor tries to find out the best means, within the situation, to realize his aims. Hence, the concept of situational logic is a way of understanding how people attempt to achieve goals or aims with limited means. Jarvie does not suggest that the actor perfectly scrutinizes the situation to find one uniquely effective move. He argues, rather, that several different moves often present themselves, although it is unlikely that the actor will be emotionally and morally indifferent between them (1972: 4). Take, for example, incidents of domestic violence where the evidence of an offence is weak or where the victim is not keen for an arrest. In such incidents, removing the suspect, arresting him or leaving the dispute without taking any direct action would all seem to be reasonable options. However, if in this situation the suspect is aggressive and confrontational the officer might, because of his emotional response to the other actors involved, consider an arrest to be the more attractive option (see discussion of the suspect's demeanour below).

When we discuss the police response to domestic disputes we are, in effect, discussing their negotiation of temporary solutions to chaotic and often intractable interpersonal disputes. The main goal of the operational officers in this study, prior to the identification of criminal offences and suspects and assistance to victims, was to restore order. This does not mean that the police simply were pursuing their own agenda: the identification of suspects and, more importantly, the implementation of the criminal law sometimes facilitated the establishment of order. In turn, the restoration or maintenance of order usually assisted the victim. They focused not on the long term problems of disputants but on identifying immediate conflicts and facilitating their resolution and preventing their reoccurrence in the near future (usually for the duration of the shift) where possible. As Bayley and Bittner (1984) have argued, the police view appropriate goals as establishing control, immediately protecting lives and property, tending to the injured, but not correcting social problems like marital discord which might result in future episodes of violence.

There are essentially three outcomes which can result from the police attending a domestic dispute: one of the disputants can be arrested; one of the disputants can be removed from, or voluntarily leave, the scene; or both disputants can remain together after the police leave the scene. The first outcome might indicate that the police have sufficient evidence of a criminal offence, or that the negotiation process between the police and the disputants has broken down, whilst the latter two might be the result of successful negotiation. In many of these types of cases attended by Thames Valley officers, arrests could have been justified in order to prevent further breaches of the peace. However, where this was not considered to be necessary, attempts were made to restore the peace and negotiate a course of action considered agreeable to the victim whilst avoiding unnecessarily provoking the other party. It will be shown that these outcomes were the product of a two-stage negotiation process.

At the first stage the police gathered and interpreted information and arrived at certain 'working assumptions' about what had gone on and what was likely to ensue. At the second stage they considered the 'options' available and took action, that is, they applied certain 'working rules'. Hence, arriving at a certain working assumption would result in the choice of a certain working rule. Both stages involved a certain amount of interaction in order to move successfully on to a conclusion. Typically, if there were two police officers present, the disputing parties were separated so that each could be spoken to alone. However, this did not always mean that the information-gathering stage was free from problems. Poor communication between the various actors, for whatever reason, could frustrate officers' attempts to gather information and this, in turn, could reduce the options available. Also, officers in the process of taking action might have found that they had to return to the information-gathering stage if one, or more, of the parties, challenged the appropriateness of the action and made further, or counter, allegations which necessitated the officers abandoning or modifying their initial assumptions. Not once did I observe an officer challenging a decision arrived at by another officer. Even when two officers were present at the scene and they spoke separately to one or other of the disputants, they always seemed to reach the same decision. Consensus was arrived at without any apparent negotiation between the two officers (see Chapter 4 for an explanation of how 'canteen culture' secures unanimity on the streets). The two stages of gathering and interpreting information and acting on it cannot be discussed discretely, as there were sometimes 'feedback loops' whereby the assumptions and rules were renegotiated—sometimes more than once. They need to be understood as a dynamic process. This chapter will, therefore, examine the various types of information available to officers at the scenes of domestic disputes and show how they interpreted this information and how decisions regarding arrest were made according to these interpretations.

Information relating to the offence

Evidence

This section will examine the extent to which officers were presented with or gathered information which could be used as evidence of a criminal offence, and the influence of this evidence on their decisions regarding the arrest of the perpetrators. As discussed in Chapter 4, some critics of the police have argued that, when officers respond to incidents of domestic violence, legal criteria, that is whether or not an offence has been committed, are frequently superseded by 'moral' criteria. In particular, it has been argued that when police officers feel that the woman is to blame for the violence they are dissuaded from arresting the suspect (see, for example, Stanko 1985; Hanmer, Radford, and Stanko 1989). To put it crudely, it is argued that officers sometimes ignore evidence of criminal offences arising from domestic disputes. This study provided some evidence to support this assertion. However, disregarding evidence did not appear to be correlated with perceptions of victim blameworthiness, or according to any other moral criteria. Furthermore, in the majority of cases there was a strong correlation between the existence of evidence and the decision to arrest (see also Feder 1996).[2] Where there was incontrovertible evidence that an offence had taken place the police tended to make an arrest, although they were sometimes persuaded against such action by women who were opposed to an arrest (see the discussion of victim preferences, below). Similarly, where there was no evidence of a criminal offence

[2] The variable 'evidence' is constructed from my own evaluation of which incidents involved evidence of a criminal offence. All of the available information on each case (details gathered from officers, crime complaint forms, and victims statements, where available) was considered and evidence of violence or criminal damage was noted. This was regardless of whether the officer thought that a 'crime' had been committed. This definition does not include breaches of the peace. Many of the cases included in the 'no evidence of an offence' category did involve such breaches. Methodological triangulation, in particular interviews with victims, provided sufficient proof of the reliability of this definitional process.

TABLE 5.1.   Evidence of an offence: number and percentage arrested

	Suspect not arrested	Suspect arrested	Total
No evidence	141 (76%)	45 (24%)	186 (48%)
Evidence of an offence	78 (39%)	123 (61%)	201 (52%)
Total	219	168	387

$X^2 = 53.8$ (p < 0.001 significance)

having been committed the presumption was against arrest, as table 5.1 illustrates.

The suspect was arrested in almost two-thirds of the incidents where there was evidence of an offence, but in less than a quarter of those where there was no evidence. In the vast majority of cases the victims and the officers were in agreement as to the availability of evidence. Furthermore, the decision to arrest was consistent with their assessments about evidence. In only forty-eight of the 387 cases the victim alleged that an offence had taken place but there was no evidence to corroborate their allegation. Nevertheless, in seventeen of these cases the suspect was arrested for breaching the peace.

Any assertions about the relationship between evidence and the decision to arrest need to be qualified. Evidence is not always a clear cut entity waiting to be recognized or discovered by the police. There are, of course, two types of evidence: legally relevant evidence, for example a black eye, and information which can be gathered and constructed to serve as evidence. The amount of evidence available to the police at different disputes varies greatly. Therefore in some cases evidence is harder to miss or ignore than in others. It seems that in cases of domestic violence when other factors point against arrest as the preferable outcome, less obvious evidence of an offence is 'missed'. More importantly, the effort which police put into finding or generating evidence also varies across cases.

Often the police have to go to great efforts to find information which can be turned into evidence. As McConville, Sanders, and Leng explained: '...at each point of the criminal justice process "what happened" is the subject of interpretation, addition, subtraction, selection and reformulation.... Case construction... involves not simply the selection and interpretation of evidence but its *creation*' (1991: 12). In the case of domestic disputes, they have argued, certain types of fact would *not* be sought and so the incidents would be constructed in such a way that 'no further action' would be the obvious result (1991: 34) (see also Cooney 1994). Similarly, Sanders (1988a) argued that domestic cases are generally regarded as trivial per se, and are therefore presumed to be unsuitable for prosecution. Since 'triviality' is not an objective fact capable of simply being reported by investigating officers, he argued that officers decide against police action and justify this in organizational terms by selecting and interpreting the 'facts' to suggest that there had been no offence, or not a serious offence. Cooney has reviewed various studies and argued that: 'As the victim's social status declines, the probability that . . . investigatory measures will be undertaken decreases. Thus, in cases where victims are of decidedly low status, even the most obvious investigative leads may not be pursued, regardless of the legal seriousness of the incident' (1994: 840). He found that victim respectability was also correlated with the pursuit of evidence (see also Stanko 1981). He further claims that the status of the victim similarly affects perceptions about the quality of the evidence as well as the amount the officers are prepared to gather (ibid.: 848).[3]

It is probably true that during the 1970s and 1980s domestic violence was regarded by the police as fairly trivial, and that the complaints of victims were not taken seriously. However, this does not describe the response of the majority of Thames Valley officers in the 1990s. These officers claimed to take domestic violence seriously and sometimes made great efforts to assist victims, who were not, in the main, considered to be undeserving. However, this does not mean that the police investigated all cases thoroughly. They almost certainly failed to investigate some of the forty-eight incidents where there was an allegation, but apparently no evidence, of an offence. It will be argued that their failure to investigate such cases is grounded in their working assumptions. For example, perceptions about the likelihood of the victim refusing to testify against the suspect can dissuade officers from making the effort required to secure sufficient evidence for a charge.

Officers do not need conclusive evidence of guilt before they arrest a suspect. But they do need evidence sufficient to create a 'reasonable suspicion' that an offence has taken place.[4] This could

---

[3] Baumgartner also writes about the 'strong and persistent association between discretion and discrimination . . . in the legal response to domestic violence' (1992: 159).

[4] Police and Criminal Evidence Act 1984 (s. 24).

amount to a 'hunch', and need not include legally admissable evidence (referred to henceforth as 'evidence'). While a bruise caused by an attack would constitute strong evidence of assault occasioning actual bodily harm, a bruise is not necessary in order to arrest for this offence. However, many of the officers spoken to in the Thames Valley Police argued that they needed both evidence and a co-operative witness in order to make an arrest. Some even argued that the force policy stated this. This policy explained: 'if it is clear that offences have been committed e.g. there is *evidence of an injury,* [my emphasis] the perpetrator *should be arrested*' (original emphasis).[5] Read carefully it does not say that the police need evidence in order to make an arrest but it could, on a superficial reading, imply just this. Officers seem to focus on the evidence necessary for charging suspects rather than arresting them. Even if the police believe that a domestic dispute has taken place and believe that they know who has committed an offence, they cannot charge the alleged perpetrator if they can gather no evidence to support their beliefs. So, whilst officers can arrest persons without evidence of a criminal offence, these are not likely to be 'good arrests'. In other words, they are not likely to result in a prosecution and consequently are often seen as a waste of finite resources (see the discussion of organizational factors in Chapter 4). In incidents of domestic violence, officers seem to create a no-win situation. As the law stands it would be easy to charge a suspect with violence even where there is no injury if the victim and the suspect both made statements which said that the victim had been assaulted by the said suspect. However, officers would only be likely to get such evidence if they initially made an arrest. They are only likely to do this if they are presented with legally relevant evidence. The best evidence of an offence is physical injury. Not surprisingly, therefore, evidence of injuries to victims was correlated with the decision to arrest (only a third of cases where the victim was not injured resulted in an arrest as compared to over half of those where the victim was injured) as table 5.2 shows.[6]

Allegations of criminal damage can also easily be substantiated but allegations of relatively minor assaults are more difficult for the victim to substantiate. Bruising is unlikely to be visible until a few

---

[5] Thames Valley Police, 'Y' Area Memorandum, No. 7/92, para. (d).
[6] See also Edwards (1996); Waaland and Keeley (1985), and Feder (1996).

TABLE 5.2. Victims' injuries: number and percentage arrested

	Suspect not arrested	Suspect arrested	Total
Victim not injured	140 (67%)	69 (33%)	209 (54%)
Victim injured	79 (44%)	99 (56%)	178 (46%)
Total	219	168	387

$X^2 = 19.9$ (p < 0.001)

hours after the injury has been sustained, by which time the police have usually attended and left the dispute. Even in cases where they believed the woman's allegations, and the woman was willing to make a statement, the absence of corroborative evidence usually meant no action, as the following comments from two different officers illustrate[7]: 'I believed the woman's allegations of violence but there were no visible injuries, so I couldn't arrest him'. 'A woman called us to say that she had been hit in the face by her ex-boyfriend. There were no visible injuries. . . . so he couldn't be arrested.' The officers could have returned to visit the victims the following day and sought corroborative evidence or they could have arrested the suspect in the hope of securing a confession. But they did not do either. In fact, officers rarely did this. In the main, they invited victims to contact them the following day if visible injuries appeared and occasionally they made a provisional appointment for the victim with the scenes of crime officer. Victims rarely kept these appointments.[8] As McConville, Sanders, and Leng argue, in domestic disputes it seems that sometimes the police make little effort to 'construct' a case. However, it will be shown that this is not because domestic disputes are considered to be 'trivial' (Sanders 1988a) or because these victims are less influential than others (McConville, Sanders, and Leng 1991). Organizational factors such as resources and policing style—in particular, the shift system—might have impeded the investigative process, but the main reason why the police failed to investigate some complaints thoroughly was that victims frequently refused to support the prosecution of the

[7] These quotations, and others presented in this chapter, are taken from interviews with police officers about specific incidents which they attended.
[8] Edwards (1989) was critical of officers' discretionary powers which allowed them to use informal 'cooling off' periods (a delaying tactic based on the belief that women frequently withdraw their statements in the hours immediately following an allegation) in an attempt to discourage them from demanding positive action.

perpetrators. Officers' working rules dissuaded them from pursuing a case involving an unco-operative victim (see below). However, this does not mean that failure to support prosecution or an absence of evidence always meant that the police would not make an arrest. Various other types of information relating to the offence and the suspect are considered by police in making decisions regarding arrest.

The seriousness of the offence

Information gathered by police officers relating to evidence of an offence is likely to inform them about the seriousness of the offence. However, the perceived seriousness of an offence is not only a product of evidence, it is also a product of working assumptions. Serious cases of domestic violence, such as grievous bodily harm, usually involve fairly strong evidence that an offence has taken place. Therefore they are likely to result in an arrest. However, other serious cases, such as threats to kill, rarely produce corroborative evidence. In such incidents seriousness is a product of the police searching for facts from which they can construct a case (Sanders 1987; McConville, Sanders, and Leng 1991). The social context of the incident can persuade them or dissuade them from making this effort. In other words, the working assumptions (which might tell them that a man might threaten his wife in a row but not really mean to carry out the threat) can dictate the effort towards securing evidence. And, more importantly, working assumptions about threats being more serious if they come from someone other than an intimate partner, can mean that available evidence is interpreted in one way or another. Hence, McConville, Sanders, and Leng (1991) argued that 'seriousness' is not an objective reality but is a construction.

In cases where a serious offence involved legally relevant evidence, the police were more inclined to arrest a suspect. This finding challenges that of another study of policing disputes. Cretney and Davis (1995) found that offence seriousness had little influence on police decision-making processes: 'There appears to be an almost random relationship between seriousness and the investigation and prosecution of assault' (1995: 13). This quotation requires close scrutiny. The authors are asserting two things: first, that seriousness does not influence the *investigation* of assault and, secondly, that it does not influence the *prosecution* of assault. In the Thames Valley study, seriousness of the offence was a predictive variable in the decision to arrest. But it seemed to have little effect on the decision to prosecute (once the suspect had been arrested, the victim's choice was the only important variable that shaped police and prosecutors' decisions—see Chapter 6).

Whilst observing officers on patrol, I attended a dispute which had resulted in quite serious injuries to a woman's face and arms (as well as damage to various items of property). Both she and her child were visibly disturbed and afraid. The officers did not wait to find out what she wanted and whether or not she was prepared to make an evidential statement—they immediately arrested her husband. There was clear evidence of two criminal offences but it was not clear whether their decision was influenced by evidence or by working assumptions regarding the seriousness of the offence and the risk of further violence (as the husband was still agitated). Serious offences of violence usually mean strong evidence and it is probably the case that *both* evidential and working assumptions influence police decisions in such cases.

In some cases, however, the seriousness of the crime and the police abhorrence of brutal violence, especially sexual violence, persuades officers to take action even when the evidence may be considered to be insufficient or controversial. In one case involving rape and grievous bodily harm[9] the victim sustained head injuries which resulted in a long period of hospitalization and permanent brain damage. When the police were first called, by a nurse, to the hospital the woman was adamant that she did not want to make a statement, explaining that she and her boyfriend normally engaged in violent sex and that, therefore, this incident was not extraordinary. The Family Protection Unit[10] was informed and they provided advice and support for months after the initial report, even though she maintained that she would not press charges. Eventually the victim made a statement and the suspect was prosecuted.

---

[9] Grievous bodily harm is contrary to sections 20 and 18 of the Offences Against the Person Act 1861. Wounding or grievous bodily harm, where no intention to cause grievous bodily harm needs to be proved, is contrary to section 20; committing wounding or grievous bodily harm with intent to do so is contrary to section 18.

[10] A police unit specializing in the investigation of sexual offences and all cases of child abuse.

The police had pushed for a prosecution in this case despite the initial wishes of the victim, and the less than perfect evidence (the issue of consent concerning the rape allegation was problematic) because of their working assumptions relating to the seriousness of the offence. However, whilst the evidence would not have been 'watertight' without the complainant's statement, there was certainly sufficient evidence to charge the suspect. Therefore, whilst the working rule relating to the seriousness of the offence shaped the officers' decisions, the strength of the evidence was also important. Hence, as in most cases, this decision reflected the interplay between evidential and working rules.

Like evidence, seriousness is not an objective phenomenon waiting to be noted by attending officers. It is, in part, a social construction. Whilst few would dispute that a murder is serious, or that minor criminal damage is not so serious, the majority of domestic disputes result in injuries which could variably be labelled anywhere on the scale from 'minor' to 'serious'. The construction of seriousness can be affected by other working assumptions derived from information about the suspect—in particular, information relating to the suspect's demeanour and the perceived risk of further violence.

Information relating to the suspect

Threats to order and police authority

There is evidence from various studies to suggest that the attitude of the suspect is crucial in determining whether or not an officer will charge a suspect. Research has demonstrated that if a suspect challenges the authority of the police and is hostile to the officer he is more likely to be arrested (Choong 1997; Worden and Pollitz 1984; Smith and Klein 1984; Buzawa and Buzawa 1993; Feder 1996). Indeed it has been suggested that an arrest nearly always occurs if an assailant remains violent in the officers' presence (Ferraro 1989b). The Thames Valley study lent some support to these findings: when the suspect was 'aggressive'—either verbally or physically confrontational and threatening the police officers' authority—the police were more likely to arrest him, and when he was calm they were more likely to decide not to arrest him. Whilst only one in three of all suspects were 'aggressive' towards officers, over two-thirds of

TABLE 5.3.   Suspects' demeanour: number and percentage arrested.

	Suspect not arrested	Suspect arrested	Total
Suspect calm	182 (66%)	92 (34%)	274 (71%)
Suspect aggressive	37 (33%)	76 (67%)	113 (29%)
Total	219	168	387

$X^2 = 39.9$ (p < 0.001)

them were arrested. Hence, they accounted for almost half of all those arrested (see table 5.3).

Some critics have suggested that the demeanour of the suspect takes precedence in the decision-making process over other variables such as the evidential criteria or, more pertinently, the wishes of the victims (Dobash and Dobash 1980; Dolon, Hendricks, and Meagher 1986). Quantitative analysis of the Thames Valley data did not support this. Both evidential criteria and the wishes of the victim were more highly correlated with the decision to arrest than the suspect's demeanour. However, as with all of these determining variables, there was, in many cases, an interaction between the suspect's demeanour and other situational factors.

As the suspect's demeanour presented a source of variance in the outcome of the negotiation process, it affected the arrest decision in many cases. Challenges to police authority, provocation of individual officers, or unwillingness to calm down enough to respond to questions, all meant poor communication between officers and the men involved in the disputes. Just as a calm victim can expedite a smooth and successful negotiation of the pertinent issues (see below), a hostile suspect can impede this process. The frustration of officers' attempts to facilitate a smooth resolution to messy disputes was particularly evident in incidents where the suspect was not only hostile but also under the influence of alcohol. In a conflict situation when people are drunk they are more likely to be belligerent and volatile and less likely to be calm upon request. Consequently, arrests are more likely (Bayley 1986; Buzawa and Buzawa 1990; Smith and Klein 1984; Waaland and Keeley 1985).[11] The suspect being under the influence of alcohol was highly correlated with the suspect being 'aggressive' and, therefore, with the

[11] Again, research has suggested that suspects who are drunk and belligerent to the police are most likely to be arrested whether an incident is a domestic in a home or a non-domestic out in the street (Sanders 1988a).

breakdown of the negotiation process and the decision to arrest (three-quarters of those who were aggressive were under the influence of alcohol). Less than one-third of the 'sober' suspects were arrested, compared to over a half of those considered by the officers to be drunk.

These data suggest that working assumptions regarding what is confrontational, challenging, or even threatening in certain contexts automatically result in the application of the working rule which tells officers to arrest belligerent suspects. However, the dynamic negotiations of the various significant actors sometimes cannot be reduced to this simple deterministic model. There are, in a number of cases, 'feedback loops' (see Chapter 1). Hence, options are suggested—based on the officers' working assumptions—and 'suitable' outcomes are negotiated. Whilst the most belligerent suspects were almost automatically arrested, many of those men who initially threatened or challenged the police authority were given a chance to contribute to the achievement of a 'solution' to the dispute.

In just under a quarter of all incidents the suspect was asked to leave the scene of the incident. Men who were initially resistant to officers' suggestions that they leave were threatened with arrest in an attempt to make them co-operate, as in the following incident, described by one of the attending officers:

This woman called us because her ex-husband arrived at her home causing a disturbance. He was drunk and refusing to leave. According to the woman, relations between them were normally good. I asked him to leave explaining that this was an unreasonable hour to call uninvited. He argued with me for a while and so I threatened to arrest him to prevent a breach of the peace, after which he left.

When men were reluctant to leave the scene of the incident officers sometimes spent considerable amounts of time trying to persuade them to go peacefully, as the following interview excerpt shows:

They needed separating so we told the man to get dressed and go and spend the night with a friend. The man was procrastinating, hoping that if he took a long time to get ready that I would leave and he'd stay in the house. I warned him that if he didn't leave soon I would arrest him to prevent a further breach of the peace. He soon got moving then and I escorted him out of the house.

In these situations the original working assumption about the belligerence of the suspect persuaded the officers that the man needed to be removed from the scene to secure the victim's safety. However, they did not automatically arrest the man. Instead, they negotiated alternative options. Once the suspects showed that they were prepared to calm down and leave, the officers' evaluation of them changed and arrest was no longer considered to be necessary.

The suspects in fifty-six incidents were told that if they did not leave they would be arrested. Some were further warned that if they returned within a given period of time they would also be arrested. Sometimes suspects were offered a 'deal': 'leave peacefully, promise not to return tonight, and you won't be arrested. Play up, and you'll spend the night in a cell.'

Twenty of these fifty-six suspects who were threatened with arrest refused to comply with the officers' requests. All were consequently arrested. Their behaviour did not alter and so the officers' original assumptions did not alter. Hence, the working rule, which urges officers to arrest confrontational and aggressive suspects, remained. The suspects' pugnacity, often coupled with their being disinhibited by alcohol, meant that they were not willing or able to co-operate in the negotiation process. The following excerpt shows an attempt by an officer to negotiate with a suspect, despite the officer's obvious irritation at being provoked. As was usual, the man was given a few chances to co-operate before the police officer asserted his authority:

A woman called us up to say that she wanted her 'ex' removing from the house as he was refusing to leave. They had recently split up and he had come round to see the baby. She had allowed this although they have a history of domestic disputes. She wanted him to leave after a while but he told her to 'fuck off' and said he would not go. . . . There had been no violence but she was afraid. I tried to talk to him and reason with him but he was very arrogant and very condescending. I told him to leave. I gave him a couple of chances to leave, and eventually he went. He then went outside and sat in his car and would not drive off. I again told him to leave. He swore at me, drove 100 yards and parked up again. I then went to his car and arrested him to prevent a further breach of the peace. I thought enough's enough!

Officers tended to be most willing to negotiate with truculent suspects when they sympathised with their emotional plight, as the following example shows:

This was a very young couple with young children. She had thrown him out on many occasions. He kept returning and pressurising her to take him back—pushing his way into her home and hitting her. On this occasion he had forced his way in. After we arrived he left amicably saying he had only come to see his baby. But then he stood outside her home and refused to leave. He kept calling out and saying he wanted her back and he wanted to be with his baby. He was very distraught, crying and shouting and generally harassing her. I went out and spoke to him for fifteen minutes and offered to take him anywhere he wanted to go. He refused to go anywhere. I warned him three times that if he did not leave voluntarily I would have to arrest him to prevent a breach of the peace. In the end he was arrested. I used the breach of the peace to give me the power to get him in my car and take him away. He was kept in custody only for long enough for me to call his mum and then I took him to his mum's home on the other side of town. I wanted to get him away from the house as he was carrying four Stanley knives on him. He had a fairly plausible excuse to do with his work, but I was concerned for the woman's safety as the man was so upset. I would rather not have arrested him but it was a busy night and I could not spend any more time trying to persuade him to leave voluntarily.

In this incident there was not one uniquely effective move. The officer was faced with two options and neither seemed to be ideal. In the end he responded to the woman's predicament and arrested the man.

This last excerpt shows that suspects' demeanour, whilst highly correlated with the decision to arrest, is typically one part of a more complex negotiation process where the needs and predicaments of all significant actors are of consideration. Whilst some factors weigh more heavily in the equation than others, it is the interaction of the various sources of information and the working assumptions regarding such information that leads officers towards certain decisions. One of these sources of information is the factors which point to a high chance of further immediate violence.

Risk of further violence

Some critics of the police have argued that even when victims are in danger and request an arrest, officers consistently refuse to make arrests (Buzawa and Buzawa 1990; Davis 1983; Black 1980). This was not borne out by the Thames Valley study. In a few cases the police believed that to leave the suspect in the home would have put the victim at a significant risk of further serious violence.[12] In these cases they arrested the suspects in order to neutralise that risk, even

[12] The risk had to be *significant*. On occasions the police considered that there was a slight risk of further violence and yet took the chance of leaving the alleged suspect at the scene (see below).

if they did not believe that they had a good prospect of securing a conviction. Even when victims were adamant that they would not make a statement about the incident, the dangerousness of the situation shaped the police response—they arrested first and asked questions later. Details of two cases will serve to illustrate this point. In both of them the victim was unwilling to co-operate, the offences were serious, and there was sufficient evidence to charge the suspect. However, in only the first case did the police consider that there was a risk of further serious violence and so only in this case did the officer arrest the suspect:

She'd called us to this incident saying that her husband was trying to kill her. She's been attacked on many occasions but never wants him charged with anything. He's in and out of prison. He's got form for violence to others as well as his wife and for firearms offences. When we arrived we saw him dangling her over the balcony. The front door was open so we went straight in and arrested him, even though she was telling us to leave him alone. Had we not got him out he might have killed her. He'd punched her and thrown her across the room before he held her over the balcony, threatening to kill her. She had a split lip and was very badly bruised and very distressed. I stayed with her after he was arrested. Her doctor was there as well. I spent several hours with her taking a statement. At the end she refused to allow it to be used in court. She told me that she did not want him charged. She then made a withdrawal statement, as she has done four times before. So he was never charged for the ABH [assault occasioning actual bodily harm] or the threats to kill.

The officers' priority in this case was to remove the suspect, by arresting him, to ensure that he could not inflict any more damage on the victim. Once the immediate danger was over, because the suspect had been removed and put in a police cell to calm down, the victim's wishes came back into the equation and took precedence in the decision of whether or not to charge the suspect.[13]

In the second case, when the police arrived there was no longer any immediate danger of further violence as the suspect had left the scene and the woman had been admitted to a hospital:

This lady's husband had beaten her up and then left. She had blood pouring from the back of her head where he'd thrown an ashtray at her. There was a history of violence and it was a clear GBH [assault occasioning grievous bodily harm]. She was taken to hospital. She was totally incoherent and not prepared to make a statement. She blamed the alcohol and minimalized the

---

[13] See chap. 6 for a discussion of the victim's wishes influencing the decision to charge.

violence, and blamed herself for provoking him. I explained the options to her later when she was more coherent but she would not make a statement. With no statement there was no point in arresting him.

As the period of immediate danger was over the officers deferred to the wishes of the victim and the suspect was not arrested. The majority of incidents in the Thames Valley study did not involve officers negotiating information relating to the risk of immediate further violence considered serious enough to affect police decisions, although in most cases information about the suspect's demeanour, fed into officers' perceptions about danger, as well as their own prejudices against aggressive citizens threatening their authority. Indeed, all of the types of information discussed so far can be seen to be interrelated. For example, perceptions of strength of evidence feed into notions of seriousness, and perceptions about suspects' demeanour feed into notions of risk. For this reason, whilst the various types of relevant information have been discussed discretely, they should be considered as a more fluid interaction between everything officers see, hear, and think in relation to specific disputants and domestic disputants in general. Having said that, there is one rather more discrete type of information which officers receive at the scene of disputes. Whilst feeding into and being translated through notions of victims of domestic violence in general, this type of information stands rather more separately (although not entirely so) from the other types of information discussed above. It is information relating to what victims want from the police and feel about the dispute.

Information relating to the victim

Victim Preferences

In the literature on domestic violence it is recognized that the single greatest impediment to criminal justice intervention is the victim's failure to report the incident to the police (see Chapter 7). However, a discussion of the role played by victim non co-operation in the police decision-making process, and in the prosecution process once the incident has been reported, has been largely absent from this literature. Many critics have asserted that victims want the police to arrest their partners and rarely withdraw their statements once made. They have argued that victim preferences by themselves do not significantly affect police decisions because of an overwhelming police bias against arrest.[14] And, further, that victim withdrawal and unreliability is a 'myth', promulgated by police to excuse this bias (Stanko 1985; Faragher 1985). McConville, Sanders, and Leng (1991: 32–4) have argued that some victims are more influential than others and that the police are more likely to be willing to arrest those who have committed crimes against more influential victims. They further argue that whilst parties to any domestic dispute are by definition non-influential, female victims of violence in general are especially non-influential (see Chapter 1). Other writers have been more inclined to acknowledge the influence of victims of domestic violence on the police decisions to arrest and charge suspects. Some British and American research has found that victim preferences accounted for the largest variance in arrest rates (Feder 1996; Berk and Loseke 1980; see also Buzawa and Buzawa 1996b; Smith and Klein 1984).

The writers cited above are not necessarily contradicting one another. McConville, Sanders, and Leng, for example, were referring to the influence of different types of victims who *wanted* the police to take positive action, rather than victims who did not want the suspects in their cases to be arrested. They are undoubtedly right in arguing that certain, more powerful, victims have a greater chance of persuading an officer to arrest, if the officer is uncommitted to that course of action, than a victim of domestic violence, who may have no 'power' or 'influence' within the community and who is perhaps less willing to make a formal complaint against the suspect. Those who have argued that victims of domestic violence are powerful are those who have considered the influence of victims on the police decision *not* to take positive action. They have been more concerned with police decisions not to arrest than McConville, Sanders, and Leng, who were primarily concerned with how and why police exercise their powers of arrest and detention because their research was based primarily on a sample of arrests.

The focus of this section will be on the influence of victims who prefer that their assailants are not arrested. It will show that even when there is evidence of an offence, and even when the officer would prefer to arrest the suspect, victims' hostility to this course of action will more often than not result in no further action against

---

[14] Indeed Bayley (1986) reported that victims' wishes were not even correlated with the arrest of assailants.

the suspect. In other words, the police usually regard the victim's complaint (rather than the existence of evidence of an offence) as a necessary precondition of arrest. Other research has shown this to be true of victims involved in non-domestic disputes. It seems that the police often fail to arrest people involved in disputes regardless of the gender of the disputants or the type of relationship between them (Stanko 1995). Cretney and Davis (1995), who interviewed ninety-three assault victims admitted to an accident and emergency department, found that at the initial victim-police encounter the victim largely determined the progress (if any) of the case. This was almost regardless of whether the injuries had resulted from a domestic dispute or a dispute between non-intimates and regardless of offence-seriousness. These authors have argued that the police do not respond to 'crimes against society', but, instead, to 'complaints by the aggrieved'. They will usually only take action if the aggrieved is committed to the prosecution process, even in respect of very serious assaults. If the victim is reluctant to co-operate, whether this is because of fear of retaliation or for another reason, the police will not pursue the case.

When the officers were considering the options they questioned the disputants to discover what they wanted the police to do: 'So what do you want us to do?' was the most common response to the disputants' revelations of violence, intimidation, or discord. Consequently, information on victims' preferences was obtained from each police officer. Some victims were very clear about what they expected from the police. Others made more than one request. However, almost all expressed a primary wish: over a third wanted the suspect to be removed from the scene; a third wanted simply to be advised or for the officers to restore the peace; and just under a third wanted the suspect to be arrested (see Chapter 7).[15] Looking more closely at the secondary or alternative requests, it was found that there was substantial overlap between the victims' requests for the suspect to be removed and their requests for him to be arrested. In other words, in many of the incidents the victim had wanted the police to do either of these things. Also, in many cases where the woman had initially only wanted the police to remove the suspect, he was arrested because the negotiation process had broken down

[15] Other studies have similarly found that many women do not want their partners to be arrested and charged, with the majority wanting support and advice (see Bourlet 1990; Cleveland Refuge and Aid for Women and Children 1984).

TABLE 5.4. Victims' preferences regarding police action: number and percentage arrested

	Suspect not arrested	Suspect arrested	Total
Preference for *no* police action	120 (81%)	29 (19%)	149 (38%)
Preference for police action	99 (42%)	139 (58%)	238 (62%)
Total	219	168	387

$X^2 = 56.56$ (p < 0.001)

(see above). Most of these women were satisfied that arrest was the only option left. Hence, for quantitative analysis of the data, these two variables were combined to create one variable of victims' preferences regarding police action (the removal or arrest of the suspect). Table 5.4 shows that both victims' preferences for police action were correlated with the decision to arrest, and also their preferences for *no* police action were highly correlated with the police decision *not* to arrest the suspect.

In a third (sixty-nine) of the 219 incidents which did not result in an arrest, the victim had either refused to make a statement or initially made a complaint but then refused to sign it, or withdrew it, before the suspect was arrested. Furthermore, in seventy-one (42%) of the 168 cases where the suspect was arrested the victim withdrew her statement at some stage—either before or after the suspect had been charged (see Chapter 6). These victims were considered by the officers to be unreliable; that is, they could not be relied upon to support a prosecution. Many of the Thames Valley officers spoke about this 'victim unreliability'. They argued that the victims, along with other problems inherent in implementing the criminal law in disputes between intimates, made domestic violence cases more prone to failure. Examination of the interview data supports this. It shows that 'victim unreliability' is not a myth postulated by police officers to justify their inaction, as was suggested by Stanko (1985) and Faragher (1985) (see above).

Some critics have suggested that the police are themselves sometimes responsible for 'persuading' victims to withdraw their complaints by allowing a 'cooling off' period and by their behaviour towards victims (Edwards 1989; Faragher 1985; Chambers and Miller 1983). There were only twelve cases in which Thames Valley officers gave the victim a 'cooling off' period, and in four of these cases the suspect was eventually arrested. Some of the other eight incidents involved women who were too drunk to make a statement and were told to contact the police the following day when they were sober. Similarly, some women who alleged assault but had no visible injuries were asked to call the police the following day if any bruising appeared. Needless to say, these women rarely did make further contact with the police. The majority did not involve grave allegations. However, four of the twelve cases were more serious, involving hospital treatment. The police were prevented from taking statements by the women's condition and their need for medical attention. In all these cases the officers left the woman saying that she should contact them the following day should she decide to make a statement. The excerpt below shows the most alarming example of this type of 'leave the ball in her court' response:

This woman had been assaulted by her partner and she had a broken nose. He'd left and she was rather unco-operative—more concerned for the welfare of their child, who was only one year old. She was worried about who would look after it when she went to hospital. She was also pregnant with his child. The ambulance took her to hospital. I did an area search for the suspect but could not trace him. She was not in a fit state to give a statement and so I decided I'd pass the job over to the next turn [the team of officers who would be starting patrol duty after this officer's shift ended].

In fact the 'job' was not passed on at all. No-one was told about this incident.[16] The woman did not make any further calls to the station and she was not seen by another officer.

Those officers who had left victims with no intention of making further contact had, in fact, usually dealt with the initial incidents effectively and sympathetically. Their failure was in not following them up. When questioned about this some made weak excuses about shift work, arguing that as they might not be on duty the following day, or might be working a night shift, they were not best placed to make further contact. It is certainly true that shift-based reactive policing is not conducive to officers taking ownership of problems. But efforts can be made to ensure that someone makes further enquiries, whether that is another patrol officer or a CID officer. It is clear that if women do not initially request, or agree to,

---

[16] Every constable and sergeant on the next shift was asked if he had knowledge of the incident. When reapproached about which officer he had passed details to, the original officer in charge said that he could not remember.

police action, for whatever reason, they usually do not get a second chance. Hence, the probability of an arrest is reduced when the victim is unwilling or unable to make an initial statement and when organizational factors conspire against further contact between a police officer and the victim (see Chapter 4). This incident supports McConville, Sanders, and Leng's assertion about non-influential victims. Whilst the organization of policing, in particular the shift system and the reactive policing style, might make 'errors' such as this more likely, it is unlikely that had the victim been a powerful businessman or a police officer the case would not have been followed up.

Only occasionally did an officer make great efforts to continue with a case after the victim had decided to withdraw, and when they did it was not appreciated. One officer who told me that he thought prosecuting a particularly violent man would be the only way of stopping him repeatedly assaulting his wife, threatened the wife that he would persuade the Crown Prosecution Service to compel her to testify if she did not co-operate with his efforts. The woman could not be persuaded. She explained to me that: 'The policeman was angry with me for not signing my statement. He said he was going to send the papers to the CPS anyway. He kept going on and I wanted him to leave me alone. I'd made my decision!' A handful of other women were not only unwilling to make a statement about aggressive partners, but were angry with the police for trying to intervene in the first place.

Police were called to an incident by a fifteen-year-old boy who claimed that his father was attacking his mother. When the officers arrived the mother told them, in no uncertain terms, to leave. They insisted on seeing the boy and tried, in vain, to persuade her to talk to him. In interview, this officer explained that:

She kept telling me that this was nothing to do with me and telling me to leave. I made sure that the boy was okay and told him to call again if he was frightened. Then the woman threw a plate of food at me and so we left, covered in gravy. My partner slipped in the gravy on the way out. Thinking that we were not leaving quick enough she grabbed me by the jacket and told me to 'fuck off'.[17]

I interviewed this woman at a later date and she was still outraged that the officers had insisted on checking on the welfare of her son.

[17] This incident was referred to in chap. 4.

Angry with me, for being 'yet another busybody', she nevertheless offered an explanation for her affront:

> They asked if I was okay and tried to come in, and then insisted on speaking to my son. I didn't want the copper to speak to my son. He shouldn't be allowed to speak to him without my permission ... it had nothing to do with my son or the police.

Whilst these types of incident were few and far between, they served to reinforce the police cultural perceptions of victims of domestic violence being unco-operative and sometimes hostile in the true sense of the word (see Chapter 4). As one officer said: 'In some domestics you know when to leave well alone, when you feel like an intruder.' Such cases reinforce the police working rule that when victims are unwilling to co-operate it is best to leave well alone. In other words, cultural assumptions about victims' preferences and the working rule which says officers should not arrest if the victim is unco-operative are re-forged in such situations. Officers choose not to arrest when a woman does not wish to make a statement and in the majority of cases they get called out again at a later date. But, as McConville and Shepherd (1992) have argued, instead of thinking that failure to arrest did not end the violence and was therefore the wrong choice, they decide it was the right choice because the couple are still together.

Officers' reluctance to arrest a perpetrator when the victim would not make a statement or agree to testify seemed to apply to victims of domestic violence, regardless of gender, as the following incident shows:

> We were called out by an Asian woman who'd had an argument with her husband. He was a postman and had just got in from work and was calmly sat eating his breakfast. She said that he'd threatened to hurt her and she wanted him removed from the home. He agreed to leave once he'd finished his breakfast. We thought this was the best course of action as she was nine months pregnant and had three children all under five years with her. We left but then five minutes later we were called back: the wife had stabbed her husband in the back. He was bleeding very heavily and we thought that he might die. He claimed to have fallen backwards onto the knife, and when we said that we didn't believe this he said he'd stabbed himself. This would not have been possible due to the position and depth of the wound. It was a very serious GBH [assault occasioning grievous bodily harm], probably an attempted murder, but he would not make a complaint against his wife and when we spoke to her all she would say is 'it's an Asian

problem', and she refused to answer any questions. No one was arrested. What can you do?

In another case a woman had been viciously attacked by her husband, who had smashed a blunt object on the back of her head. The police spent hours by her bedside in hospital after she had received medical attention but she refused to make a statement. A few hours after the attack, her son, having seen his mother's injuries, retaliated by stabbing his stepfather. The stepfather survived the attack but was taken to the same hospital as his wife, with even more serious injuries. He was also asked to make a statement but refused. Neither of the suspects were arrested. Of course in this case, as in others, the police did not *need* the co-operation of the victims. They could have collected evidence even without initial complaints but the working rule about victim co-operation shaped their response. When officers were asked to what extent they had tried to persuade a victim to make a statement, or not to withdraw a statement previously made, many insisted that they had gone to great efforts. But most then went on to say that once a woman has made up her mind it is near impossible and probably not desirable to change her mind. They spoke of respecting the victims' wishes and recognizing her responsibility for her own life. Furthermore, they seemed to be sensitive to the problems women faced in prosecuting their partners or ex-partners.

The victim's demeanour

In some cases, the dispute continued, although victims did not want their assailant arrested, or then there were no legal grounds for an arrest. The police had to decide if they should terminate their intervention or if they should try to negotiate an alternative resolution. One solution was for the victim to leave. If she was willing to do this the officers invariably performed a 'social service' type of role by assisting her in this endeavour—usually driving her, and any children, to an alternative address. If neither disputant was willing to leave, or be taken away from the scene, a 'truce' had to be negotiated, even if the officers recognized that this was likely to be only temporary. In most of the disputes the victim had marginally more bargaining power than the suspect. Her wishes typically superseded those of the suspect and her demeanour sometimes affected how seriously officers took her wishes. The police tended

TABLE 5.5.   Victims' state of mind (calm): number and percentage arrested

	Suspect not arrested	Suspect arrested	Total
Victim not calm	143 (51%)	138 (49%)	281 (73%)
Victim calm	76 (72%)	30 (28%)	106 (27%)
Total	219	168	387

$X^2 = 13.6$ (p < 0.001)

to resist removing women from their home, especially if they had young children and if they were extremely upset or afraid. This means that the options open to suspects were often dependent upon the choices made by, and the state of mind of, the victims. If the police and the victim agreed that arrest was a desirable outcome the man would usually be arrested. If it was decided that the suspect should leave the home, he would usually be given the option of leaving or facing arrest.

The victim's state of mind clearly affected the success, or otherwise, of this negotiation process. When victims were calm, suspects were less likely to be arrested, but when victims were 'hysterical' suspects were highly likely to be arrested.[18] The suspect was not arrested in almost three-quarters of the incidents where the victim was calm (see table 5.5).

If we compare these data with those presented in table 5.6, we see that the opposite of being calm—that is, the victim being hysterical—is correlated with the decision to arrest. The suspect was

TABLE 5.6.   Victims' state of mind (hysterical): number and percentage arrested

	Suspect not arrested	Suspect arrested	Total
Victim not hysterical	196 (60%)	129 (40%)	325 (84%)
Victim hysterical	23 (37%)	39 (63%)	62 (16%)
Total	219	168	387

$X^2 = 11.4$ (p < 0.001)

[18] 'Hysterical' was the term used by the majority of officers describing women who were extremely upset and agitated. The term tends to be used only to describe highly agitated *women* and has pejorative overtones which the majority of officers almost certainly did not intend.

arrested in almost two-thirds of those incidents where the victim was hysterical compared to just over one-third where she was not.

There are a number of reasons why this is so, all of them inter-related. If the victim is calm it is likely that she is not afraid that she is in immediate further danger and that she has not suffered a serious injury. However, the main reason why the victim's state of mind impacted on the officers' decisions regarding arrest concerns the negotiation of a temporary solution. Women who were calm were more likely to be able to engage in discussions, not only with officers but also with the suspects, and contribute towards the achievement of a peaceful solution, avoiding the necessity of an arrest. It might also be the case that calm victims are less likely to want their partners or ex-partners to be arrested.

In this way, the two types of information discussed in this section, as with the other two sections, can be seen to be interrelated. The above three sections have shown how the various significant actors come together at disputes and bring with them their own 'stories' about what has happened and what should ensue. The job of the police officer is to interpret these, often conflicting, accounts and agendas and negotiate temporary solutions which would be satis-factory to as many of the parties as possible—not least themselves. In arriving at these solutions, officers 'rationally' consider the pos-sible outcomes and probable impact of the various choices avail-able. Sometimes there seems to be only one choice available and then the only task is to convince the disputants of the appropriate-ness of their decision. However, at other times several options present themselves. It is then that we see the clearest process of negotiation between the various actors and the various sources of information discussed above.

A model of police decision-making

Chapter 4 presented a model of the negative concept of 'cop culture' and discussed its limitations in explaining the police response to domestic violence. That chapter concluded that such a narrow concept alone could not explain the police decision-making process. Qualitative assessment of the data collected during the Thames Valley study suggested that 'cop culture' interacted with other factors, such as organizational criteria, force policies and training and procedural law, to create a set of working assumptions. These

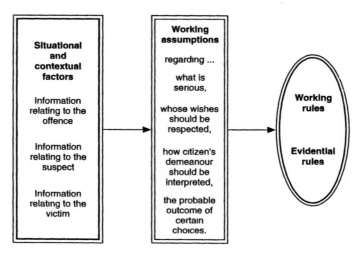

FIG. 5.1.   The influence of situational factors and working assumptions on officers' decisions

working assumptions helped officers at the scene of domestic disputes to make sense of, and respond to, information presented to them or gathered by them. Hence, the working assumptions shaped the exercise of police discretion and determined the application of certain working rules. In other words, it was found that officers' responses were not arbitrary and that discretion was not exercised according to negative stereotypes about victims, as has been suggested by some writers, but, rather, according to working assumptions and working rules. Figure 5.1 summarizes the types of information presented to, or gathered by, police officers and the working assumptions which help them to make sense of this information.

Close examination of the police decisions made in nearly 400 cases of domestic violence has shown that the working assumptions of police shape their interpretation of various types of information gathered at the scene of domestic disputes, and the police working rules tell officers how to respond to this interpreted information. Hence, the study identified five main working rules which guide officers' decisions in domestic disputes. These relate to the perceived seriousness of the offence (arrest if the offence is serious); the risk of further violence (arrest if there is a significant risk of immediate

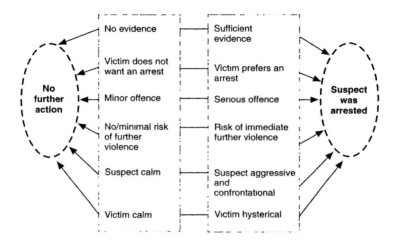

FIG. 5.2.   An explanatory model of the police decision-making process

further violence); the suspect's demeanour (arrest confrontational and aggressive suspects who try to challenge police authority); the victim's demeanour (if the victim is very distressed arrest the suspect); and, most importantly, the victim's preference (if a victim does not want the suspect to be arrested, do not arrest him).

Of course, it is not only working rules which shape police decision-making. The substantive law plays a part. As was shown above, evidence of a criminal offence was highly correlated with the decision to arrest. Hence, an explanatory model of police decision-making needs to recognize the influence of both working rules and evidential rules. Figure 5.2 shows the working rules and evidential rules which apply in cases of domestic violence.[19]

The remainder of this section will assess (quantitatively) the relative explanatory strength of this model. First, as the majority

[19] The model illustrates the factors which were most influential in the officers' decisions of whether or not to arrest the suspect in domestic disputes. Of course, each incident is a unique event and the particular outcomes are contingent on a range of factors, including particular situational and biographical details. For this reason no model can, or should, attempt to provide a deterministic recipe for action. However, it does identify those factors which are strong determinants of police behaviour when responding to domestic disputes, and for this reason the model is more than just an heuristic device.

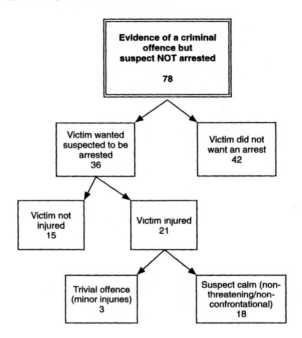

FIG. 5.3.   Reasons for non-arrest in cases where there was evidence of a criminal offence.

of critics have been concerned with police decisions not to arrest in domestic violence cases, it might be helpful to examine those incidents where there was evidence of a criminal offence but the suspect was not arrested. Table 5.1 showed that whilst evidence of an offence was correlated with the police decision regarding arrest in the majority of incidents, there were seventy-eight cases in which there was evidence of an offence but the suspect was not arrested. Figure 5.3 shows that forty-two of these seventy-eight cases did not result in an arrest because the victim did not want the perpetrator to be arrested and would not make a statement. This leaves thirty-six cases where the failure to arrest, despite evidence of an offence and despite the victim wanting the suspect to be arrested, needs to be explained. Of these thirty-six cases, fifteen did not involve injuries to the victim (the offences were property crimes where the offence was not considered to be serious and where the victim was not thought to be at risk of further violence). Hence there were twenty-one cases where there was evidence of a violent offence and where the victim wanted the perpetrator to be arrested. In eighteen of these incidents the suspect was calm and did not behave in a threatening or confrontational way with the police officers, and the other three incidents were relatively trivial with the victim having sustained only minor injuries.

Of course, the simplest way of discovering why officers arrest some men and not others is to ask individual officers to provide reasons for their actions in specific cases. This was done in relation to all of the 387 incidents charted in this study. Officers' explanations were not taken at face value but tested against all of the information gathered, from the officers, the victims, and from direct observation. An examination of these data provided support for the qualitative analysis of the interview data.

In over half of the cases where the officer had decided not to arrest the suspect the decision was justified by reference to the lack of evidence of an offence. In a third of the incidents where no-one had been arrested the officer explained that the victim had been unco-operative, that she had not wanted them to arrest the perpetrator and had refused to make a statement. And in 13 per cent of non-arrest cases it was explained that the officer had managed to calm the parties involved. That is, they had negotiated a temporary resolution to the conflict. In only a handful of cases did the officer explain his decision not to arrest by a derogatory reference to the victim, either blaming her for provoking the dispute or stating that she was a 'bad' wife or mother and implying that she did not deserve police protection. In a few of these cases the officer explained that both the suspect and the victim were equally to blame for the dispute.

Questioning officers about their decisions to arrest suspects provided compatible data. In 42 per cent of the incidents where the officer had arrested the perpetrator he explained this action by reference to evidence of a criminal offence. In over half of these cases the officer pointed to victim injuries as evidence. In almost a third of the incidents the decision to arrest the suspect was justified, by the arresting officer, in terms of protecting the victim, and some-times her children, from further harm. In one in five of the incidents which resulted in an arrest the officer spoke of the influence of the suspect's aggressive demeanour. The majority of these officers referred to the suspect being under the influence of alcohol.

There was, of course, some overlap between this reason and the explanation about protecting victims from further harm. Other explanations for arrest, such as an injunction being in place, the dispute taking place in a public setting or information about a history of disputes, were offered in only a handful of cases.

Quantitative (logistic regression) analysis of the data was carried out in order to further test the extent to which the identified working and legal rules, as well as other variables, increased the probability of being arrested. It was found that the odds of being arrested increased dramatically if the victim wanted this, if the suspect was aggressive towards the police officer(s), and if there was evidence of an offence. The victim's preference was the strongest predictor of an arrest, followed by the suspect's demeanour, the available evidence of an offence, and the victim's demeanour.[20] These variables successfully predicted the decision to arrest or not in 77 per cent of the 387 cases examined (no other variables were significant). Hence these variables would accurately predict whether or not a man would be arrested at any one time within the two police areas under study (if the external conditions, such as force policy, were the same as during the fieldwork period) in over three-quarters of all cases.[21]

There are two factors discussed above which did not feature in the logistic regression: 'the seriousness of the offence' and 'the risk of further immediate violence'. These explanatory variables were not considered suitable for statistical analysis. The 'seriousness of the offence' was not included because the data gathered for most of these incidents was filtered through the subjective perceptions of officers and was, therefore, not considered detailed or rigorous enough to be able to apply a seriousness scale test. And to use the offence for which a suspect was arrested as a guide to seriousness would be useless in an analysis which is aimed at testing the factors

[20] All four variables had a significance level of 0.0000 based on the Wald test.

[21] Certain interactional effects (non-additive combined effects) were tested in cross-tabulations with the arrest variable (choices were theoretically informed) to see if some of the variables became stronger in relation to others, rather than assuming that they all worked independently of each other or in addition to each other. The only interaction effect which was considered to be strong enough to test logistically (according to log odds ratios) was the interaction of the victim's wishes concerning arrest and the aggressive/confrontational demeanour of the suspect. However, whilst this was significant in a cross-tabulation, it was rejected from the logistic regression model (significance statistic 0.2066).

influencing the decision to arrest. In other words, it is not an independent variable.

The other factor, 'the risk of further immediate violence', could not be added to the regression analysis as there were too few cases where it applied.[22] However, in the few cases that it did occur it appears to have been the most influential factor in the decision to arrest. The impact of the specific factors influencing officers' decisions can be measured in two ways: by their frequency and by their power. First, quantitative analysis of the data can show the number of incidents where a specific factor was influential, and, secondly, qualitative analysis can reveal how powerful an effect a specific factor had on the decisions made. The variable 'victim wants police action' was the strongest predictor of arrest in the logistic regression analysis, and victim non co-operation was the second most often cited reason officers forwarded for non-arrest. However, in some incidents other factors, such as the victim being in immediate and serious danger, prevailed over the wishes of the victim as more powerful determinants of the police response.

There were many cases where working rules and evidential criteria both pointed towards an arrest. However, there were some cases where the police wanted to arrest the suspect (either perhaps because the victim wanted or needed such an action, or because the officer wanted to reassert his authority over a suspect who had challenged him in some way) but there was no evidence of an offence. In order to understand decisions to arrest in such cases, we need to consider the use of the criminal law, in particular police powers, as a resource upon which the police can draw.

The criminal law as a resource

When the police believe that an infraction of the criminal law has occurred, or is about to occur, they are entitled to use certain powers to apprehend and detain suspects, with a view to commencing criminal proceedings.[23] Their belief is a matter of judgement and discretion. Officers are given discretion by the law and by the

[22] If there are any cells which are empty, or contain extremely small numbers, in a cross-tabulation between the dependent and independent variables, the independent variable should not be included in the regression analysis as the estimates which would be recovered from the model would be unreliable.
[23] See the discussion of police powers in chap. 4.

organizational structure. There is no-one 'policing the police' when they respond to incidents away from public, and sometimes away from peer, scrutiny. This is, as Hawkins puts it: '. . . the point at which the legal system touches the people or problems it is intended to address, [it is] where the tensions, dilemmas, and sometimes contradictions embodied in the law are worked out in practice' (1992: 12). Early sociological research argued that the low visibility of everyday police work allowed the police to operate working rules with little relation to legal rules (Goldstein 1960; Skolnick 1966). As Smith and Gray (1983) have argued, decisions made by officers on the street are not governed by legal rules, although issues of legality informed the way that officers explain their actions to others. Hence, they are able in practice, if they consider it expedient, to use legal powers in cases where there has been no criminal offence, just as they can decide not to use legal powers in cases where there has been a criminal offence (see Hawkins 1992).

When officers, at the scene of domestic disputes, had gathered relevant data and interpreted the events which had precipitated their attendance, they needed to decide on the 'appropriate' action. In those cases where an arrest was considered to be legally justifiable, the officers had to decide whether such action would facilitate or constrain their realization of their goals. However, there were many disputes amongst those recorded in this study which involved either no criminal offence or only minor infractions of the criminal law. Where both parties had a different 'story' to tell and conflicting expectations of the police, the police had to decide whose expectations to try to realize. This does not necessarily mean that they did precisely what that party wanted. However it does mean that they took more seriously their hopes concerning the resolution of the dispute and took action which in their own opinion was to the benefit of that person.

Police officers chose to arrest suspects when there was no evidence of a criminal offence in forty-five cases (none of these cases resulted in a criminal charge) (see table 5.1). As figure 5.4 shows, the majority of these arrests were for breach of the peace. Most of these cases involved suspects who were confrontational and threatening towards the officers. The police used the criminal law to remove confrontational suspects and give victims some brief respite. When 'aggressive' suspects behaved in a way which was not illegal

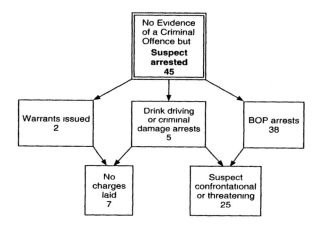

FIG. 5.4. Arrest decisions in cases where there was no evidence

but was, in the officer's opinion, 'unacceptable', officers usually used public order powers to remove the belligerent suspect. As Bittner (1990) has argued, the law provides a resource for officers—legal categories are often available within which to place a socially unacceptable activity. It was often possible for them to label the action of 'aggressive' suspects as 'likely to cause a further breach to the peace' without being challenged, as this is such a subjective response to a given situation. Very often, however, the peace had not actually been breached in the first place. Although disputes had taken place, most were not in the public domain and so there were no likely public ramifications. In a broader context, it has been noted that the police use their arrest powers to bolster their authority by invoking the Public Order Act where the evidence of specific offences is very thin (Brown and Ellis 1994). Therefore, the use by police officers of arrest powers as a resource for broader crime control aims is used in the domestic context, but also more widely.

In many of these forty-five cases the officers explained that they had made an arrest because the woman wanted the man to be removed from the scene and arrest seemed to be the only option for achieving this. The following excerpt provides evidence of one such example:

The husband had damaged the wall but it was his home. . . . He was drunk, but completely calm. . . . She made no complaint of violence and did not seem to be injured. . . . I asked her if she wanted to leave and I'd take her somewhere but she had nowhere to go. . . . The woman wanted him removing but the house was in both of their names. I asked him if he was prepared to leave and stay somewhere else for the night but he was not. I told her that we would arrest him for breach of the peace and he would be out of the house for a few hours to give her the chance to decide what she wanted to do. I did this because the woman said if he stayed there she would attack him! I felt that if I had not removed this man from the house one or other of the partners would have got hurt and I did not want them fighting in front of the children.

In other cases the officers arrested suspects to prevent a 'further' breach of the peace when there was no evidence that the peace had been breached previously. In explaining such actions it was apparent that the officers felt that the moral justification for removing the male outweighed their equivocal legal powers. They redefined incidents which had initially been reported as 'service' matters into 'criminal' incidents because it turned out to be desirable to use the criminal law to reach satisfactory resolutions.[24] It was desirable because the victims in such cases wanted the suspects to be removed temporarily from the home. They wanted a few hours 'breathing space' to consider their options or to pack their bags and seek alternative accommodation.

In some cases officers insisted that men leave their own homes for the night, although they sometimes admitted that they had been unsure of their legal powers to do so. Concerned about the potential repercussions of complaints, they were usually careful not to aggravate the men unnecessarily. Hence, when they drove men to other addresses, as they often did, it was not only to ensure that they did indeed leave the vicinity, but also partly to placate them. Some explained that if they were going to insist that a man leave his own home, the least they could do was to give him a lift somewhere else.

Such behaviour on the part of police officers not only raises questions about the influence of law and policies, in relation to other factors, on police decisions, it also raises questions about the role of policing. It seems that the contrast drawn between 'law enforcement' and 'social service' police work in some of the literature on policing disputes is, to some extent, a false dichotomy (Ekblom and Heal 1982; Morgan 1984). As Kemp, Norris, and

[24] Ericson (1982) has made the point that officers frequently do this.

Fielding (1992: 86) argue, the contrast serves to obscure the help-control continuum. Some of the incidents dealt with by the police using 'peacekeeping' negotiation processes in this study did involve infractions of the criminal law. Conversely, as discussed above, the police did threaten to invoke the criminal law and in some cases use it where there was no evidence of a criminal offence in order to resolve a dispute successfully. Clearly, specific incidents do not dictate *either* a law enforcement *or* a social service response. The social service functions, such as providing transport for disputants to relocate temporarily, are not only examples of benevolence but also serve a 'crime control' function. Similarly, spending time with disputants talking through their 'troubles' is not only fulfilling a social service role, but is also an attempt at preventing further violence, and as such is a 'crime control' measure.

Most of the time the police are 'keeping the peace', and only some of the time does this involve making arrests. But, as will be shown later, whilst order maintenance can sometimes be achieved without using the law coercively, this does not mean that officers do not use the law in other ways. Their legal authority, their presence in uniform, is often enough to resolve a difficult situation. The law is ever present during police-citizen encounters. The threat of coercion in an adversarial encounter is there without being articulated, and this is often enough to resolve the dispute successfully. Furthermore, many disputes which did not result in an arrest might have turned out differently if circumstances had been only slightly different.

The successful negotiation of some incidents was threatened by the suspects challenging the decisions, and indeed the authority, of the officers. The threat by the police to use their powers was enough in most situations to 'persuade' the men to co-operate with the officers. The police are the only ones with a legitimate claim to intervene in the affairs of citizens, to enforce the law and keep the peace and to exercise force in carrying out their duties (Bordua and Reiss 1966). Indeed, as Bittner (1980) argued, their legitimate claim to legal force is the central characteristic of the police role. This means that when an officer wants a man to leave his own home for the night he usually only has to ask him to do so. In asking the men to leave their homes, these officers were not doing anything that the women, or any other private citizen, could not have done. They were simply making a request and yet, despite the fact that sometimes they had no more *rights* to do this than the women had, their 'authority' frequently led to compliance. Even though officers do not always have the legal powers to guarantee the achievement of their goals, their possession of the ideological weight of the law usually sufficed (Kemp, Norris, and Fielding 1992).

As Dixon, Coleman, and Bottomley (1990) have found, from research on the legal regulation of police powers under the Police and Criminal Evidence Act 1984 (PACE), police officers frequently achieve their objectives not by using a legal power, but by securing the 'consent' of the suspect. An officer does not usually have to arrest someone or physically grapple with him in order to make him comply with his demands. Police officers are symbolically distanced from the other actors by their uniforms, their technology, the law which they represent, and the force at their command. Hence, what might superficially appear to be compliant consent to an officer's suggestion might, in fact, be unwilling acquiescence, submission, or co-operation or compliance rooted in ignorance of the possibility of acting differently (Dixon, Coleman, and Bottomley 1990). When suspects in the Thames Valley study were asked to leave their own homes they generally had neither the knowledge nor the power to refuse. Their agreement was not 'voluntary' in any true sense of the word.[25] Hence, the criminal law allows officers to manage disputes even when they do not enforce the law or directly threaten to enforce it. No laws give the police these dispute management powers, but there are no laws preventing them either.

Choong (1997) has looked rather more critically at the use of the criminal law as a resource. Studying suspects who had been arrested and detained in police custody, he assessed and evaluated the fairness of criminal justice procedure. He also found that officers sometimes arrested suspects and held them in custody when they had no intention of charging them with a criminal offence. He found, as did the Thames Valley study, that belligerent suspects who challenged the authority of police officers were much more likely to be arrested than those who respected and complied with police authority. He argued that detention in the police station, rather than prosecution, was the goal of officers in such situations. The police station was the site of summary justice. The only objectives which he identified in the decision to arrest were punishment, humiliation,

---

[25] Disputants rarely ask officers what *rights* they have to enter their homes and demand that they disclose personal details about their relationship.

and control over certain 'suspect communities', people who were considered by police to be 'nuisances', 'troublemakers', and likely to be 'factually guilty' of something, even if not legally guilty of anything at that time. Hence he has referred to this behaviour as the 'social discipline model' of policing. In the same way, this Thames Valley study found that the police station was at times detached from the judicial process. It was used to allow men who were under the influence of drink or drugs, or just exceptionally agitated, to calm down. It was also used to teach some aggressive men a lesson. However, in the main, when officers arrested men who had been involved in a domestic dispute, they did so for the benefit of the victim. They did it to give her some breathing space and allow her a few hours free of abuse to make important decisions about her course of action. Hence, whilst Choong and I found similar practices, I found different or additional motivations for such behaviour. This could be because we were examining different types of suspects. The law was used with belligerent men as 'summary justice' but this was to help the victims as much as to avenge frustrated officers. A few officers admitted that they wanted to issue some summary punishment. As one said: 'I put him in a cell for a few hours so that he could reflect on his behaviour. I wanted to teach him a lesson.' However, the majority justified these 'resource' arrests in terms of using the law to prevent a further dispute—as an immediate crime prevention measure, or to provide the victim with much needed breathing space.

The influence of working rules and evidential rules

In trying to analyse the data gathered in this study I have considered a number of different approaches to understanding police dispositions: the impact of legal versus 'working' rules; police discretion; 'cop culture'; police organization; and the role of victim preferences. As discussed in Chapter 4, these concepts are, to some extent, interrelated, since 'cop culture' and the police organization inform the use of police discretion, and the adoption of working rules.

The statistical analysis of the data gathered in this study, as is evidenced above, has shown that officers are, to some extent, bound by legal rules and organizational factors, and, more importantly, they do not exercise discretion in a random or patternless way.

Their discretion is structured according to working rules developed by policing on the ground. Further, it has shown that citizens enter the criminal justice system not only as alleged violators or victims, but also as, to a certain extent, enforcers of the law.

This chapter set out to assess the extent to which evidential rules and force policies can explain police decisions regarding arrest and the extent to which these decisions can be explained by working rules. It showed that decisions to enforce the law are the result of an interpretative process, with negotiation usually being more important than the law or the current policy. It has been shown that evidence of an offence does not necessarily produce an arrest (although the force policy indicated that it should), and the lack of it does not necessarily prevent officers from making an arrest. Clear, incontrovertible evidence of an offence often led to an arrest, but not because the police pursued rigorously all cases where there was evidence of an offence, but, rather, because evidence facilitated police action when the working rules pointed towards an arrest. In other words, when the police had other reasons for wanting to arrest someone (either because the suspect had challenged their authority, or because the victim wanted him arrested, or was in further danger), and they felt that it would be to the benefit of the victim, evidence of an offence allowed them to do this. Hence, the criminal law did not determine arrests but, rather, it often facilitated them.

Commentators such as McConville, Sanders, and Leng (1991) and Kemp, Norris, and Fielding (1992) have questioned whether it is the 'law in books' or 'law in action' which best explains police handling of incidents. They have argued that, to a large extent, the 'law in action' takes over from the 'law in books' when police are at the scene deciding on the appropriate response (Fielding 1989). The 'law in action' refers to the 'working rules' which determine much police behaviour. For these authors, discretion is structured according to a set of informal working rules developed by policing on the ground. The working rules adopted by patrol officers shape the interaction between the officers and disputants and hence influence decisions.

Thus, to paraphrase McConville, Sanders, and Leng, the substantive law makes arrests possible, but it does not dictate that arrests should be made: the reason for the arrest has to be sought elsewhere (1991: 17). Whilst the criminal law and force policies can both enable and constrain police choices, as Reiner (1992) acknowledges, it does not determine practical policing, as officers have wide discretionary powers. However, law and policy are not rendered powerless by cop culture. They are reworked and invoked when they resonate with the dictates of the working rules (see also Holdaway 1989). In the Thames Valley Police, in the case of domestic violence, both working rules and evidential rules had some influence on police decision-making.

Police powers and the criminal law are mediated through the subcultural norms and values of policing so that they provide a resource for the police to act in a way which they believe to be most appropriate. In some cases officers decide what response is most helpful to themselves and to the victim, or other interested parties, and then fit their legal powers around their decision. In other words, the choice of response often came before the assessment of the position of the criminal law (Bittner 1967). Hence the criminal law was often used as a means of controlling one or both disputants, invariably to impose order and to assert authority over the disputants, and as a measure of temporary relief for the victim. This is the way that the 'law in books' is translated into the 'law in action'. An understanding of this negotiation process shows us that, prior to police assessment of the situation, disputes often cannot be objectively categorized as crimes or social service matters (Dixon 1997). These are definitions arrived at through a process of negotiation between the parties involved and the police. These definitions are also sometimes changed during this process of negotiation. The law is often only used when it is necessary to control the situation, when it is in the interests of the officer to do so—interests as defined by the organizational culture (see also Ericson 1982). Police discretionary powers make this possible.

The idea that discretion is subjective justice has provoked criticisms from those who believe that the law should be applied rigorously according to objective legalistic criteria. It has been argued that such discretion leads to inconsistency in decision outcomes, with apparently similar cases not being treated in the same way by decision-makers, whether they be police officers, or judges. As Hawkins has noted, an obvious corollary is that '. . . discretion can impose similar outcomes upon apparently different cases' (1992: 16). This study of policing in the Thames Valley fits within this latter criticism. For example, various different cases were treated similarly, vis-à-vis the decision to arrest, simply because the victim did not wish to make a formal complaint.

In the literature on the negotiation process one important aspect has been underplayed. This is that there is little or no on-site negotiation between the police officers where there is more than one at the scene. This study found the decision to arrest was not influenced by the gender of the attendant officers. Officers who were generally more sympathetic to domestic disputes made, in the main, the same choices as officers who were less so. This is because of shared working assumptions which represent a collective consensus on how to deal with certain types of situation. Within this consensus extreme positions tend to get lost as solidarity amongst officers is more important than being honest to one's own convictions. Hence whilst officers negotiate with members of the public in order to establish which working rule should take precedence over another or over the 'rule of law', they do not, in the main, negotiate with each other. Hence two officers at a dispute operate in much the same way as one as far as decision-making is concerned. They 'read' the scene in much the same way and come to the same decisions about how to respond because they have a shared understanding. The officers are comfortable that their colleagues will not challenge them, unless they step way beyond the boundaries of acceptability, because the boundaries have already been worked out in the canteen. This shared understanding, as was argued in Chapter 4, derives from the police culture.

This chapter has shown that in understanding what officers do at the scene of domestic disputes, the principal explanatory variables are contextual. However, the influence of these variables can only be understood when they are considered within the context of the occupational sub-culture of the police. It is the working assumptions—which are culturally informed—that make sense of the contextual factors presented to officers. Hence, we need to remember the organizational context which officers take with them to any incident. As discussed in Chapter 4, this context brings with it procedural law and force policies. Officers are aware of the 'rules' which should apply in any given situation. Whilst the working rules were found to be much more powerful explanatory variables, it is not helpful to conceptualize discretion as decisions made unhindered by rules. The rules-versus-discretion dichotomy is, to some extent, a false one. The evidential rules and the working rules interact and emerge during the process of negotiation at the scene. In other words, the situational context is not determined for the officers. It is determined by them and by the other significant actors interacting. Different situations involve different weightings and the varying persuasiveness of both working rules and evidential criteria.

6

Understanding Prosecution Decisions

When the police make an arrest the suspect is taken to the police station so that detention can be authorized by the custody officer.[1] Detention in custody allows the arresting officer, and sometimes his colleagues, to interview the suspect. When the officer believes that he has sufficient evidence to prosecute he is supposed to stop the investigatory process[2] and put the facts before the custody officer, who can then decide whether or not to charge. However, even when the custody officer believes that he has sufficient evidence to charge the suspect with the alleged offence there are a number of choices: he can decide to caution him; he can release him with no further action; he can delay the decision either by releasing the suspect on police bail to return at a later date or by reporting the suspect with a view to a summons; or he can charge the suspect. If the decision is to charge, the case file is sent to the Crown Prosecution Service where a prosecutor must decide whether or not to continue with the prosecution.[3]

An original intention of this study was to interview custody officers about their decisions, but during the pilot study it was decided not to continue with this part of the fieldwork. This decision was reached in part because custody officers, while easy to

---

[1] The Police and Criminal Evidence Act 1984 (PACE) created this new role for the police. Custody officers need to hold at least the rank of a sergeant. They are responsible for suspects' rights and welfare whilst in custody. The custody officer has to decide whether or not to detain a suspect and, if so, on what grounds (see Sanders and Young 1994 for a discussion of the extent to which they are in fact responsible for these decisions).

[2] PACE Code of Practice C, para. 11.4.

[3] The Crown Prosecution Service, set up in 1986 by the Prosecution of Offences Act 1985, is an independent prosecuting authority headed by the Director of Public Prosecutions and responsible for the prosecution of most of the criminal offences brought by the police in England and Wales.

locate, were invariably too busy to devote sufficient time to an interview.[4] However, the main reason for not continuing with these interviews was that the responses obtained from custody officers suggested that they did not, in any real sense, make decisions. Rather, decisions were made by the arresting officers (see below). Hawkins understands this phenomenon by taking a 'serial view of discretion' (1992: 28). He explains that where cases are processed over time by means of a referral system, effective power to decide the outcome of the case is frequently assumed by actors other than the person allocated formal authority to exercise discretion: 'What is described as a "decision" reached is sometimes nothing more than a ratification of an earlier decision made in the handling of a case, even though that prior decision may appear in the guise of an opinion or a recommendation.' (Ibid.: 29.)

McConville, Sanders, and Leng similarly found that the custody officer is not an independent decision-maker, as the wording of PACE implies. They cite examples of custody officers admitting that they would go along with whatever the arresting officer said: 'I'm dependent completely on what the officer says happened' (1991: 122). On this basis, Sanders and Young (1994) have argued that it is very rare for custody officers to caution or release a suspect with no further action when the arresting officer wants to charge, and vice versa. The Thames Valley study supported the findings of these critics. Indeed, as far as I was aware, the custody officer challenged the decision of the arresting officer in only one of the 387 cases.[5]

This chapter will examine the factors which shaped the decisions made by officers regarding charging and the processes by which cases came to be prosecuted or discontinued by the Crown Prosecution Service. As with the decision to arrest, the relative power of legal criteria and working rules in making prosecution decisions will be assessed. In discussing these decision-making processes, two themes which emerged in the previous chapter will be further developed: first, the role of the victim in the criminal justice system; and secondly, the use of the criminal law as a resource.

---

[4] The few interviews which were conducted were hindered by constant interruptions.

[5] This was an unusual case involving a man who voluntarily attended the police station to report that he had strangled his wife. The wife survived the attack but refused to make a statement. The officer in charge of the case requested that the man be charged, but the custody officer decided against this as there were no independent witnesses and no complainant. This case is discussed below.

Factors shaping police decisions regarding prosecution

Of the 1318 cases reported to the two Thames Valley Police areas under study, the suspect was arrested in 224 cases. Of these 224 suspects arrested, 27 per cent (sixty-one) were charged with a criminal offence and 61 per cent (137) were refused charge. Ten per cent (twenty-three) were cautioned, or dealt with by the county court (usually for breaching a county court order), or charged with breaching the peace and bound over to keep the peace by the magistrates' court.[6] The remaining three suspects were released on police bail whilst the police sought advice from the Crown Prosecution Service. In all three cases that advice was against prosecution and the suspect was released from police bail with no further action taken (see figure 2.1a.).

As police decided not to charge domestic violence suspects in almost three-quarters of cases, it is important to understand what factors shape police officers' decisions not to charge a man arrested for an offence involving domestic violence. This is especially so when we consider that, of all arrests, in general only around one-quarter end in no further action (Sanders and Young 1994: 214). The Thames Valley study found that there were essentially just two factors—the prior intention to arrest suspects for reasons other than prosecution and the failure of the victim to either make a statement or to testify in court.

As discussed in the previous chapter, 168 of the 387 cases which comprised the interview sample resulted in an arrest. In seventy-one of these 168 cases the victims withdrew their statements after the suspect had been arrested (see table 6.1). Custody sergeants refused to charge the suspect in 75 per cent of these seventy-one cases (although in six of these cases the suspect was put before the magistrates' court and bound over to keep the peace). In the remaining eighteen cases the suspect was charged because the victim did not withdraw her support until the case had been sent for prosecution. Hence, in all cases where the victim withdrew her support prior to the decision to charge, the police refused to charge the suspect.

---

[6] These bind-overs were civil resolutions. The defendant must not breach the peace for the period of the bind-over, usually six or twelve months. Failing to keep the peace can result in a penalty of usually £50 or £100.

TABLE 6.1. Victim withdrawal: number and percentage of suspects charged

	Refused charge	Suspect charged	Total
No withdrawal or no statement	54 (56%)	43 (44%)	97
Victim withdrew	53 (75%)	18 (25%)	71
Total	107	61	168

Examination of all of the cases where the police refused to charge the suspect showed that in almost half of these cases the victim had withdrawn her statement after the arrest and before the decision to charge was made. The majority of the remaining 'refused charge' cases were arrests for breach of the peace where the victim had made no statement at all and where neither she nor the police intended for the suspect to be charged with a criminal offence. Only three cases did not fall into one of these two categories. These three cases were sent to the Crown Prosecution Service for advice but, as stated above, none were prosecuted. Hence, the data show that when suspects are arrested for breach of the peace or when witnesses withdraw their statements suspects are highly unlikely to be charged.

Prosecution was never the intention

There were 101 arrests for breach of the peace and in the majority of these cases charges were refused. Occasionally, after the suspect had been arrested, it transpired, from talking to the victim, that he had committed an offence and that she was willing to make a statement so he was charged with a criminal offence. However, eighty-eight of the men arrested for breaching the peace (typically the arrests were common law arrests 'to prevent a further breach of the peace') were released with no further action. In the majority of these cases prosecution was not the intention of the arresting officers. Instead, arrest was used as a resource to terminate domestic disputes: to maintain order and prevent further trouble; to provide the victim with a little 'breathing space' to consider the options and take initial action if desired; to give the suspect a few hours in a cell to calm down (an immediate crime prevention measure); or to issue some summary punishment (see Chapter 5).

Under PACE (s. 37) a custody officer can only agree to a period of detention if the arresting officer intends to keep the suspect at the station in order to gather evidence, to preserve evidence of an offence, and if it is necessary to detain the suspect in order to achieve these objectives, or in order to charge. In many of the arrests made in this study the officer clearly had no such intentions, and yet custody officers allowed the suspects to be held in detention for up to six hours.[7] Whilst these arrests were lawful, the legality of these detention decisions was rather less clear. Custody officers could have justified the detention of suspects without charge by arguing that they intended to put each suspect before the magistrates' court in order to achieve the civil resolution of a bind-over to keep the peace. But once the suspects had calmed down it was no longer necessary to have them bound over.[8] However such justifications were not considered necessary as the law in this area, the 'necessity rule', is virtually unenforceable. Consequently, many researchers have found detention decisions to be automatically endorsed by custody officers (Sanders and Young 1994: 121–4). Thus, detention is used by officers as a resource for aims other than prosecution. If these suspects were to be released immediately (whilst still agitated and possibly under the influence of alcohol or drugs) they might return to the scene of the dispute and cause damage or harm to persons or property. Unlike disputes in public—for example fights in the street, where disputants can usually be released immediately after arrest without the likelihood of the dispute starting up again—domestic disputes require that one party be removed from the presence of the other for enough time for the antagonist genuinely to calm down. PACE does not authorize detention for these purposes, but it could be argued that it is a common sense use of the powers contained therein.[9]

Critics have tended to assume that if an arrest does not result in a prosecution the police have failed the victim. But a different interpretation can be made of the high attrition rate. The fact that many suspects who were arrested, especially for public order offences, were not charged is not necessarily a sign of police failure. It may often have been a sign that the police used the law in order to resolve

---

[7] A suspect can be held without review for six hours or until he has been charged with a criminal offence.

[8] A bind-over is in effect a suspended fine since an offender stands to forfeit a specified sum of money unless he or she abides by an undertaking to be of good behaviour and keep the peace (Cavadino and Dignan 1997: 208).

[9] An honest debate on possible exceptions to s. 37 of PACE is long overdue.

a dispute even when they had no realistic prospect of getting a conviction. In other words, they did not *fail* to charge—they *never intended* to charge, for in many cases there was no evidence on which to base a charge. But they used the law as a resource for their own or the victim's benefit.

Some feminist researchers have suggested that men who are violent towards their partners are frequently charged with crimes of lesser seriousness than would appear to be justified by the facts. Edwards (1986) found that often men were charged with breach of the peace or being drunk and disorderly rather than with assault, and when an assault charge was made it was often a common assault charge, with the victim being advised to prosecute privately. This practice, known as 'criming down', like the failure to arrest in cases of domestic violence, has been explained in terms of 'undeserving victims' and cultural attitudes regarding the privacy of the home and the acceptability of certain behaviours (Smith 1989). The majority of the arrests for breach of the peace in the Thames Valley study were not examples of the police under-enforcing the law. Rather, they were examples of the police engaging in law enforcement for 'social service' ends when, because of unco-operative victims or insufficient evidence, they believed that they had little hope of achieving a conviction (see Chapter 5).

Unco-operative victims

Sometimes police officers arrested suspects even though the victim was unco-operative because they considered the violence to be serious and the victim in danger of further harm (see Chapter 5). However, the decision to charge—even in very serious cases—was shaped almost entirely by the victim's preferences, as the following case illustrates:[10]

This couple were arguing in public.[11] Both were injured. He had cuts and abrasions to his fists, from punching her, and scratches on his face. She had bleeding from her mouth, some teeth had been knocked out and her left jaw was very swollen. She was asked if she wanted to press charges for GBH [assault occasioning grievous bodily harm] but she said no. I arrested him anyway. She tried to prevent us making the arrest and when her

[10] As with the quotations presented in Chapters 5 and 6, all excerpts from interviews recorded in this chapter are the words of the responding patrol officer unless otherwise stated.

[11] There were independent witnesses to the dispute.

partner was put into the car she tried to pull him from it. The ambulance had arrived but she had refused medical attention. Both of them were taken to the station but the custody officer was worried about her state and so we took her to the hospital. When I followed up the case, I found out she had a broken jaw, which is now wired up with plates. Her teeth were braced and wired. She had to have an operation the next day for internal injuries. I phoned her again a week later and asked her to make a complaint, but she kept saying no because she loved him.

Although arrested for assault, the man was released without being charged because the victim refused to make a complaint.

Police officers often referred to the difficulties inherent in achieving a successful prosecution, particularly for a crime of violence. They argued that they wanted to be sure of the victim's commitment to such action before they used scarce resources in preparing a case for prosecution. In practice, they never attempted a prosecution when the victim withdrew her statement, even when there was corroborative evidence. In one example there were both photographic evidence of injuries and the victim's original statement. In another case they argued that the woman's learning disability meant that a prosecutor would be unlikely to compel her to testify. In other cases there were other justifications, even when the violence was extreme. For example, a woman who had been married for only six weeks, and had been assaulted by her husband on four separate occasions since the wedding, had been brutally attacked by him. After the attack he had voluntarily gone to the police station and told the station duty officer that he had strangled his wife and that she might be dead. The responding officer found her alive but injured and very distressed. He explained the decision not to charge the husband:

She was adamant that she did not want to make a complaint. I tried to persuade her to but she would not budge. I asked the custody sergeant if he could be interviewed for a bind-over but the sergeant said no as she was not making any complaint.[12]

When asked why he did not leave this decision to the Crown Prosecution Service, the custody sergeant argued that 'there would have been no point because they wouldn't have taken it on without any witnesses'. As with the decision not to arrest, the wishes of the victim not to proceed seemed to be crucial in the decision not to

---

[12] This was the only case where a custody officer made a decision which was different from the action suggested by the officer in charge of the case—see above.

charge. It was decided to test this conclusion, arrived at through analysis of the qualitative data, by statistical analysis of all of the cases which resulted in an arrest.

Logistic regression analysis was carried out with the dependent variable being 'criminal charge' (sixty-one of the 168 arrests resulted in a criminal charge being laid).[13] The independent variables were those which had been tested against the decision to arrest (except for the variables 'evidence' and 'victim injured').[14] This analysis created a model with just two variables as predictors of the decision to charge: the victim requested police action (either for the suspect to be arrested or to be removed from the scene—see Chapter 5); and there was a history of disputes between the couple.

The first, and strongest, of the two predictive variables in the model was also one of the strongest variables for predicting an arrest. In the main, what women wanted was what they got. Of course, it is not surprising that if a woman wanted her partner to be arrested in the first place, she would be more likely to want to see him charged and prosecuted. Qualitative analysis of the data shows that the police value a co-operative witness above almost anything. As stated above, most of the suspects who were arrested but not charged have their victims to thank for their exit from the criminal justice system at that early stage.

The second predictive variable, history of domestic violence, was not sufficiently highly correlated with the decision to arrest to be included in the logistic model for arrest. It might have been absent at that stage because in half of the cases when the police were deciding whether or not to arrest they did not know about the history of violence (see Chapter 4). However, it was a strong predictor of the decision to charge. There are two possible explanations for this.

First, in cases where there was a history of violence it is more likely that the police involved in the decision-making process would have had prior contact, or at least knowledge, of the suspect and might, therefore, be more inclined to lay charges. Knowing that he had been violent or caused disturbances on previous occasions, officers might have decided that previous warnings, or conciliatory

---

[13] In three of these cases the charges were subsequently dropped.

[14] It was considered inappropriate to use these two variables to measure the factors influencing the decision to charge as there is very little chance of someone being charged when there are no injuries or other evidence of an offence.

approaches, had not deterred him and this time they needed to take criminal action.

Considering the strength of the other variable in the model, there is a more plausible explanation: that the victim having suffered similar abuse in the past had finally decided that she had had enough. Research suggests that women will often suffer numerous acts of violence before engaging with the criminal justice system (Smith 1989). Hence it is probably the case that the victims in this study who had experienced such abuse before were more willing to see the suspect prosecuted than were those for whom the incident was the first such event. Qualitative analysis of the data from interviews with victims as well as with police supports this hypothesis. Therefore, both variables in the regression model point in a similar direction—to the importance of victim co-operation in the decision to charge domestic violence offences.

Factors shaping prosecutors' decisions

A total of sixty-one cases were sent for prosecution. Four of these were prosecuted on reduced charges. In over a third (twenty-three) the prosecutor discontinued the case or offered no evidence at court (under section 23 of the Prosecution of Offences Act 1985).[15] Although the suspect in half of the discontinued cases was bound over to keep the peace, this left only just over half (thirty-four) of the charged suspects who were prosecuted on the initial charge.

The majority of the cases which were discontinued failed because the victim withdrew her complaint (although there were four cases which were discontinued despite support from the victim). Indeed, of the eighteen cases where the victim withdrew after the file had been sent for prosecution, sixteen were discontinued because of the withdrawal (six of these suspects were bound over to keep the peace) and two resulted in a prosecution for a reduced charge.[16] Both of these suspects had initially been charged with assault occasioning actual bodily harm but the charges were reduced to common assault when the suspects were persuaded to enter guilty pleas to the lesser charge. As Cretney and Davis (1996) have argued, victim withdrawal presages discontinuance.

[15] Both of these dispositions are identical in effect to acquittals.
[16] The charges were reduced in the other two 'reduced charge' cases because there was insufficient evidence.

The decision to discontinue a case

The data collected from prosecutors in the Thames Valley Police support the conclusion arrived at through analysis of the police data, that is that 'victim unreliability' is the main explanation offered by criminal justice agents for the high attrition rate of cases of domestic violence. When victims of domestic violence withdraw their complaints, prosecutors, like the police, rarely proceed with the case (see also Quarm and Schwartz 1983; Edwards 1986; Crisp and Moxon 1994). Indeed, Cretney and Davis have argued that in *all* cases of assault, 'It is difficult to overestimate the importance of witness evidence' (1995: 107). In most of the incidents they followed it was only the availability of independent witnesses which made a prosecution viable, even in cases where the victim had not withdrawn his or her statement. In cases of domestic violence, because of the very private nature of the violence, the police often do not have the luxury of independent witnesses:[17]

As far as 'domestic' violence ... [is] concerned, the low conviction rate is a direct result of victims' inability or unwillingness to make a formal complaint or to give evidence when called upon to do so. In other words, this high failure rate is not necessarily reflected in the trial: most cases do not get that far. (Cretney and Davis 1995: 144.)

The Crown Prosecution Service is supposed to review all cases referred to it in accordance with the principles set out in the Code for Crown Prosecutors (hereafter referred to as 'the Code'), issued pursuant to section 10 of the Prosecution of Offences Act 1985,[18] and then decide whether to prosecute or drop the case.[19] In order to decide which cases to prosecute and which to dismiss, prosecutors should apply the tests set out in the Code. The first is the strength of the evidence.[20] They should be satisfied that there is 'admissible,

[17] Furthermore, they do not seem to make the effort to locate and interview those who could provide corroborative evidence (see below).
[18] Under section 10 of the Prosecution of Offences Act 1985 the Director of Public Prosecutions issues a Code for Crown Prosecutors giving guidance on general principles to be applied by the Service in determining whether cases should proceed or not. The Code forms part of the Director's Annual Report to the Attorney General, which is laid before Parliament in accordance with section 9 of the Act.
[19] The Crown Prosecution Service is entitled to discontinue a case as soon as it has examined it or at any time thereafter (s. 23, Prosecution of Offences Act 1985).
[20] Although the slim Code for Crown Prosecutors is publicly available, the Crown Prosecution Service makes most of its day-to-day operational decisions on the basis of 'manuals' which contain detailed guidance about what might constitute enough evidence for proceedings, for example.

substantial and reliable evidence that a criminal offence known to the law has been committed by an identifiable person [and that] there is a realistic prospect of a conviction' (Crown Prosecution Service 1992, para. 4). Where the case satisfies the evidential criterion, the prosecutor should go on to consider whether the public interest requires a prosecution. Only if the public interest criterion is also satisfied should the case proceed to prosecution. These criteria apply to offences committed in domestic circumstances as they do to any other offence. However, when the case is one concerning domestic violence prosecutors follow additional guidelines in deciding on the disposal of cases.

In April 1993, before prosecutors were interviewed for the study reported in this book, the Crown Prosecution Service updated and published a comprehensive guide issued to staff for dealing with domestic violence cases: the Statement of Prosecution Policy (hereafter referred to as 'the Statement') (Crown Prosecution Service 1993a). The main tenet of this guide was a recognition of, and an endorsement of, the principle that violence in a domestic context is not a factor which reduces the seriousness of the offence. The Statement insists that in cases of domestic violence prosecutors should, first and foremost, review the case 'In accordance with the principles set out in the Code for Crown Prosecutors' (para. 2.1). In other words they should ensure that the evidential and public interest tests are applied before proceeding to prosecution. They are advised against reducing the seriousness of charges; recommended to seek bail conditions or remand in custody to protect victims from further harm or intimidation; and to consider opting for a bind-over when the witness has withdrawn her support and the case is to be discontinued. As far as the public interest considerations are concerned the statement points out that:

If there is sufficient evidence to offer a realistic prospect of conviction, and the victim is willing to give evidence, it will be rare for the public interest not to require a prosecution for offences of domestic violence. (Para. 6.3.)

The proviso concerning the victim's willingness to give evidence was backed up by the Code which asks prosecutors to consider if the witness is 'either hostile or friendly to the accused, or may be otherwise unreliable' in evaluating the evidence (s. 5 (iii)).[21] Referring

---

[21] The Code is regularly updated. The Code referred to in this book is the one which was in use in 1993 when the fieldwork for this study was being conducted. In

specifically to the problem of hostile witnesses, the Statement aims for a balance between victims' wishes and public interest:

Whilst the victim's wishes will be taken into account when determining whether to proceed with a prosecution, prosecutors must balance an individual's wishes with the wider public interest in prosecuting perpetrators of domestic violence. (Para. 6.4.)

In some circumstances, it states, 'an assessment of the public interest might prevail over and above the wishes of the individual victim' (para. 6.7).

In deciding whether or not to pursue a prosecution when the victim has withdrawn her statement, prosecutors are asked to consider the seriousness of the offence, the history of the relationship and the effect on children of living in a violent household (paras. 6.7, 6.9, 6.10).[22] One suspect in the Thames Valley study had been charged with assault, but his wife, with whom he was still living, withdrew her statement soon after he was charged, leaving no other witnesses to the offence. In explaining her decision to discontinue, the prosecutor made reference to the fact that the couple were still living together, but placed most emphasis on the fact that the injuries were not serious and that this was the first time he had assaulted her. In this case the prosecutor seemed to have followed the guidance laid down in the Statement and the Code. However, it will be shown that prosecutors' decisions regarding prosecution when the witness has withdrawn her statement usually reflect the cautious tones of the Code rather than the more encouraging approach of the Statement.

One prosecution for serious assault was discontinued because the victim withdrew, even though it was clear that there had been a history of violence (Social Services had forbidden the suspect to contact his children because of his repeated violent outbursts). For cases like this, the Statement suggests that alternatives should be considered before the decision to discontinue is made. It provides steps to be followed when victims withdraw their complaints referring to the supervision of the case, communication between the

1994 the Code underwent substantial revision and this cautionary note about 'unreliable' witnesses was omitted. This might have the effect of strengthening the presumption in favour of prosecution in cases of domestic violence.

[22] The 1992 Code did not refer to the history of the relationship. However, the revised Code (1994) does state that the public interest is in favour of prosecution if 'there are grounds for believing that the offence is likely to be continued or repeated, for example, by a history of recurring conduct' (para. 6.4 (m)).

defence and prosecution, and establishment of the veracity of original allegations. The prosecutor must follow specific criteria in assessing why the victim has withdrawn her support for a prosecution. If the veracity of the original allegations is confirmed but the victim refuses to go to court a number of options are open to the Crown Prosecution Service: the victim can be compelled to give evidence in relation to violence against herself or her children;[23] the case can proceed without her testimony (provided that the public interest requires a prosecution); and her statement can be read out in court as evidence without her having to testify (under section 23 of the Criminal Justice Act 1988).[24] The Crown Prosecution Service guidelines state that 'discontinuance of the proceedings on evidential grounds should only take place when all options have been considered and found to be inappropriate' (para. 3 (g)). It was found that the prosecutors almost invariably discontinued cases of domestic violence when the victim withdrew her statement without considering any of these options.[25] Other empirical studies have similarly found that a woman's expressed wish no longer to co-operate with the prosecuting authorities determines the outcome of the case (Cretney and Davis 1997).

One woman who had been raped by her partner encountered the defendant in the waiting room at an 'old style' committal hearing. She became hysterical and refused to go into the courtroom. Consequently, the case was adjourned. Two weeks later the victim made a statement saying she could not go through with a court case,

[23] Up until 1978 spouses were compellable witnesses against their married partners in cases where they had been assaulted. However, in that year the House of Lords (*Hoskyn v Metropolitan Police Commissioner* [1978] 2 All ER 136) ruled that a wife should not be treated as a compellable witness against her husband in a case of violence on her by him. Partly in response to rising fears about wives being pressured by partners not to testify, this position was reversed by the enactment of s. 97 of the Magistrates' Courts Act 1980, and later by s. 80 (3) (a) of PACE. PACE made a wife a competent and compellable witness against her spouse where the offence charged involves an assault on, or injury or a threat of injury to the wife of the accused. A wife who refuses to give evidence may be punished for contempt.

[24] This provision permits a statement made by a person to be admissible as evidence of any fact of which direct oral evidence by that person would be admissible, as long as the statement was made to a police officer and as long as the witness refuses to give evidence through fear (para. 3.4 (f) (i), (ii), (iii)). The Home Office Circular (1990/60) drew attention to this provision as something which might help the police and Crown Prosecution Service in dealing effectively with domestic violence.

[25] Original fears that s. 23 would open up the floodgates to victims of violent crime have not been borne out. It appears, as Edwards has argued, that s. 23 is not the panacea it was intended to be (1996: 207).

although she did not withdraw her original complaint. She claimed that she was too afraid of the defendant to face him in court. As she did not retract her original statement the prosecutor should, it could be argued, have considered compelling her to testify or, less controversially, used her original testimony as evidence (discussed above). Needless to say, the prosecutor discontinued the case, arguing that, as it rested on the issue of consent, her testimony was needed if the case was to succeed. When asked why this woman had not been compelled, the prosecutor, who admitted that he had not previously considered this option, suggested that it would not have been fair to compel her as 'she [was] obviously terrified of going to court'.

In all of the cases which were discontinued the suspect had initially pleaded not guilty to the offence charged. It is possible that the victims withdrew their complaints *because* the case was contested, and that they would not have done so if the suspect had entered a guilty plea. There are various reasons why victims of domestic violence fail to support a prosecution (see Chapter 8). However, the prospect of having to testify is a major factor, especially for victims who feel that the outcome of prosecution (usually predicted to be a minor sanction imposed by the court) would not be worth the process.

Charge bargaining

Charge bargaining and charge reduction (the dropping of the most serious charge in return for a plea of guilty to a lesser offence) is a widespread practice for all offences. It usually involves the defendant agreeing to plead guilty in exchange for the prosecution proceeding on a less serious charge. The law does not effectively constrain this practice and indeed the Code seems to encourage it, especially as it emphasizes the 'resource advantages both to the service and the courts generally' (para. 11). At mode of trial hearings the defence counsel, the prosecutor, and the magistrates must determine whether the offence is more suitable for summary trial or trial on indictment.[26] Often it is in no-one's interest to have the case heard in the Crown Court: the costs of such a trial are far greater than a magistrates' hearing; the defendant risks a higher sentence if

---

[26] The procedure followed at such hearings is prescribed by the Magistrates' Courts Act 1980.

found guilty; and the prosecutor might not have sufficient evidence, or might be unsure about the reliability of the evidence, fearing an acquittal. Furthermore, prosecutors are concerned about resources: cases for the Crown Court require counsel, and a good deal of preparation. Hence, defence solicitors have good reasons for persuading their clients to plead guilty to lesser offences which can be tried summarily, and prosecutors have good reasons for agreeing to this.

Fears about evidential sufficiency might persuade a prosecutor to initiate such a deal or agree to the defendant being bound over in exchange for dropping all criminal charges. This, of course, sometimes means that defendants will be encouraged to plead guilty to offences for which there might not be sufficient evidence to convict them in a contested case. Clearly this practice does not reflect due process values and adversarial principles.[27] Conversely, it could be argued that this practice 'sells the victim short', that it does not acknowledge the seriousness of the crime committed against her and that, as such, she will not see justice done.

With regard to charging practice, the Code for Crown Prosecutors recommends that 'the charges laid should adequately reflect the gravity of the defendants' conduct and will normally be the most serious revealed by the evidence' (s. 12 (iii)). Dealing more specifically with the acceptance of pleas, it repeats this advice, stating that 'the over-riding consideration will be to ensure that the Crown is never left in the position of being unable to pass a proper sentence consistent with the gravity of the defendants' actions' (s. 11).[28] In the Thames Valley study none of the suspects charged with assault occasioning grievous bodily harm were convicted on that count. Cretney and Davis also found 'a substantial use of the plea-bargain'. For example, out of eleven initial charges of wounding with intent[29] only one suspect was convicted on that count (1995: 138). Superficially, these data suggest that prosecutors are not doing their best for victims when they agree to reduce the charge or when they agree to drop charges in return for the suspect agreeing to be bound over to keep the peace.

[27] See Sanders and Young (1994, chap. 6, s. 3) for a discussion of the gap between 'due process rhetoric' and 'crime control reality' in pre-trial negotiation.

[28] The revised Code (1994) states, more precisely than the 1992 Code used at the time of this fieldwork, that 'Crown Prosecutors must never accept a guilty plea just because it is convenient' (para. 9.1).

[29] Contrary to s. 18, Offences Against the Person Act 1861.

There appeared, from examining the Thames Valley data, to be two main reasons for prosecutors making deals with defence solicitors: first, a lack of sufficient evidence—often caused by victims withdrawing their statements; and, secondly, limited resources. It was not always clear which took precedence in any one case. In one case the reduction of the initial charge of assault occasioning grievous bodily harm to assault occasioning actual bodily harm was due to a bargain between the defence solicitor and the prosecutor. Prior to this negotiation the prosecutor had been warned by the police officer in charge of the case that the victim was considering retracting her statement. Both reasons seemed operative here, but the prosecutor considered no harm to have been done to the victims' interests anyway: 'It will probably not need to go to the Crown Court now, which is a good thing. There's such a backlog of cases. Besides, it makes no difference which you go for. ABH and GBH are both punishable by five years.'

McConville *et al.* (1994) looked at how defendants are often persuaded to enter a guilty plea (often for cases with very weak evidence) in order to secure a sentence reduction. They found that prosecutors often reduced charges likely to require trial at the Crown Court to offences which could be dealt with cheaply in the magistrates' court. For example, wounding or grievous bodily harm with intent (s. 18) can only be tried in the Crown Court, but acts of wounding and grievous bodily harm contrary to section 20 or actual bodily harm offences are 'triable either way').[30] And when a Crown Court trial seems unavoidable the more serious charges may be dropped in return for a guilty plea to a lesser offence. Such 'bargaining' can eliminate the necessity of a trial. Their research found that prosecutors and defence solicitors were daily to be seen haggling over charges outside the courtroom. This bargaining process often seemed to be little more than a casual chat and rarely involved the prosecutors fighting for the retention of the initial charges. There seemed to be little regard for the impact of decisions on either defendant or victim. At the Crown Court McConville *et al.* found

---

[30] Similarly, dropping an actual bodily harm charge to a common assault is one example of avoiding the possibility of an expensive trial as the defendant in a common assault case cannot elect to be tried in the Crown Court—common assault is a 'summary' (magistrates only) offence, the penalty for which is a bind-over or a trivial fine.

that even more hasty deals were made between the prosecution and defence (see also Baldwin 1985).

Deals can be made between the prosecutor and defence lawyer in order to spare the victim the ordeal of having to testify or because of fear of her not attending court on the day of the hearing. One victim arrived in court on the day of the trial but told the prosecutor that she was petrified and did not want to give evidence: 'she kept asking me if she could go home'. The prosecutor negotiated with the defence lawyer and the actual bodily harm charge was reduced to a common assault, with the defendant then also pleading guilty to the criminal damage. Hence, instead of abandoning the case the prosecutor made a 'deal'. This deal saved the victim the trauma of testifying and resulted in her receiving compensation and the defendant being conditionally discharged.[31]

Often when victims withdrew their initial complaints and refused to testify the prosecutors did not have a realistic prospect of conviction. In one case the witness withdrew and the defendant would not plead guilty to the initial charge of assault occasioning actual bodily harm. The prosecutor, rather than discontinuing the case, offered the defence lawyer a reduced charge of common assault, to which the defendant pleaded guilty. As the prosecutor explained, 'a deal was the best we could hope for once she'd withdrawn'. Indeed, with no witness and no plea the assault charge may well have led to an acquittal. In other cases the defendant was 'persuaded' to plead guilty to offences for which, without the testimony of the victim, there was probably insufficient evidence. Whilst the victim's withdrawal of her statement was the primary reason for most of these 'deals', resource implications almost certainly encouraged both sides into hasty deals.

Negotiating a bind-over

Bind-overs were sometimes agreed upon as alternatives to total discontinuances when victims withdrew at 'the eleventh hour'. These practices meant that some suspects who were initially charged with very serious offences left the court with nothing more than a bind-over. One grievous bodily harm charge was

---

[31] A conditional discharge means that if the defendant appears before the court again within the next twelve months he might be sentenced more severely for this offence.

reduced to a charge of assault occasioning actual bodily harm after medical evidence failed to support a degree of injury to justify the initial charge.[32] However, the victim decided, whilst at court on the day of the trial, that she would not testify and so the prosecutor accepted that the charge would be dropped in return for the defendant agreeing to a bind-over. The policy of the Crown Prosecution Service regarding the use of bind-overs in relation to domestic violence states that such a disposal might be appropriate '... in some minor cases, e.g. cases without a history of violence, where the incident is believed to be an isolated occurrence and the parties are reconciled' (1993a: para. 9.1). However, some of the cases in the Thames Valley were more serious than this.

Whilst it might be argued that serious cases should not result in only a bind-over, this may have been the only disposal available to prosecutors if they were not prepared to compel hostile witnesses. It was certainly the case that less serious charges which did not have the support of the victim might be considered to be successes if the defendant ended up bound-over. This seemed to be true for one case involving a charge for criminal damage and affray. The defendant had already paid for the damage to be repaired and the victim had told the police that she was scared of going to court. The prosecutor, afraid that she would not attend court on the day, agreed, in advance, to a bind-over. He also argued that, as the defendant had made good the damage and had no previous convictions, even if prosecuted for the offences he was initially charged with he would have got no more than a conditional discharge which, he argued 'is not much better than a bind-over'. In this case the prosecutor followed the guidelines pertaining to non-serious offences.

In assessing the public interest criteria the Code asks prosecutors to consider discontinuance if 'the circumstances of an offence are not particularly serious, and a court would be likely to impose a purely nominal penalty' (s. 8 (i)).[33] However, seriousness is, in part, a construction and, in part, a subjective assessment. Similarly, appropriateness is highly subjective. Prosecutors can make decisions based on *their* ideas of 'appropriate punishment' and the likely impact of a particular sentence. In one case a charge of threatening

---

[32] Assault occasioning grievous bodily harm has to be a 'really serious' assault where a bone (or an equivalent) has been broken (Smith and Hogan 1996: 439–40).

[33] Crisp and Moxon (1994) found that half of cases discontinued because of public interest were explained by reference to an expected nominal penalty.

behaviour was dropped in return for the defendant agreeing to be bound over. The prosecutor explained: 'She'd withdrawn her statement . . . and the officers were on rest days. It was not worth getting them in. He'd have only got a conditional discharge or a small fine anyway.' It may be that a conditional discharge or even a fine would have dissuaded this man from committing further acts of violence against the victim. However, the prosecutor made a decision based on his own ideas about the usefulness of the process and the possible sanctions. Public interest criteria are not prioritized. Hence, the prosecutors can decide which factor, offence seriousness or likely penalty, should influence their decision regarding prosecution. This means that if they wish to pursue a prosecution they may be able to justify it according to one or other criteria, but if they wish not to do so they can also easily find justification in the Code. Hence as McConville, Sanders, and Leng argue, the decision, based, it will be argued, on working rules, comes first and the policy justification follows (1991, chap. 7).

In the above case resources undoubtedly were of consideration. The prosecutor argued that he had balanced the costs which would be incurred by a contested case resulting in a light sentence at best, with the probability of an acquittal at worst. Similarly, another suspect charged with assault left the court with a bind-over after the prosecutor discontinued the case because: '. . . there was no history of violence, and the penalty was likely be a conditional discharge. So, I agreed to the defence's offer of a bind-over. . . There was nothing that could be achieved by a trial.' When asked if there were any other factors considered in the decision to accept a bind-over the prosecutor admitted that 'the cost of running a trial was *obviously* taken into account' (my emphasis).

In many other cases it was remarkable that the defendants agreed to be bound over, as the prosecutors were sometimes left with no reliable evidence against them. In practice, if the victim was unwilling to testify, the prosecutors believed that a bind-over was all they should try for (see also Cretney and Davis 1996). However, this does not have to be the only conclusion. Whilst the prosecutors have to consider whether there is sufficient evidence of an offence before proceeding with a prosecution, evidence is not always an objective entity which is either present or absent. As McConville, Sanders, and Leng show, evidence is a construction. When victims withdraw their statements, prosecutors could look closely for any other evidence which corroborates their original statement. This could be photographs of injuries or statements from other family members, friends or neighbours. However, they do not seem to make much effort in this direction. And, more importantly, such efforts would be likely to be frustrated by the police failure to construct a case for the prosecution.

Police officers in these cases of domestic violence did not make much effort to seek corroborative evidence: they rarely interviewed other potential witnesses; and they rarely sought confessions, both of which are the expected aims of the police when they are trying to construct a case. It is often said that police investigation consists primarily of the search for a confession.[34] Yet in the Thames Valley sample many of the arrested suspects were not interviewed with the intention of securing a confession. One officer asked if a particular suspect had confessed to assault, explained that he had not done so and added: 'Most of the time in these cases we don't waste much time interviewing the bloke because she's (the victim) bound to withdraw and then it'll go nowhere.' When pushed further on this point he added: 'Of course, we asked him if he'd thumped her but he said she fell and really, whilst I didn't believe him, in domestics it's his word against hers. They're bloody difficult.' An informal conversation with a custody officer elicited support for this attitude. He explained: 'They [arresting officers] don't go flat out for confessions in these cases because they know these women will withdraw and once she pulls out CPS won't want to know.' The fact that prosecutors might be more inclined to proceed with a case with the suspect's confession if the victim withdraws her statement did not seem to enter into this 'logic'.

Other empirical work has found that some cases of violence between non-intimates are prosecuted even though the witness has withdrawn, although usually only when there are public interest implications or when the police's authority would otherwise be undermined (Sanders 1988a).[35] This is probably because the police

---

[34] Over the last decade there has been less emphasis on confession evidence. This is, in the main, as a result of restrictions imposed on police behaviour regarding interviews with suspects—restrictions imposed by PACE. Police are turning increasingly to informants as a source of information which might help them prosecute suspects (see Dunninghan and Norris 1995).

[35] Cretney and Davis (1995) provide a counter-argument.

in such cases make great efforts to gather as much evidence against the suspect as possible.

In cases of domestic violence, police and prosecutors seem to assume that the case must end when the victim withdraws her support for a prosecution. It is perhaps for this reason that the police rarely caution domestic violence perpetrators. If a victim wants the perpetrator warned about his behaviour, sanctioned in some way, but does not want him prosecuted, a formal caution might be an ideal choice. Cautions can punish offenders and go some way towards protecting victims. A caution does not count as a criminal conviction but does go on the offender's criminal record. If later the victim wants him charged and prosecuted for another assault then evidence of cautions can be useful. Furthermore, cautioning may be a good way of showing men that such behaviour is unacceptable. On average 24 per cent of adults found guilty or cautioned for indictable offences were cautioned in 1992 (Sanders and Young 1994: 228). By contrast, in the Thames Valley study, conducted just one year later, only two men (approximately 4 per cent of those cautioned or found guilty (forty-one)) were cautioned.[36] In one of these cases the man was cautioned because the victim had withdrawn her statement and the prosecutor recommended a caution. In the other it was the choice of the police. In both cases a caution was justified by reference to the suspects' fears of losing their jobs.

Cautions are supposed to be an alternative to prosecution, rather than to no further action, and so must only be given in cases where there is sufficient evidence to prosecute. As is explained above, in the majority of the Thames Valley cases there was not sufficient evidence; in particular, there was rarely a confession. However, research has suggested that in cautioning practice, as in other areas of criminal justice, there is a gap between the 'law in books' and the 'law in action'. Police officers sometimes *do* caution when there is insufficient evidence (Sanders and Young 1994: 231). Indeed, Sanders found that some cautions were administered

[36] Of course, there is always variation between forces and without data for the cautioning rates in the Thames Valley Police it is impossible to know how the cautioning rate for offences arising from domestic disputes fares in comparison with other offences. However, of the five forces examined by Sanders and Young (1994), whilst the variation was great (from 12 per cent in Cumbria to 36 per cent in Devon and Cornwall) the lowest figure of 12 per cent was still much higher than the 4 per cent found in this study.

precisely because there was insufficient evidence (Sanders 1988b). Of course suspects should also agree to be cautioned. However if a suspect was not told that his victim was considering withdrawal or had already withdrawn her statement he might be happy to accept a caution rather than risk the penalty that a court might impose. Also, research has suggested that cautions are sometimes issued in the absence of consent or an admission (Sanders 1988b).

There is clearly a 'catch 22' situation regarding cautions. The police do not caution suspects because they do not have a confession. However, they do not appear to seek confessions in these cases because they anticipate victim withdrawal from the process, and because they do not envisage a caution as an appropriate disposal. It appears that in the case of domestic violence, the police do not commit to the goal of obtaining a formal sanction. It is difficult to understand why this is so. It could be argued that the typical 'incentives' to caution are absent in cases of domestic violence. These are what Sanders and Young (1994: 234) call 'the unofficial police interest criteria'. For example, cautions are sometimes given as an alternative to prosecution as a favour to the suspect, providing, or maintaining, the basis of a relationship on which future 'deals' can be built. Thus, informers are frequently cautioned rather than prosecuted as part of maintaining a mutually beneficial relationship (ibid.: 235). Perpetrators of domestic violence are unlikely to make good informers.

Another reason for the police wanting to caution a suspect is to punish suspects in cases where there is insufficient evidence to prosecute (Sanders and Young 1994: 234). When suspects' offences impact on local businesses or local residents, for example, there are likely to be demands, through community liaison departments, for the police to take some sort of positive action. Yet it might be that there is no pressure from the community to 'do something' about men who commit acts of violence or damage property within their own homes. For juvenile offenders cautions are often used as a form of crime prevention or deterrent: a warning of what will happen next time they are arrested. There seems to be no logical reason why cautions are not used for this purpose with perpetrators, of offences within a domestic context, when bind-overs and conditional discharges, as well as arrests with no further action, seem to be used, in part, with crime prevention in mind. It would seem that in cases of domestic violence the police and prosecutors are only prepared to commit to using their powers when the victim is also committed to supporting such action.

The influence of evidential rules, working rules, and public interest criteria on decisions to prosecute

One critical question which arises from the data reported in this chapter is whether the refusal to charge and prosecute a suspect when the witness was unco-operative was a product of the law or a product of police and prosecutors' working rules. In other words, whether it was an evidential rule (they could not charge or prosecute because legally they had insufficient evidence) or a working rule (cases without a co-operative witness had come to be classified as 'unprosecutable' so that officers and prosecutors automatically dropped them without considering whether or not there might have been alternatives)? This is, of course, creating too crude a dichotomy. Both evidence and working rules influence police and prosecutors to a greater or lesser extent. Furthermore, there is necessarily a close relationship between working rules and public interest criteria, as criteria such as offence seriousness can be both objective and subjective. Therefore, the question should be the extent of influence of evidential criteria and working rules.

It might be thought that reported assaults involving acquaintances or intimates are very easy to process, because detection is almost guaranteed. However prosecution is not made more likely, because of this: rather, the relationship undermines the chance of a prosecution because witnesses cannot be relied upon to translate their report into evidence in court. This has been found to be so in all social relationships, especially where there is a power imbalance, and not just in domestic disputes (Cretney and Davis 1995: 99).

Essentially, if a witness withdraws her evidential statement, and the suspect is likely to plead not guilty, the police have two options. If there is evidence other than the testimony of the witness they can charge the suspect. Similarly, if there is no corroborative evidence they could still charge the suspect in the hope that the prosecutor will compel the witness or allow her original statement to be presented to the court without her oral testimony (see above).[37] Or they could choose to take no further action.

---

[37] Since PACE the Crown Prosecution Service has had the power to ask a court to issue a summons or warrant of arrest in order to compel a reluctant witness, whether

Clearly, as has been shown above, in cases of domestic violence the police rarely pursue a prosecution when the victim is reluctant to proceed. Officers who argued that the police cannot prosecute without a co-operative witness implied that this was a 'rule' based on legal constraints. But other officers who argued that the police *will not* proceed because of the harm such action might visit on a victim, or on the family as a whole, offered a more convincing argument. Their reluctance to compel a hostile witness in cases of domestic violence seemed to be influenced more by a working rule than an evidential rule. The working rule, which points to no further action when victims withdraw, is based on working assumptions about the sanctity of the family unit, the likelihood of further repeat violence, and the unhelpfulness of the criminal justice system in such cases.

Their comments about the unhelpfulness of the system reflect, in part, public interest criteria which ask prosecutors to weigh up the 'costs' of a prosecution, economic and otherwise, against the likely outcome. Police, as well as prosecutors, are influenced by the Code —not least because the cautioning guidelines are very similar. However, the majority of police officers justified their decisions not to prosecute by reference to the damage such a decision might visit on victims and their families. They suggested that they preferred not to initiate proceedings in cases where they felt that it would not help the family or would have a negative impact on the family (see also Moody and Toombs 1982). The officer in the following incident, for example, alluded to such concerns:

Within an hour of arresting him she phoned the station and withdrew the statement. We visited her for an official withdrawal to see if she was being pressured. We believed that she may have been 'persuaded' by a relative of the aggressor. I did not think that the Crown Prosecution Service would have compelled her, and *I feared the implications if they had done.* (My emphasis.)

---

a partner or ex-partner, to attend court and give evidence at a trial. If a woman refuses to give evidence at a trial, whether or not she has been compelled to attend, she can be imprisoned for contempt of court. In the infamous case of Michelle Renshaw (cited in Edwards 1989) a woman was sentenced to seven days for contempt of court when she refused to give evidence against her partner who, it was alleged, assaulted her. More recently, Sophie Bird and Sarah Holt were imprisoned for contempt of court arising from similar circumstances (*The Guardian*, 24 October 1996). As Edwards has argued, courts have been insensitive, obtuse, and heavy-handed in the few cases where attempts at compelling witnesses have been made (1996: 204).

Others were adamant that they would not force a victim to testify against her wishes. They talked about not wanting to deny women their autonomy and control over their lives and about how a prosecution could not help women who genuinely want to continue or re-establish their relationships with the perpetrators. One officer spoke for the majority when he explained: 'It's up to her. I'll not push a woman if she doesn't want to make a complaint. She had all the options explained to her but she didn't want to prosecute.' Similarly, in the following case the officer was concerned about the whole family. He spent some time talking with the victim considering the options and decided that in this case the civil options were preferable to criminal proceedings:

When I went to see the aggrieved the next day to take a statement she was not sure that she wanted to make a complaint. She was confused as to what to do. Her concern was for the safety of the children. She wanted to do what was best for them. I told her that there were agencies other than the criminal law to help her sort out the best for the children. I have visited her twice since the assault and eventually she decided to file for a divorce instead of going for a prosecution. She also said she would get an injunction. I thought this might be the best as I didn't feel that this family was at the end of its road. It's no good pushing the criminal law when the courts typically give such weak sentences for domestic dispute which leave the victim feeling alienated. The courts do not take domestic disputes seriously enough.

Prosecutors similarly rarely proceeded with a case once the victim had withdrawn. However, just as victim unreliability should not always preclude the police commencing a prosecution, nor should it necessarily preclude prosecutors from taking a case to court. As with police decisions, prosecutors' justifications for reduced charges and discontinued cases need to be examined in order to ascertain the influence of the law and the influence of working rules. Whilst a few cases were undoubtedly casualties of stringent evidential criteria, many seemed to be products of a working rule which equates hostile victims with unwinnable cases, a working rule based on the same working assumptions as the police working rule.

Prosecutors become aware of the likelihood of a victim withdrawing either through the information provided by the police on the original file (usually on the confidential information form) or through further communication after the file has reached the prosecutor. This further information may be conveyed to the prosecutor directly from the victim, through the police officer in charge of the case, or through the defendant's solicitor. Alternatively, some victims fail to attend court on the day of the hearing. The aim of police, prosecutors, and magistrates or judges should be to determine whether or not the victim has withdrawn her support through duress, through fear of retaliation or for other reasons. However, they rarely did this.

One victim, a pregnant woman whose boyfriend assaulted and threatened to kill her (there had been a history of abuse), contacted the police to ask them if she could withdraw her statement. The police suspected that the boyfriend might have been putting her under duress to withdraw her complaint and so contacted the Crown Prosecution Service before taking a withdrawal statement. When a decision was made to proceed with the case the woman wrote directly to the Crown Prosecution Service and later followed up this communication with telephone calls on two separate occasions to request that the case be discontinued. Eventually the defence solicitor suggested his client would accept a bind-over instead of going to court to face a charge of assault. The prosecutor accepted this and did not demand that the police investigate further the possibility that the victim had withdrawn under duress.

Another serious assault charge was discontinued after the victim withdrew. This woman had made a full statement about this and other incidents but whilst the prosecutor was considering the case she withdrew the statement. She told the officer in charge of the case that she was afraid of retaliation. This information was passed on to the prosecutor dealing with the case. Later, in interview, this same prosecutor said that he could not be sure whether she really was withdrawing under duress. Earlier in this same interview the prosecutor, discussing domestic violence cases in general, had argued that: 'If injuries are serious and the witness has been harassed and threatened and withdraws we should try to push for a prosecution. The police should find out why they withdraw—it's very important.' In this case it was clear that the woman had withdrawn her statement through fear of retaliation but this did not persuade the prosecutor to continue with the case. In none of the cases where it was not clear why a victim withdrew did a prosecutor make serious attempts to assess the likelihood of duress.

In many of the cases discontinued in this study there was some evidence apart from the testimony of the victim. Hence witnesses could have been compelled to attend court and testify. However, none of the reluctant witnesses in this study were compelled. And in none of the cases had the prosecutor considered using the witness's testimony as evidence when the witness was afraid to testify. It seems, from examining the files, that this was not because these cases had insufficient evidence to compel the witness, but, rather, that the prosecutors, like the police, did not think that it would have been in the victims' interest to compel them to testify.

Prosecutors would not have been encouraged by the cautious tone of the Statement on the issue of compellability. It insists that a decision to compel a witness 'must always be exercised with sensitivity and discretion' (para. 4.2). It recommends effective liaison with support services, in particular Victim Support, to provide women with the confidence and determination needed to go ahead with a prosecution (para. 4.4). But it warns prosecutors of the risks involved with compelling 'hostile' witnesses (para. 4.3) (my emphasis).

Witness intimidation affects witnesses to various types of crimes, not just interpersonal violence. However, it is particularly likely in offences between persons known to one another. According to Edwards, this practice of victims writing directly to prosecutors has, in the past, led to 'some prosecutors and courts [accepting] victim statements and pleas made by victims on behalf of aggressors, resulting in a more lenient treatment of the offender' (Edwards 1995: 147). She argues that these pleas should not be taken into account because they are unlikely to be made voluntarily. Whether she is right or not cannot be known from interviewing prosecutors as it seems that they rarely make the necessary checks.

The Statement on domestic violence suggests that in cases which are discontinued, as a result of the victim's withdrawal of support, it may be appropriate to require the victim to attend court to confirm on oath that the initial allegations are true, but the victim has voluntarily and without duress decided not to support the prosecution (para. 3.4 (h)). And it recommends also that a case should be adjourned pending police investigation if there is any suspicion of duress (para. 3.4 (i)). Cretney and Davis (1996) found that in the area covered by their study the woman's decision to withdraw was handled in a rather 'ad hoc' fashion. Whilst some form of 'checking up' (which is recommended by the Code) generally does occur, both the Thames Valley study and that carried out by Cretney and Davis found that the degree of vigour employed varies considerably.

One woman, for example, refused to speak or give any evidence regarding an assault charge against her boyfriend. The judge decided, with no reason apparent to me, that she had not been interfered with and, in the prosecutor's words, this was 'a standard case dismissal'. Cretney and Davis (1996) found that whilst requiring a victim to make a retraction statement from the witness box is meant to be a safeguard against intimidation, none of the prosecutors they interviewed could recall an occasion when intimidation had been revealed as a result of this procedure. Hence, they conclude that such a procedure is a cosmetic exercise, designed to protect the court, prosecutors, and police officers, rather than the victim.

Occasionally prosecutors argued against compelling witnesses because of evidential problems: 'You can compel her to go to court but you can't actually make her speak. If she gave a different story in court and said the defendant wasn't the one who had injured her this would invalidate her original statement.' Many cases sent to the Crown Prosecution Service in the Thames Valley study rested on the complainants' statements. This meant that if complainants withdrew their statements prosecutors believed that they were left with little else to build a case on. This was an evidential judgement, but one based on the evidence put together by the police (that is, generally without confession evidence). One prosecutor put it this way:

Police should pursue the reasons why the victim has withdrawn and they should improve their interviewing skills as far as the defendants are concerned. As for us, we'll go on whether we've got a witness or not. They usually testify at court even if they've been hostile previously. Also we can use section 23 of the Criminal Justice Act . . . But if she's really against this we shouldn't do it. It's a moral dilemma.

This belief is a moral judgement. However, it is bound up in public interest considerations, in particular expectations of a nominal penalty were the case to go to court.

When a prosecutor suspects witness intimidation, but does not compel the witness or recommend that the case proceed without the witness being required to attend court, it appears that he is more influenced by working rules than evidential rules. This is proven by the fact that occasionally prosecutors did have corroborative evidence yet still discontinued because of reluctant witnesses. For example, in one serious assault which was discontinued because the victim withdrew her statement, there was a detailed statement from a neighbour who had heard the attack, photographic and medical evidence, and a partial admission from the defendant. It was withdrawn, according to the prosecutor, because 'The couple got back together and it wouldn't have helped their relationship'.

The working rule that prosecutors will not proceed with cases without a co-operative witness seems to be founded on genuine consideration for the harm that compelling a witness to testify might visit on that witness. It is also rooted in concern about the message that such control over witnesses would give out to a wider victim population, as the following quote from a prosecutor shows: 'We shouldn't compel. If hostile witnesses go to court it sends out a bad message to the victims—that they can't get protection by the police without having to co-operate.'

In a similar case, the prosecutor stated in a letter to the police, in which he proposed to discontinue, that 'a magistrates, court appearance could only lead to the situation being further inflamed'.[38] And a more serious assault charge was dismissed when the witness withdrew her statement because she had moved back in with her husband. The prosecutor decided against going to court 'because it would have been damaging for their attempt at reconciliation and the sentence would not have made it worthwhile.'

In the light of these explanations, prosecutors were asked if they believed that the public interest is best served by prosecuting men who assault their wives. The majority agreed that it was, mentioning that it might be a deterrent to further violence, or that it was symbolic—sending out the message to society that such behaviour was unacceptable. Many of them said: 'we need to be seen to be taking it seriously'. However, most also argued that the victims' interests were not necessarily best served by a prosecution. They tended to argue that 'at the end of the day it does little for her'. One interviewee explained his concern with prosecuting domestic

[38] In all cases in which a prosecutor concludes that the case should be discontinued he is meant to consult the police wherever possible before the discontinuance is effected. This enables the police to comment on the proposal to discontinue and to provide any possible additional information and evidence. In the Thames Valley the prosecutors almost always did this. However, they rarely decided against discontinuance on the basis of the information provided by the police even when it suggested that the victim had withdrawn under duress.

violence offenders: 'The criminal justice system doesn't really provide any answer to the complex problems these women suffer from.' Another explained: 'It might send the right message to society but it does little for the man and woman who need help.' While a third put it in the following way:

> If they only get a paltry sentence—a conditional discharge or a fine (as most do) then you must weigh up the trauma and the costs of a court case for the victim. Putting her on the witness stand against the disposal. If the couple want to reconcile, I don't think it's worth prosecuting.

It could be argued that because officers and prosecutors feel that in many cases to continue with a prosecution would not be helpful to the victims involved, they fail to identify those few cases where to compel a victim or to proceed without the victim's testimony (with independent evidence) might be of long-term benefit to the victim. As Edwards argued: 'It has been more expedient to drop cases at the onset than try to support prosecution witnesses who even if compelled may be hostile' (1996: 201).

In conclusion, it would appear that both police and prosecutors rarely initiate proceedings in cases where the victim refuses to cooperate. Whilst Cretney and Davis are right to argue that '... victim ambivalence and withdrawal is a fundamental reality...' they are not correct in arguing that it is '... something which, in the end, the police can do very little about' (1995: 74–5). It is not necessarily true that victim withdrawal has to mark the end of a case. It is the influence of working rules which leads police and prosecutors to this decision. Whilst the police see themselves as distinct from the Crown Prosecution Service, and express concern when prosecutors discontinue cases which they consider to be strong, the prosecutors who were interviewed appeared to share the same concerns and express similar opinions to the police. Both shared the same working rules. This finding inevitably raises the question of the independence of the Crown Prosecution Service from the police.

Does the Crown Prosecution Service provide independent scrutiny of cases?

The Crown Prosecution Service was set up in response to a recommendation of the Royal Commission on Criminal Procedure, which had reported in 1981. The Royal Commission had been concerned about the inefficiency, lack of openness, and inconsistency of police procedures in prosecuting cases. The Crown Prosecution Service was intended to provide independent scrutiny of cases which had been instituted and investigated by the police as a prerequisite to deciding whether a prosecution should take place. However, the finding that the police share the same working rules as prosecutors would suggest that the two organizations are not so independent.

There seem to be two arguments pertaining to the independence of the Crown Prosecution Service. Edwards, writing soon after its inception, believed that the Crown Prosecution Service would provide independent scrutiny of cases, and would be 'another level of discretion [which] will interfere with justice' (1989: 220). Indeed, she saw the Crown Prosecution Service as providing 'another selective mesh through which cases have to pass in order to reach prosecution' (ibid.). Hence she was worried about low prosecution rates.[39]

McConville, Sanders, and Leng (1991), on the other hand, developed their argument about how the police 'construct' cases, with prosecutors making decisions according to the information fed to them by the police. In other words, they only know what the police choose for them to know. McConville, Sanders, and Leng (1991) thus argued that the prosecutors sometimes pursued evidentially weak cases where to do so served some police imperative. It was claimed that the prosecutors often felt that the public interest was best served by uncritical acceptance of police decisions to charge. Hence their argument was that prosecutors 'rubber-stamp' police decisions and that this necessarily leads to a low discontinuance rate.[40] An important corollary of this argument is that where it is *not* important to the police that there be a prosecution, prosecutors are usually happy to discontinue. Since one of the working rules which they identify is that the interests of non-influential victims ar not pursued as a priority, they argue that domestic violence cases tend to get 'constructed down' (that is, not prosecuted or undercharged).

There is therefore no contradiction between McConville, Sanders, and Leng, and Edwards on the Crown Prosecution Service

---

[39] Edwards has, more recently, described the role of the Crown Prosecution Service in domestic disputes as 'determining the police's hand' and 'the tail that wags the dog' (1996: 198–201).

[40] Sanders and Young (1994: 247), writing a few years after McConville, Sanders, and Leng (1991) acknowledge that the discontinuance rates have increased since the fieldwork was conducted for this publication.

treatment of domestic violence cases. As they all predict, it seems that there is a vast differential between the general discontinuance rate and that for domestic violence. In 1994 the Crown Prosecution Service had a national 11 per cent discontinuance rate (Crown Prosecution Service 1995). An independent study conducted by the Home Office found that termination rates throughout the thirteen branches studied ranged from 10 per cent to 20 per cent (Crisp and Moxon 1994). Even if the two Crown Prosecution Service branches investigated by the Thames Valley study were areas of very high discontinuance rates,[41] the 34 per cent of domestic violence cases discontinued in this study would be much greater than the rates discovered by the Home Office, and three times as great as the national average.

There is, however, a difference between McConville, Sanders, and Leng, and Edwards on the issue of the independence of the Crown Prosecution Service. Support for the argument put forward by McConville, Sanders, and Leng would seem to be provided by a comparison of Edwards' work with the data collected in the Thames Valley. Edwards' (1989) study was conducted before the establishment of the Crown Prosecution Service when the law allowed the police to prosecute if there was a prima facie case. This was a low threshold—it was necessary only to have some evidence to indicate that there was a case to answer. Now a suspect should only be prosecuted if the prosecutor is satisfied that there is 'a realistic prospect of conviction' (Crown Prosecution Service 1992, para. 4). Further, not only must there be sufficient evidence but the prosecutor must also believe that it is in the public interest to prosecute. Therefore, all things being equal, if the Crown Prosecution Service is providing an independent scrutiny of cases, prosecution rates, as a proportion of those suspects who are arrested, should have decreased.

Whilst Edwards did not provide data on the number of charged suspects whose cases were subsequently dropped, she did have statistics on the number of arrested suspects who were subsequently charged. Although some cases were dropped after charge prior to the establishment of the Crown Prosecution Service this was rare. Therefore, Edwards' figures provide a point, although not a reliable

---

[41] I was told by the branch prosecutors that this was not the case, although no figures were obtained.

point, for comparison. In Edwards' study *all* of the arrested suspects were subsequently charged (although this was only 2 per cent of the original incidents attended), whereas in the Thames Valley study only 27 per cent of the arrested suspects were charged. In as far as it is possible to compare two studies carried out in different areas, using different research methods, this might suggest that the more stringent evidential tests resulted in the police refusing to charge more cases. It might therefore lend support to her argument about the Crown Prosecution Service being yet another filter through which cases can be rejected. However, an alternative and more plausible explanation is provided by the data reported above. The interesting point of comparison is not the stage at which the decision to charge is made, but the stage when officers decide to arrest. Comparing the attrition rates of the two studies suggests that officers in Edwards' study only arrested suspects when they had the intention (and, therefore we must presume, the evidence) to prosecute. In the Thames Valley study officers often arrested suspects when they had no such intention (see Chapter 5 and above).

Hence, superficial examination of the attrition rate (in particular, the discontinuance rate) might suggest that Edwards was correct in believing that the Crown Prosecution Service would provide not only an independent, but also rigorous scrutiny of cases. However, as this chapter has shown, if we look behind the figures we can see that the main reason for the majority of the discontinuances in cases of domestic violence was that the victim withdrew. This was also, of course, the main reason why the police failed to proceed with cases earlier on in the criminal justice process. Thus, the majority of the cases discontinued in this study would have been prosecuted if the victim had been co-operative. But, more importantly, most of these cases would never have got to the Crown Prosecution Service if the victim had withdrawn earlier. They are no different in substance to the numerous cases where the police refused to charge, or even to arrest the suspect, when the victim was 'hostile'. Therefore prosecutors were doing simply what the police would have done had they known the victims' responses at an earlier stage. As McConville, Sanders, and Leng found, the Crown Prosecution Service usually discontinued cases in the same circumstances as the police would have done.

McConville, Sanders and Leng (1991) argue that the police influence prosecutors, whilst Cretney and Davis (1997) argue that the prosecutors influence the police. There are, of course, examples of both, but the important thing to note is that both agencies are going in the same direction. In most cases they are prosecution-orientated whilst in cases of domestic violence the presumption seems to be against prosecution.[42] This would appear to lend some support to McConville, Sanders, and Leng, and Sanders' arguments about the lack of independence of the Crown Prosecution Service from the police.

However, McConville, Sanders, and Leng (1991, chap. 7) are ambiguous on this point. Sometimes they suggest that prosecutors *follow* automatically the police, without making their own decisions whilst, at other times, they suggest that the prosecutors and police come to similar conclusions about cases. This is because they are also 'prosecution-orientated', because they follow the same working rules and because the information the police give them is designed to point to only one decision. This second, rather more sophisticated, argument is supported by the data reported in this chapter. Of course, one might argue that it is not surprising that prosecutors and police come to similar conclusions about cases. After all, they both follow the Crown Prosecution Service Code in making their decisions about the strength of cases and the public interest, which means that they both screen out cases for the same reasons.

Officers who decided not to charge a suspect because the witness refused to support the prosecution were effectively making decisions based on what they believed a prosecutor would or would not do. Officers screened out cases that they thought their own Administration Support Unit (the police department responsible for processing cases) would reject, in accordance with the criteria set out in the Code. Crown prosecutors use a 'reasonable prospect of conviction' test, so the police have to measure their evidence against this before initiating prosecution proceedings. The police 'second guess' the prosecutors and magistrates, weeding out cases which they believe do not have a realistic prospect of conviction.

Not only do the police refuse to charge suspects in anticipation of the likely decisions of the Crown Prosecution Service, but they also make decisions in anticipation of how the courts would respond even if the Crown Prosecution Service were to proceed, as the following explanation from a police officer shows:

---

[42] Temkin (1995) found that cases of rape are similarly seldom prosecuted.

The victim claimed that her partner had come home drunk and 'high' and assaulted her. The bruising was only faint. In the statement she said that she had hit him first and he had retaliated. Whilst the CPS might have taken it on, the courts would see it as a 'blow for a blow'. It would have fallen down in court. I explained this to the victim who said she understood and agreed not to bother.

Clearly the police, in following the Crown Prosecution Service Code, screened out the cases which would probably have been discontinued by a prosecutor. Hence, when police officers argued, as they often did, that they would usually not send files to the Crown Prosecution Service when the victim had withdrawn her statement, because prosecutors would reject the case, they were right. Prosecutors were asked if the police were correct in this assumption and all but one said yes. As one claimed:

They're right—with hostile witnesses it's very hard to get much from a magistrate. With no witness there's no offence with most domestic violence cases. They have to select the strong cases because we couldn't cope with dealing with them all and the weak ones would be thrown out by the magistrates.

Another argued similarly:

We can't take on a case without a witness. If she won't make a complaint or withdraws it will go nowhere. We shouldn't waste time with hostile witnesses. The police are right to sift cases—they shouldn't send us rubbish. If there's no victim, there's no evidence—that's it!

Even those prosecutors who said that they would not mind if the police sent them more of the 'weak' cases acknowledged that 'they sift out the ones we'd reject anyway—the ones where there's no evidence.' The consensus was that 'there needs to be a cut-off point or we would get swamped with work', and the prosecutors had faith in the police deciding where that cut-off point should be. This consensus points not only to the influence on decisions of the Code or any other official Statements, it points to the influence of a similar culture and working rules.

Clearly, for both the police and crown prosecutors, working rules, which are, in part, related to public interest criteria and, in part, related to their perceptions of what is in the interest of the victim, are more important than evidential criteria. In cases of domestic violence it had become an almost inviolable working rule that victim withdrawal marked the end of the case. However, this does not mean that the criminal law had no role to play. The response of police officers could not have been fully understood without reference to both legal and working rules. As discussed above, often officers decided how to respond according to working rules, but then the criminal law was used to achieve this desired outcome. Prosecutors were even more bound by the criminal law, because without evidence of an offence (even though both evidence and its absence can, in itself, be a police construct) they could not pursue a case. However, what is more important is that even with strong evidence of an offence they can choose not to prosecute a suspect.

The criminal law and policies aimed at criminal justice agents do not dictate the behaviour of police officers or prosecutors. However, these agents do not disregard policies or law. Their choices are influenced by both to a degree. The disagreement amongst academics, as well as between academics and practitioners, is over the *extent* to which the legal rules and policies shape decision-making. The Thames Valley study suggests that, as far as domestic violence is concerned, policy changes do not have a dramatic impact on decisions to arrest and prosecute offenders. And whilst this study suggests that McConville, Sanders, and Leng (1991) placed insufficient emphasis on the impact of the criminal law, their conclusion about the role of the law and the role of working rules is only slightly more 'pessimistic' than that of this study.

Clearly police and prosecutors follow the same official guidelines and share the same working rules. Hence they evaluate cases in the same way. With regard to incidents of domestic violence the main factor which shapes the response of both agencies is the victim's preference. The following chapter will look more closely at these preferences and explain why victims of domestic violence so rarely choose to support the prosecution of their partners or ex-partners.

7

In the Victim's Interest?

As the previous chapter showed, police and prosecutors do not think that it is in the victim's interest to prosecute offences arising from domestic violence when the victim is opposed to this solution. Some feminist writers have disagreed with the practice of allowing a victim of domestic violence to withdraw a statement once it has been made and, thus, advocate that reluctant witnesses should be compelled to testify (Edwards 1989). The Victim Support Inter-Agency Working Party on Domestic Violence (1992) similarly argued that the decision to proceed with a prosecution should not be the responsibility of women who report the crime as they may sometimes be pressurized by violence to withdraw. If necessary, the report recommended, victims should be compelled to give evidence, provided that protection and support can be offered.

Arguments in favour of arrest, prosecution, and compelling witnesses have surfaced within a social and political climate which has rarely questioned the appropriateness of the criminal justice system as a way of dealing with domestic violence. Indeed, in describing and criticizing the response of the police and the wider criminal justice system, writers have tended to assume that to take punitive legal action against perpetrators is both an effective and desirable way of dealing with domestic violence (see, for example, Horley 1988). This chapter will question such preconceptions from the viewpoint of the victim. It will draw on interviews conducted with a sample of women who had recently had a visit from the police in response to an incident of domestic violence;[1] on interviews with women in the Women's Aid refuges; as well as data gathered from patrol officers and prosecutors.

[1] As detailed in chap. 2, the sample of 'victims' was chosen from the sample of incidents about which officers were interviewed. There were forty-nine such incidents and the researcher gained access to thirty-nine victims. Interviews were also conducted with the perpetrators in five cases.

As discussed in Chapter 6, over a third of the victims in the Thames Valley study chose, at some stage, not to co-operate with the criminal justice process (almost half of the victims in incidents which resulted in an arrest withdrew support for prosecution after the arrest).[2] These victims were referred to as 'unreliable', 'non-co-operative' or 'hostile'. These labels not only indicate police and prosecutors' perceptions of the victims but, more interestingly, what they consider to be the purpose of the police response. Women who do not give, or who withdraw, their support are considered ultimately to be acting against their best interests. This chapter will look critically at this assumption. It will examine the perspectives of women who have been victims of domestic violence: asking why they often do not support prosecution; what they expect of the police and the criminal justice system in general; and the extent to which they have been satisfied with the police response. It will be shown that many interventions between the police and the disputants were, in the victims' opinions, successful, rather than failures, despite the fact that the majority did not result in a prosecution.

Victims' reasons for not seeking prosecution

The literature on non-reporting suggests that some of the reasons why women will not testify are the same as their reasons for not reporting in the first place (see Dutton 1988; Morley and Mullender 1994). Some feminist writers have attributed women's reluctance to request assistance or support to the statutory agencies' ineffective response or refusal to deal with domestic violence (Dobash and Dobash 1992). They have argued that women's perceptions of the inappropriate response of the police discourage them from reporting, except in cases where the violence continues for a long time and becomes intolerable (Carlson 1977; Pahl 1985; Flynn 1977; Stanko 1995).

Two recent studies found that between a half and two-thirds of victims told no-one about the first time they experienced violence, the average time before telling anyone being one to two years (NCH Action for Children 1995; Mooney 1994). Many of the respondents

---

[2] In Cretney and Davis's (1995) study 81 per cent of assaults were reported to the police but in only 63 per cent of these did the victim make a formal statement (although all had needed hospital treatment).

explained that they felt embarrassed or thought it was too private a matter to discuss, whilst some thought that to inform anyone would lead to further, retaliatory, violence. Some were unaware that help was available, others were worried about not being treated seriously or, conversely, about being compelled to take legal action against their wishes, and a few of the women were worried about their children being taken into care. Others expressed feelings of worthlessness, and lacked the self-confidence to believe they were deserving of assistance. The responses for the Thames Valley study were broadly consistent with these findings.

Just under a half of the sample of 387 Thames Valley incidents were not reported by the women (in one-fifth of the incidents a neighbour called the police, and in 13 per cent a relative, or the male disputant himself, alerted the police). In twelve of the thirty-nine incident about which I interviewed the victim, someone other than the victim had alerted the police (in seven incidents a neighbour had called, in four a member of the victim's family, and one call was anonymous). Hence, it was possible to discuss reasons for non-reporting with some of the victims in the sample.

Some women had not reported because they did not think that the police had a role to play in their dispute. As one explained: 'If I thought I needed the police I'd call them. They've been okay in the past when I've called them for other things. They do a good job generally, but this was a domestic—nothing to do with them.' Other women were embarrassed or agitated by police interference, insisting that they could look after themselves—that: '. . . this is private—it's nothing to do with [the police]'. Whilst it might be argued that they demonstrated pride and independence, it is also clear that they felt that the police could not provide effective support.

Conversations with women, and observations of women interacting with police officers, suggested that victims made rational choices, within the constraints as they perceived them, regarding the decisions to involve the police or support police action. Three main reasons for non co-operation emerged: first, some women did not want to break up the relationship or the family unit; secondly, some were afraid of further retaliatory violence; and, thirdly, some did not think that the likely sentence would be worth the 'costs' incurred by the process. All three reasons concern the high 'costs', of various sorts, that victims can incur by supporting a prosecution. These reasons are, of course, interrelated: one often impacts on another, but for ease of explanation they will be dealt with separately. No attempt has been made to assess in quantitative terms which reason most accounted for women's refusals to co-operate with the criminal justice system. This is because the sample of interviews with victims was too small (n = 39) to allow for any meaningful generalizations. Also it could not be so easily supplemented with officers' views because for many of the cases discussed with officers the reason was not apparent, or the officer's interpretation could not be relied upon. Also, many women cited more than one reason for their non co-operation and even after fairly in-depth interviews it was not always apparent which particular reason was most influential.

Women don't want to break up the relationship or the family

Chapters 5 and 6 showed that if a woman does not want to end her relationship with her violent partner, it is very difficult in practice for the criminal justice system to intervene effectively. There are, of course, various reasons why some women do not want to end their relationship with their violent partners. Mooney (1994) identified a number of factors which included economic dependency, lack of affordable accommodation, children (they did not want to break up the family), and hopes that their partners would change and stop being abusive. It was not part of the remit of this study to explore the reasons why some women chose to stay with violent men, but in discussing the police response to their victimization, women often referred to this reluctance to break away.

In one case the victim, an Asian woman, argued that her culture worked against her. She said that it was very hard for the police to know what to do when she could not contemplate leaving her husband: 'Even though my family and his know about the violence, I can't leave him. I'd be all alone—they'd reject me.' Although this woman felt particularly isolated and unable to consider seriously alternatives to further victimization, her experiences were not unique. Other women who did not have specific cultural barriers to making certain choices felt equally trapped in abusive relationships because of familial ties. One woman, indignant that the police officer had told her that she should divorce her husband, explained: 'Yes, I was scared of him and he is a bully, but how dare she tell me I should divorce him. He's my husband and the father of my kid—there's no way I'm leaving him.'

Of course, for some ethnic minority groups police intervention can have very serious repercussions. Men with insecure immigration status might find themselves deported as a consequence of an arrest (Southall Black Sisters 1989). One of the arrests in the Thames Valley study resulted in the deportation of the offender. In this case the victim considered this to be a satisfactory result as she had already ended the relationship. However, for women who want to remain in the relationship, and in particular for those who have children, deportation might be a tragic consequence of a request for help. In addition, it has been suggested that police sometimes investigate women's immigration status as a condition for receiving assistance, and may even arrest these women while their status is being checked (Mama 1989).[3]

Recent research suggests a high correlation between physical abuse of wives and physical abuse and neglect of children (NCH Action for Children 1995). There is also an emerging literature on the long-term effect on children of living with repeated episodes of domestic violence which, until recently, was given only scant attention (Carroll 1994; Hurley and Jaffe 1990; Jaffe, Wilson, and Wolfe 1990). However, many of the women I spoke to believed that even though their partners were aggressive to them, they were 'good fathers'. Just as non-violent families sometimes stay together for the sake of the children, so do violent and dysfunctional families. One woman explained, 'He's assaulted me before but I wouldn't press charges because of my twelve-year-old son.' Another woman changed her mind about supporting police action because her husband had booked a holiday for the following week and she did not want to break up the family 'for the sake of the kids'.

Many of the women spoken to in the refuges stated that the worst thing about leaving their partners was being uprooted from their local support networks. A few women encountered practical difficulties regarding rehousing. However, for many the pain and inconvenience of moving away from their home, taking their children

---

[3] No attempt was made in this study to try to examine the extent to which different ethnic groups or different socio-economic groups varied in their experiences of domestic violence and the response of the statutory agencies. This was because the sample of women interviewed was not considered large enough to make any comparisons and the information on these variables provided by the police interview data was not considered to be sufficiently reliable. For an interesting look at the experiences of abused Pakistani women in Great Britain see Choudry (1996) and for black women see Mama (1989).

away from their fathers, and sometimes from schools, friends, and other relatives, and trying to establish a new life for themselves and their dependants, were the overwhelming factors. These had caused a number of them to return to violent partners, even if only temporarily. One woman who had suffered from a long history of domestic violence withdrew her statement after a particularly nasty attack 'because [she] couldn't stand being separated from [her] children'. This was despite the fact that she had received a lot of help and guidance from the Women's Aid refuge.

One woman, who had alerted the police when her husband, who has a history of violence, had set fire to their bed, said she did not want to take any criminal action against him but wanted him out of their home. He was removed and she was taken, upon request, to the refuge. I attempted to speak to her a few weeks later. Refusing to be interviewed, she explained that her husband had returned to their home and that he was in the house at that time. She explained that she did not want to risk aggravating him as she was 'trying to make it work'. As we were leaving she called after us: 'He's changed, honest he really has'. Another woman, who was frequently assaulted by her boyfriend, told the officers that, whilst he occasionally abused her, she had a good relationship with him most of the time. When the police advised her to make a statement she replied: 'I'd feel so guilty if he got in trouble. I still love him.'

Occasionally women's justifications for refusing to make statements suggested that they considered that a certain amount of violence by a partner was acceptable or that they blamed themselves. One woman, who claimed to have been assaulted by her partner (although she had no visible injuries), informed the police that there were committal warrants out on him. Pleased to have the opportunity to arrest him, the police kept him in a cell overnight and had decided that a short spell in prison would give her time and space to terminate the relationship. However, in the morning she arrived at the station and paid off his warrants, which obliged the police to release him. She told the custody officer: 'I thought about it and I think I caused the row—I wind him up'. In another case, a woman called the police to complain that her daughter had been hit by her boyfriend. However, the daughter, a teenager with a three-week-old baby, did not want to make a complaint. The officer explained:

She did not welcome our interfering and resented her mother for sticking her nose into her business. She told me that she deserved to be slapped by him and did not blame him. She said she loved living with him and wouldn't go back to her mother's.

Bush and Hood-Williams (1995) found, from their study of relationships on a housing estate in London, that some women normalized the violence.[4] They did this largely because they thought that it was better to be in an abusive relationship than no relationship at all. None of the women used the local self-referral counselling service for victims of domestic violence because they could not make the transition from seeing the violence as part of their everyday lives to identifying themselves as abused women. The authors argued that: 'This climate of acceptance ensures that few will seek the assistance of statutory agencies and that those who do will first have to overcome their conviction that they brought the violence on themselves' (Bush and Hood-Williams 1995: 17). Like some of the women in the Thames Valley study, they feared loneliness and not being able to cope on their own, and spoke of their partners in terms of love, regretting the changes in their relationships since they first met. Missing the companionship and respect they had received at the beginning of the relationship, they wanted the violence, but not the relationship, to end. Whatever the reason, for women who cannot envisage separation from their partner any call for police assistance is likely to be a call for immediate emergency help to halt a particular incident, rather than an attempt to get the man prosecuted.

All the evidence suggests that men who are violent to their partners do not stop being violent, but, rather, increase the frequency and severity of the attacks.[5] This suggests that women who stay in the hope of a future free from violence are likely to be disappointed. However, and this is where their decisions might be considered rational, if they do leave the probability of further abuse does not necessarily diminish.[6] Indeed, some studies have found that men

[4] This was an in-depth study of thirteen women in relationships with abusive men and four men who were committing this abuse.
[5] There is an emerging literature on repeat victimization in this field (see, for example, Hanmer and Stanko 1985; Lloyd, Farrell, and Pease 1994).
[6] Just under 40 per cent of the women in the Thames Valley study were involved in incidents of domestic violence with ex-partners with whom they had not been living at the time of the dispute. Clearly, they had not been protected from further violence by leaving their partners.

escalate their violence during and after separation (Morley and Mullender 1994).

Fear of retaliation

Research suggests that many women rationally choose to stay with their partners because they hope that by doing so they will avoid the retaliatory violence which frequently results from attempts to leave (Mooney 1994; Bowker 1983). Men who are emotionally dependent on their partners are often violent when they feel insecure about the continuance of the relationship, whether real or perceived (Bush and Hood-Williams 1995). The majority of women in the Thames Valley study had stayed because their partners had threatened them with violence, and sometimes death, if they left.

Some women will not even call the police for fear of retaliation. One refuge resident explained: 'If I'd called the police I'd have ended up in a worse place than this. He would have murdered me.' Others make choices concerning arrest or prosecution according to their experience of how their partner responds to intervention. One woman who did make a statement and whose partner was arrested explained that 'getting nicked made him more pissed off'. When asked whether, under similar circumstances, she would call the police again, she replied: 'I'm not sure. Before this incident I wouldn't have hesitated, but now I'm not sure it's worth it.'

Another case involved a particularly nasty assault and threats to kill. The suspect was known to the police for serious offences of violence on intimates (including the victim) as well as strangers, and for firearms offences. He had spent many years in prison. The officer explained that this man had not been charged, having been arrested for violence, because the victim withdrew her statement as soon as she had made it. This woman insisted that the police should not have arrested her partner without her agreeing to it as this put her even more at risk (when the police had arrived he was dangling her over the balcony of the house threatening to drop her on to the pavement). She explained to me:

They told me to make a statement and get him prosecuted. I wish it was that easy. I hate the bastard but he'd kill me if I got him in trouble with the police. If he went down for hitting me he'd finish me off. I dream of leaving him. I'm going to learn to drive and get a car and take off in the middle of the night sometime with my kids. I'll go where he can't find me and start again . . . but I think he'd find me wherever I went and just drag me back or kill me. I hadn't wanted him arrested as I thought it would provoke him, cause more trouble. I'm always scared he'll retaliate, and that time he did. He knocked me around again when I got back to the house. He said he was teaching me a lesson.

I had already spoken to the aggressor before interviewing his wife in private and found him to be very angry with the police:

It was a private row between me and my wife and they had no business interfering. They burst in and just arrested me straight away and took me to the nick. They're bastards—they arrest anyone given half the chance. She shouldn't have let them arrest me . . . now the silly cow deserves whatever she gets.

Knowing her husband as she did, this woman's reluctance to prosecute could be considered to be rational (although not necessarily in her best interests). Other women had made similar rational choices. As one explained: 'If I'd pressed charges he'd have been more violent in future.' A woman whose boyfriend had hit her and pushed her out of their car would not make a statement because she was afraid of her boyfriend retaliating. The officer involved in the case, like others, acknowledged that it was difficult to protect women from retaliation from intimates:

Her boyfriend is a 'toe-rag'. I told her about the available agencies who could help her going through the court case but she was adamant she would not go to court and she didn't want any further contact with us. She thought that no amount of agency intervention could protect her. In many ways she's right.

Even when women flee violent partners and seek refuge in 'safe houses' they often remain in fear of further abuse. One woman had moved into a refuge in the Thames Valley from the refuge in her home town where her ex-partner had found her and threatened to kill her and kidnap their son. She was now living in fear of him tracing her. She had initially made a statement regarding numerous violent assaults but after threats from his brother had withdrawn her support. Like many women living in refuge accommodation, she was nervous every time she heard a knock at the door. When asked if she had told the police about her fears she said:

What's the point. Him and his crowd are the law. They make the rules and they decide who'll get punished. The police can't protect me from them all. Even if they locked him away the rest of his brood would come looking for me.

As Cretney and Davis found:

> Whenever victim and assailant have an on-going relationship, whether as partners, family members, or habitués of a common social environment, it may be felt that neither the police nor the courts will be able to prevent further attacks or other threatening behaviour. (1995: 15.)[7]

How the police respond to women's reluctance to proceed with a prosecution through fear of retaliation is an important question. Examination of the cases where the police chose not to arrest revealed that the police did not seem to distinguish those cases where the victims would not co-operate because of genuine fear of retaliation, from those cases where non co-operation was due to the victim not feeling that she was ready to end the relationship, or another more 'rational' reason. In one case, for example, a woman had been 'terrorized' by her estranged husband who had kept her hostage in her home for many hours and made threats against her life. The officers recognized that she had believed the threats to be genuine and was 'very upset and shocked', and yet they accepted her refusal to make a statement, based on her fear of retaliatory violence, and did not arrest the suspect.

The sentence is not worth the process

Some women's choice about whether or not to make a statement, depended not only on fear of reprisals but also on their knowledge and understanding of sentencing. As one woman said:

> He was furious that I'd called the police in the first place. He'd have really taught me a lesson if I'd had him arrested. Besides I asked the police what he'd get for bashing me and they said probably just a fine. You weigh it all up don't you—it just wouldn't be worth the hassle.

Women who want their partners to be treated harshly are likely to be disappointed. As Edwards has argued, sentences in the domestic context, compared with the non-domestic context, have tended to be derisory. Buchan and Edwards' study of sentencing in London in 1990 found that in cases of assault the more typical sentence of the court was a fine, and even in the case of assault occasioning grievous

---

[7] Recent research has found that on high-crime housing estates, 13 per cent of crimes reported by victims and 9 per cent reported by witnesses lead to subsequent intimidation. And 6 per cent of crimes not reported by victims and 22 per cent not reported by witnesses go unreported due to fear of intimidation. It also found that in many cases, before a suspect is apprehended, intimidation of the victim is difficult to prevent where the offender knows the identity of the victim (Maynard 1994).

TABLE 7.1.　Sentences for domestic violence offenders

	Conditional discharge	Fine	Probation order	Community service order	Prison
Assault (ABH)	6	4	3	4	4
Criminal damage	6	3	2		
Assault on police	1				
Murder					2
Threats to kill					1
Rape					1
Assault (GBH)					1
Breach of injunction					1

bodily harm, very few offenders were committed to prison (1996: 207). Only 3 per cent of the Thames Valley incidents originally attended by officers resulted in a suspect being convicted of a criminal offence. And conditional discharges, community service orders, and fines were the usual sentences imposed by the courts, as table 7.1 shows.

Not surprisingly, knowledge, or previous experience, of lenient sentences leave some women with little faith in the system:

I had a previous domestic with my ex-husband [not the present disputant] who broke my arm and got off with a conditional discharge. I'm disillusioned with the criminal justice system, especially tired out magistrates who haven't got a clue.

An offender who breaches a conditional discharge by committing another offence within the specified period can be imprisoned. However, this is rarely done and many members of the public tend to regard a conditional discharge as 'getting off' as they can see no immediate penalty.

It is not only victims of domestic violence who think that most defendants are treated too leniently in court. Studies have shown that the general population underestimates, sometimes greatly, the typical sanctions imposed by the courts (see, for example, Hough, Lewis, and Walker 1988; Doob and Roberts 1988). However, in domestic violence cases it is not only that women regard the court sentences as too lenient but, more importantly, they often consider them to be at best unhelpful and, at worst, totally inappropriate. Most of the women spoken to wanted help and support for the perpetrators, as well as for themselves, and they recognized that most of the penalties available to the courts cannot address these needs. As one woman said: 'It's not worth making a statement—I've done it all before. I'm disillusioned with the whole system. He needs help rather than punishment.' This woman's partner had previously been prosecuted for assaulting her. She had supported this action and he had served a short prison sentence. However, rather than being encouraged to address his offending behaviour and his negative attitudes towards women he had become more aggressive and embittered by this experience. Hence, she no longer considered such punishment to be beneficial to her or her partner.

Other women had similarly learnt from past experiences that court sentences are often not worth the costs of proceeding. Two of the victims could not be persuaded to make statements against their partners because in both cases their partners had previously been successfully prosecuted for assaulting them and had been fined £200 and £100 respectively. As both men were unemployed and the women were in work they had to pay off the fines. These women had no intention of ending the relationship and so decided that they could not afford to risk their partners being fined again.

There are clearly many rational reasons why women do not seek prosecution. But if women do not want their partners or ex-partners to be prosecuted why do they call the police? The following section will show that women have good reasons for requesting police assistance irrespective of their desires regarding prosecution and punishment.

The expectations of victims and the police response

The majority of officers who were interviewed stressed the importance of asking victims what action they wanted them to take. According to these officers, over a third of the victims wanted the suspect to be removed from the scene, with a third wanting him to be arrested, and a third wanting simply to be advised or for the officers to restore the peace (see Chapter 5). Interviews with women explored these expectations and the extent to which the police provided these services.

Immediate protection

In the majority of cases the women wanted their partners or ex-partners to be arrested or removed from the scene for immediate protection.[8] They wanted the police to solve the immediate problem, to 'stop what was happening', 'to take the situation in hand', 'to take control'. A few women thought that the police could 'control the situation . . . calm him down without him going to the station'. But their need for immediate protection was usually met by the police removing the suspect and taking him either to the police station for a short period of time or to another location (see Chapter 5).

Many women did not mind whether the man was arrested or taken to another location as long as he was removed from the home. One woman who requested an arrest did so purely for some breathing space: 'I wanted a few days' rest from him'. When asked if she wanted him prosecuted she looked shocked and said: 'No, of course not'. Another woman explained: 'I wanted him out of the way, for the police to take him away until he'd cooled down'. In those cases where the immediate problem had been solved, by the man complying with the victim's wishes and leaving before the police arrived, usually the women wanted no further assistance from the police. In one case, for example, the woman told the police to leave as soon as they arrived, she explained: 'He's leaving so I don't need you any more. You can go.' When the officers asked her to explain what had happened she said 'It's none of your business'. Of course, for a few women the need for protection did not go away once the aggressor had left the scene of the incident. Some feared further problems and wanted the police to protect them against that possibility by ensuring that the man was not waiting around the corner until the police left: 'I wanted them to do a search of the area to make sure he wasn't hanging around still.'

There were a few disputes which had been resolved prior to the arrival of the police. Some were only mild altercations which had been resolved through effective communication between disputants. On other occasions the suspect had left after the police were telephoned. Indeed some women called the police with the sole intention of scaring the man into leaving. All of this ensured that officers sometimes had to do very little to stop a dispute. The knowledge that they had been called was enough to persuade some of the men to leave the scene or calm down.

---

[8] During interviews the women used the word 'protection' more than any other word in discussing both what they wanted and what they got from the police.

Some disputants were subdued into deferential compliance by the arrival of the police. This facilitated a reasonable discussion of the issues, as the following incident shows:

...When we arrived they stopped rowing. She had phoned because she wanted someone to speak to and to stop the row. It was late at night and she didn't know who else to phone. She was upset. I asked her what she wanted us to do. She said she just wanted us to calm the situation down. We managed to talk to them both and left them calm.

In this, as in other incidents where there had not been physical violence, the police negotiation process typically involved mediating between the disputants in a 'social service' type role rather than a law enforcement role.

The majority of those who wanted immediate protection felt that they had got this from the police and were consequently satisfied with the police response. Two of the five men interviewed who were arrested had later recognized that the women needed protecting from them. Asked if he considered that the situation could have been resolved without him being arrested, one replied: 'No—I was out of control. They had to get me out—I was very drunk and smashing the place up. She needed to be protected from me and that's what they did.'

Occasionally the police were considered to be too keen on protecting the victim. One couple regretted the officers' insistence that the woman should leave the family home to stay in a refuge overnight. Although the victim did not want to leave her home, concern for her and her child made the officers insist that they should not be left with her husband for the night. Although the man admitted to me, when pushed on the point, that he would have continued to argue with his wife after the officers had left, both he and his wife were adamant that the police had overreacted in this situation.

Suspect warning

A few of the women wanted simply for the police to tell the man off. They argued that a warning from a police officer might deter aggressors from further violence, 'to give him a serious warning...to stop him doing it again'. In some cases, where the victim agreed that the man could stay in the home, or where the police could not reasonably justify removing him, the officers gave the suspect a warning. They warned him that he would be arrested if he did not calm down and behave himself. Of the male suspects who were not arrested, one in five were warned that they risked being arrested if the police were called back to another domestic dispute.[9] This was sometimes the very response that victims had hoped for when calling the police: the majority of the victims who did not want the police to remove or arrest the suspect wanted the situation defused and the aggressor calmed down, without recourse to the criminal law. As one woman I interviewed explained, when asked what she expected from the police: 'I was looking for someone to control the situation. I hoped they'd calm him down without him going to the station. I've got a lot of faith in the police.'

According to a police officer, one woman wanted her aggressive partner warned about his behaviour because 'he was not normally violent and she thought that a visit from us would frighten him and stop him doing it again'. Other victims wanted only a confirmation that their partners' actions were unacceptable, 'I mainly wanted him to be told that his behaviour was wrong', or 'I wanted them to tell him that he couldn't get away with this'. One woman who had wanted her husband to be arrested was asked if she would have been prepared to testify against him in court. She seemed surprised by the question and replied in the negative insisting that she wanted him to be arrested only 'to scare him off—to show him that I mean business'. 'Business', it seemed, was not putting up with his violence, rather than seeing him punished for it.

Although the police said that the victims wanted the perpetrators to be warned in only twenty-nine of the 387 cases, data gathered from interviews with victims and from patrol observation suggests that this is a conservative figure. It is likely that victims requested this in more cases than officers recalled, and that they wanted this to happen in more cases than they actually requested. The disparity between what the police thought victims wanted and what victims actually wanted could be due to problems of communication between distressed women and police officers, or because officers do not like to warn perpetrators of violence if they had no intention of arresting them. They did sometimes warn men that if they did not leave the scene of the incident they would be arrested. But they did not feel that it was part of their 'job' to chastise people about

---

[9] In addition to such warnings, a few suspects were told to contemplate their unacceptable behaviour and to improve their treatment of their partners.

previous behaviour and warn them not to repeat such behaviour in the future (see Chapter 5). During the periods of patrol observation, police officers were observed warning and 'telling off' children or youths but they were reluctant to do this with adults, especially if the man was not present when the police initially attended the dispute.[10]

Police officers tended to evaluate situations in terms of dichotomies. One dichotomy was offence or no offence. If there had been no criminal offence committed, officers explained that they did not believe that they should be judgemental and tell people how to behave, and if there had been an offence they thought in terms of another dichotomy; to arrest or not. If the victim did not want her partner or ex-partner to be arrested they tended to shy away from in-depth discussions with the suspect about his alleged behaviour, even though they often spent a great deal of time listening to both sides of the story.

Information and advice

Despite the undisputed low reporting rate, many abused women do come into contact with the police at least once, and often several times. Even if the suspect is prosecuted, the police often remain the agency closest to the victim. The police should, therefore, be aware of the specific needs of each victim, as they are best placed to guide those victims towards the appropriate sources of help. Women need moral and practical support in order to make informed decisions about what type of criminal justice intervention is appropriate to their situation and needs (Brownlee 1990). Over three-quarters of the women interviewed in the Thames Valley study, regardless of any other desires, stated that they wanted advice and/or information about their short-term and long-term options. They wanted someone to talk to about their problems, someone with whom they could share their experiences who would be non-judgemental and who would not insist on taking any action for which the woman was not ready. In some cases the officer explained that the woman had called the police because 'she wanted someone to talk to, someone to act as a mediator'. On other occasions they found that they were expected to advise couples about their relationships, and even, on a few

---

[10] If the perpetrator had left the incident before the police arrived they would rarely locate him in order to 'tell him off' even if this was precisely what the woman wanted.

occasions, to try to persuade partners *not* to leave, as was the case in the following example, described by the attending police officer:

Neither would make an allegation against the other. He just wanted to leave when we arrived, and she wanted me to make him stay with her. I explained that it wasn't my job to persuade people to stay with partners against their wishes and that I had no powers to force him to stay.

The Thames Valley Police policy in place during 1993 recommended that victims be kept informed of their options, their legal rights, and the availability of practical and emotional support. However, whilst a few women were happy with the advice and information provided, most did not feel that the police provided adequate information for them to make crucial decisions regarding prosecution. They felt that the officers did not spend enough time with them, listening and discussing their problems: 'They didn't have the time to talk—they weren't here for long'; 'The officer didn't have time or the patience to sit listening to me'. They also complained about not being kept informed during the later stages of the prosecution process. As one woman explained: 'I get no information on how the case is progressing. He [her ex-partner] is still in touch—he lets me know what's happening in court.' Similarly, one woman complained: 'I don't understand the system. They [the police] didn't explain it all to me. I don't know what is meant to happen at each stage.'[11]

Victim evaluation of the police response

Whether a victim regards the police response as appropriate or not may depend on how she conceptualizes domestic violence and how she perceives her ability to take effective action to deal with it. Also what she knows about the available support and how she thinks that the criminal justice system functions, and will respond to her complaint, will impact on satisfaction levels. Unfortunately, it was not possible in all cases, given the limitations on time, to ascertain the victims' knowledge about available support, and the criminal justice options.[12] However, it was possible to gather views on their expectations about the police response.

[11] A study of burglary victims found a similar problem with communication during the investigation and prosecution process (Maguire and Bennet 1982).
[12] It was not my time which was limited, but the interviewees. I did not consider it acceptable to take up more time than was absolutely necessary and whilst some women were eager to talk for a long time others had practical constraints on their time.

The women were, of course, generally satisfied if their expectations were met. In other words, dissatisfaction generally resulted from a discrepancy between what victims wanted and what they got. Most women had fixed expectations of the police. They knew what they wanted the police to do (as discussed above, this was usually to provide immediate protection, to warn the perpetrator and/or give information and advice), and over half of the thirty-nine women were satisfied with the police response. ('The police were wonderful', 'I couldn't fault them at all', 'No complaints, they were really good and helpful', 'The police handled it very well. I was very satisfied.') When asked if there was anything that they had hoped for that the police had not done, 40 per cent of victims said no. However, whilst some women with low expectations were pleasantly surprised at the police response, (one woman, for example, who declared herself to be very pleased with the police response, explained: 'I thought that they wouldn't take him away. I guess I had low expectations'), half of them felt that there had been a discrepancy between what they wanted and what they got. A woman, who had previously 'had a lot of faith in the police', had been disappointed when her expectations were not met and her ex-partner was not arrested.

Whether an arrest occurred or not was in itself unrelated to level of satisfaction. It was not the case that more punitive responses resulted in more satisfied victims. Women who wanted their partners to be arrested were satisfied if this was done but those who were looking for some other type of assistance were left feeling very disappointed when the police arrested the suspect without providing information or advice. The majority of those who said that there had been a discrepancy between what they wanted and what they got felt that the police had failed to provide adequate advice and information. As one woman said: 'The police should reassure a person before they leave because I was left feeling very vulnerable. There was no support for me after he was arrested. I would have liked more support and more information about what I could do. I felt guilty for calling them.'

Women were satisfied when the police provided what they wanted or needed, rather than proceeding with their own agenda. Thus, writers who assume that victims of domestic violence will only be satisfied if their assailant is arrested and charged (Pahl 1982, 1985; Binney, Harkell, and Nixon 1981) overlook the range of complex dilemmas facing women who are subjected to either psychological or physical violence by their partners or ex-partners. One woman, whose partner had been arrested and kept in a cell overnight, expressed disillusionment with the criminal justice system. She wanted advice and information about sources of help, not a punitive response:

> I've done it all before, the punishment isn't worth the effort...we need help and the system doesn't help people it only punishes them.... They told me about the refuge, but that's not worth it either. I tried to get in touch with Relate before but they had a two-month waiting list. The WPC was sympathetic but too busy. I wanted someone to talk to.

This woman's partner was also interviewed. He was not angry that the police had arrested him: 'I knew they'd nick me—it's the usual thing they do. I was too drunk. I think I might have given her a smack [he had broken her nose]. I needed to cool off in a cell.' However, he was surprised that no-one had spoken to him about the violence, offered any advice or told him to seek help. His wife had refused to make a statement and so he had been released with no warning, official or otherwise. Twenty-four hours after the incident neither the victim nor the aggressor felt that they had gained any long-term benefits from the police intervention.

Two-thirds of the women felt that the officers had been sympathetic, and just over half thought that the police had understood how they felt. Sometimes what might seem to be a relatively insignificant act of kindness was sufficient to please the complainant. One woman, for example, who had wanted the police to arrest her husband, was satisfied even though he had not been arrested because 'they were sympathetic—they held my daughter's hand'. Another woman was happy because the officer had arranged for a locksmith to mend her door. Another factor which impressed women was the speed of the response. Immediate protection typically requires a quick response to a call for help, and those officers who arrived at the scene in what the victim considered to be a short period of time were appreciated for taking the request for help seriously. As one woman put it: 'The police were fantastic—they came in minutes'.

Women were most likely to declare themselves satisfied when the police had given them sufficient information both at the scene and, where necessary, as the case progressed. As one woman said: 'The police did not "rubbish" the incident. They said they'd keep calling round, keeping me informed. I worried that I was wasting their time. The refuge had told me the police had improved and it's true.' Another woman who had wanted the police 'to control the situation . . . to calm [her husband] down' was satisfied even though they had arrested her husband and she had initially hoped that they could 'restore the peace without him having to go to the station'. The officers had listened to her; discussed the problems which had led to the incident; explained their course of action; offered her advice and information about other agencies who might be able to help them; and contacted her about releasing him from custody. Not only had they fully communicated their intentions with the woman but they had also explained their response to the man once he had sobered up.

It has been argued that the manner in which the 'options' are put to the complainant is likely to determine the choices made (Faragher 1985). Whilst observing officers on patrol I saw many exceptions to this: examples of good practice. One man who had physically assaulted his wife was immediately arrested. Two constables spent over two hours with the victim taking extensive statements and offering advice and sympathy. They gave the victim the name and telephone number of the co-ordinator of the local Victim Support scheme and told her the address of the local refuge. Their response was impeccable. However, when we left the woman's home both admitted that they 'knew' that she would withdraw. Believing this to be unjustified police cynicism, I was surprised the following day when she did. The constable who visited her and took a withdrawal statement tried to persuade her to support police action, but she would not. The charges against her husband were subsequently dropped.

Another woman, interviewed about the police response to a physical assault against her, reflected back on an incident which had occurred a year earlier. She had been raped and assaulted by the same man who had attacked her on this occasion, but had decided to withdraw her statement after her partner was arrested. She explained that she had been very surprised that the police had responded so positively to her complaint that her husband had both raped and physically assaulted her:

The officers in uniform were very sensitive—they took the rape allegation very seriously. I was stunned by that. But I only wanted to complain about him hitting me, not about the rape. He'd broken my nose and I wanted him done for that, not for the rape. So I dropped the charges—it was all too much.

This woman had received assistance and support from the Family Protection Unit[13] as well as the patrol officer in charge of her case. They had all made an effort to persuade her not to withdraw her statement and yet she withdrew—for her own reasons.

The police response may, in some cases, determine the likelihood of the woman calling the police, should she be involved in a similar dispute in the future. However, only three of the thirty-nine women I interviewed said that they would not call the police again (the rest said that they would call the police again even though some of them had been dissatisfied with the police response to that particular incident). These three were dissatisfied because of the discrepancy between what they expected and what the police delivered. One explained that the ineffectual response had left her vulnerable: 'I've not got much faith in the police now. I don't think they can do much.' She said she would not bother to call them again in the future.

A few of the victims might have been dissuaded from pursuing criminal action by officers' behaviour. For example, victims were sometimes warned that they would probably have to go to court and face aggressive cross-examination. Officers justified this by explaining that if the women could not stand up to the process their cases would collapse, because the prosecution would rely on their testimony. As one officer explained:

This girl was assaulted by her boyfriend.... I discussed the options with her and told her that he could be arrested for ABH. At first she said she would support police action and then we told her that she would need to be present in court if the CPS took the case on. She then declined to give a statement.

Whilst such officers were 'preparing' the victims for what *could* happen, they were giving them the worst possible case scenario. Most defendants plead guilty, especially in the magistrates' court, and therefore most cases are dealt with quickly involving only the crown prosecutor and the defence counsel, without the victim

---

[13] The police department which handles all allegations of rape, sexual assault, and child abuse.

having to attend court.[14] Moreover, women can receive support from Women's Aid or Victim Support. Officers rarely told victims about these services.

Examples of good practice are necessary for the police to break down negative preconceptions. One woman, who had always thought that the police did not treat domestic violence seriously, deliberated over contacting them when her ex-husband was trying to break into her new home. Eventually she telephoned the police but told them that she was being harassed by a stranger: 'I didn't tell them that it was my "ex" at the door. I didn't think they'd come if it was a domestic.' The police did come and arrested the perpetrator, leaving the woman surprised, but 'very satisfied'. She told me of previous episodes of physical and sexual abuse which she had not reported, believing that the police would not respond. This incident had increased her confidence in the police to the extent that she declared: 'In future when he bashes me about or threatens to kill me, I'll call the police and get him done.' Although she added: 'I don't know about the sex though [there had been four acts of rape and numerous other serious sexual offences], I don't see that they could do him for that. We were married for years you know.'

Satisfaction with the police was, in part, related to the aggressor's response to the police intervention. The few women who had experienced retaliatory violence were, not surprisingly, less satisfied than those whose partners had ceased being disruptive or violent as a result of the police visit. One woman wished that she had not called the police because: 'After [the police] left I barricaded myself in the bedroom but he pushed his way in and carried on humiliating me. It was like he now felt he had the police's permission to harass me further.' She was the most dissatisfied of all of the victims.[15] A handful of women who felt that the police attendance had had a positive impact on the relationship were, not surprisingly, very

---

[14] Precise statistics on guilty pleas are difficult to obtain (see Baldwin and McConville 1978), but from April 1992 to March 1993, 97.6 per cent of cases proceeding to a hearing resulted in conviction and 83.6 per cent of the convicted defendants had pleaded guilty (Crown Prosecution Service, Annual Report, 1993b). Of course these figures may be higher than those for domestic violence cases. Men who have assaulted their partners are probably more likely to plead not guilty in the first instance as they believe that the victim will withdraw. But they are likely to change their plea at a later stage if they realise that the victim is likely to testify against them.

[15] In half of those incidents where the police presence had aggravated the situation the suspect had been arrested and in half he had not.

satisfied: 'He's improved since that day'; 'Everything was fine after they left'; 'It made him calm down—he was shocked'; 'It taught him a lesson. I've not had any problems since. It worked—the arrest did the trick.'

The different goals of different actors

As the above section has shown, victims' dissatisfaction arose out of a discrepancy between what they wanted and what they got. This disjunction between desires and outcome can be explained in part by the very clumsiness of the criminal justice system as a tool for solving domestic disputes, and in part by the disparity between the goals of the officers and those of the victims.

The disparity between the officers' and the victims' perceptions regarding prosecution is not a product of confusion on either side. Rather, it is a product of two groups of people coming together to find a solution but with different goals in mind. When victims choose to withdraw their support for prosecution it is not that they are being unco-operative per se, it is simply that they are not motivated by the same organizational goals as police and prosecutors.[16] As was discussed in Chapters 5 and 6, in cases of domestic violence the police often arrest and detain for 'social service' rather than prosecution purposes. But, in cases where there is clear evidence of an offence they usually believe prosecution to be the appropriate goal. Victims who do not co-operate with this aim are necessarily deemed to be 'hostile'. However, the desires of these victims often relate to social and domestic needs and desires. Hence, in practice, the police have to respond to two different sets of needs and criteria (their own, and the victims') and this can cause tension and sometimes inconsistency.

Further tensions are created by the fairly recent recognition of victims' needs and rights. The idea that services should respond to victims' needs has been established over the last decade (Shapland, Willmore, and Duff 1985; Maguire and Pointing 1988; Miers 1992) and formally recognized in the Home Office Circular 1988/20 on *Victims of Crime* and the Victims' Charter (revised in 1996) (Home Office 1990b, 1996), and government policy in general. These

---

[16] See chap. 4 for a discussion of these organizational goals which both push and pull officers in certain directions.

changes require the police to respond to the needs of victims whenever possible, rather than to pursue their own agenda or that of the feminist or political advocates of criminalization.

Some advocates have assumed that criminalization and a punitive response will meet the needs of victims of domestic violence. Thus, Edwards, writing about the prosecution of domestic violence, takes a normative stance which assumes that it is still the case that *too few* cases proceed to a prosecution (1996). She and other feminists have assumed that victims are dissatisfied because they want their aggressors to be arrested and prosecuted and the police do not do this enough. Consequently these writers have demanded tougher and more punitive measures from the police and criminal justice system. However, it has been shown that this was not what many victims wanted because the burden was so onerous and the outcome often perceived as unhelpful.

The police are generally the first, and often the only, agency to intervene in incidents of domestic violence. But when the police intervene there is considerable evidence that their intervention is not always framed by the interests of the victim (Mawby and Walklate 1994). They are highly dependent on victims to provide evidence in order that they can pursue their goal of prosecution. However, focusing on issues of criminality can mean that their style of intervention is inappropriate. Sometimes they do not provide the services which the victims expect, for example, feedback on the progress, of their case or information on other service providers (Newburn 1989; Shapland and Cohen 1987).[17] This can hinder their progress, as there is evidence that where victims perceive the criminal justice system to be insensitive or inimical to their interests, they are less likely to participate in the system (Joutsen 1987).

As with any other dispute, the police when responding to domestic disputes either maintain order or enforce the law, or both. It has been shown that these can both be effective short-term management resolutions. However, neither is seen, by victims, as doing much for the long-term problem. The police response is rarely thought to address the future stability of the relationship. At the end of the day, the criminal justice system, as it stands, is regarded by victims of domestic violence as an exceptionally clumsy and ineffective tool.

---

[17] A variety of studies have found that victims are not kept up to date on developments in their case, and that this is a major source of resentment (see Shapland, Willmore, and Duff 1985; Newburn and De Peyrecave 1988).

To return to the question raised in Chapter 1, what is the *extent* to which, and *under what circumstances*, did the Home Office Circular, and the police policies it informed, bring about change? Whilst officers did not adopt the pro-arrest position of the domestic violence policy, they did seem to be influenced by it. The policy was probably influential in alerting officers to the seriousness of domestic violence and encouraging them to be more sympathetic when dealing with victims. Hence, in the main, the women spoken to felt satisfied with the police response, even though the police had often failed to arrest suspects even when they had the legal powers to do so.

This finding on the significance of the policy contrasts with the work of the 'Warwick School' on the significance of the Police and Criminal Evidence Act 1984 (PACE) (see Chapter 1). For example, Sanders and Bridges (1990) and McConville, Sanders, and Leng (1991) have argued that the police comply with the *letter* of PACE but not the *spirit*. To return to one example provided in Chapter 1, they argued that the Code of Practice requirement for custody officers to give suspects written notice of their rights has been complied with in the main. However, their research showed that most suspects did not find written advice very useful, and would have benefited from oral advice. This the police rarely offered. They did not do the things that would have helped the suspects most, and those changes they made did not necessarily protect those more vulnerable suspects whom PACE was designed to protect. In other words, they argue that the changes have been largely presentational, and have affected little of substance in the experience of suspects (Reiner 1994b).[18] Whilst these findings suggest that rules can be ritualistically observed with little meaning, defeating their intended objectives, the Thames Valley study suggests that the intended objectives of a policy can be largely met even though the directive is not ritualistically applied. Police decisions not to arrest in the cases examined by this study were in line with the *spirit* of the domestic violence policy. They were in with the grain of the policy in that the officers were, in the main, doing what victims wanted. They were, it could be argued, applying the policies intelligently. The main conclusion of the work by the Warwick School—that rules do not necessarily translate into practice—was, however, supported by this study.

[18] See Smith and Gray (1983) and Sanders and Young (1994) for explanations of the distinction between 'working rules', 'inhibiting rules', and 'presentation rules'.

The message which emerged from this study is that it is not possible to read off police behaviour from knowing what the rules or the policies are. Soothill, Francis, and Sanderson (1997) came to a similar conclusion. They found, from examining the police response to cautioning guidelines for sexual offences, that guidelines are unlikely to make an impact when they are not clear enough or practices are too entrenched to shift by persuasion. The most interesting finding from this research was that police selectively applied parts of the Home Office guidance when it fitted with their current perspective. The guidance discouraged multiple cautions and the use of cautions for serious offences. However, the result has not been a decrease in the use of cautions across the board. The police have decreased cautioning for sex offenders, as one would expect from the guidelines, but the rate of cautions for offences of physical violence (Violence Against the Person offences) has continued to rise (as it had throughout the 1980s). This contradicted the guidance and the intentions of a hard-line Home Secretary. It is clear, as Soothhill, Francis, and Sanderson argue, that the police decided that sex offences are a special case. The guidelines were applied in the case of sex offences because they were in sympathy with the police cultural position on sex offenders at the time. This position reflected increasing public concern over sex offenders, in particular paedophiles, who were getting a lot of media coverage at the time.

The impact of the 1990/60 Circular

Gradually the police have introduced all of the recommendations of the 1990/60 Circular, except the pro-arrest position, because for most operational officers it did not seem sensible to arrest in all cases where there was evidence of an offence. These findings fit with the classic culturalist account of policing provided by Skolnick. He saw the police as skilled negotiators who do not crudely follow the rulebook. He referred to the policeman as 'a craftsman rather than as a legal actor, as a skilled worker rather than as a civil servant obliged to subscribe to the rule of law' (1975: 231). But, like most culturalists, he did not ignore the law. He looked at the extent to which officers obeyed or disregarded the law.

If law dominated policing we would expect policies to work as they are intended. But they do not. What this chapter has shown is that the partial implementation of the Home Office Circular by the police was largely a response to their perceptions of victims' needs and expectations. Not surprisingly, therefore, the police response in the 1990s, which emphasized a quick response, negotiation between all parties and, most pertinently, sympathy and compassion, but did not emphasize prosecution, was appreciated by the majority of the victims of domestic violence. It was a response to their wishes but, it might be argued, not in their interests. The following chapter reviews the empirical findings reported in this book and returns to this question of the difference between victims' wishes and victims' interests.

8

Interrogating the Role of the Victim

Feminists in the 1970s, on recognizing the enormity of the problem of domestic violence, were outraged at the state's apparent lack of interest. However they were concerned not only, or even primarily, with the inadequate response of the criminal justice system, but with the causes of domestic violence—the unequal power relations between men and women, and women's political and economic subordination. Their main goal was empowerment, encouraging women to work collectively to take control of their own lives and to avoid further victimization— hence the establishment of refuges run by women for women. Whilst some campaigns centred around legal reform, emphasizing, in particular, that domestic violence is a criminal rather than a private or a civil matter, the law was not the only institution which pressure groups attempted to reform.

Throughout the 1980s, however, the original aims of the women's movement receded. Although some 'grass-roots activists' continued to lobby for the broader agenda of women's rights, many critics focused on the criminal justice system. This shift in attention, from the wider issues to the rules and operation of the justice system, and in particular the police, is understandable. After all, it is easier to fight for specific law reforms than to tackle the fundamental basis of a patriarchal social order.

Campaigns were thus centred around 'improving' the police response, which soon came to mean more police powers, with the goal of higher arrest and prosecution rates. In the United States women's advocates used litigation, legislation, and research to press for the increased use of arrest. Approaches predicated on the assumption that crime could be reduced by arrest and sentencing policies aimed at deterring potential offenders began to be widely approved.

Many feminist writers and activists who had normally aligned themselves with progressive groups on the left, fighting for empowerment and assuagement, joined with the political right and embraced agendas of punishment at the expense of other alternatives. As Nelken recognized, it is paradoxical that feminists discussing violence against women should position themselves on the 'right side' of the law and order lobby, 'arguing for more rather than less use of the criminal law' (Nelken 1987: 108). Some feminists have also expressed concern with this developing hunger for law reform, arguing that social problems such as domestic violence can only be tackled effectively through ideological and structural change (see, for example, Stanko 1995). The formal law, they have argued, does not affect women's lives very much and, therefore, should not be thought of as a panacea (see Smart 1989, 1995; Mathiesen 1990; Stang Dahl 1986). Further, they have questioned whether or not reforms actually protect women or prevent men's violence in the first place; whether they empower women, regardless of race or class, or reinforce dependency and victimization; and whether they enhance or marginalize feminist understandings of the causes and solutions to men's violence. As Currie has argued: 'As a public discourse, wife battery has been transformed from a critique of patriarchal power, to demands for protection from male power. While the latter is a documented real need, the problem is that its satisfaction has been equated with justice for women' (1990: 88).[1]

The feminist campaigns which have embraced further criminalization have legitimized the growing emphasis on coercive control, incapacitation, and punishment at the expense of amelioration of the underlying problem.[2] In the main, their approach has been based on simplistic assumptions about the way that civil and criminal justice processes function and an inadequate evaluation of the effectiveness of the present criminal justice response. If the police attend a dispute and a woman has been assaulted, some feminist critics assume that the police have failed in their duty if they do not arrest the perpetrator. They adopt this normative stance because they believe this to be the proper police response to this crime (although this might not be their view of the proper response to crime in general). The findings

[1] On a more practical level, some have questioned the amount of public funds directed towards increased criminalization whilst refuges are battling to meet an ever-increasing demand for support.
[2] It is not, of course, necessarily a bad thing to have more criminal justice intervention. However, it would be better directed at non-punitive ends, for example at trying to rehabilitate offenders (see discussion of perpetrator programmes below).

of this study regarding the needs and expectations of domestic violence victims and the police response to them present a challenge to some feminist interpretations of non-arrest by police as a 'failure' to respond adequately to domestic violence.

This final chapter will argue that although areas of the police response need improvement, the police discretionary powers should not necessarily be removed, and should only be removed if changes are made to the criminal justice system. It will be argued that the demands for pro-arrest and pro-charge policies, in absence of other changes, may be misguided. Not all women who call the police want their violent partners prosecuted and so, before the police and the prosecution services adopt pro-arrest and pro-charge policies, we need further research to understand what women want from the police as well as the other criminal justice agencies. In particular, we need to understand why women frequently do not presently embrace prosecution and what they might want either as an alternative to prosecution, or as an alternative to the present sanctions imposed by the courts. First, let us re-visit the results of the Thames Valley study.

The findings of the study

The response of the police and the Crown Prosecution Service

This study shed light on the factors which prevented a substantial increase in the arrest rate which might have been expected as a result of the 1990/60 Home Office Circular on domestic violence. Relatively low arrest and prosecution rates were explained partly by reference to victims' preferences—in particular the frequency with which victims withdrew their statements—and partly by reference to police and prosecutors' perceptions of the effectiveness and appropriateness of the criminal justice system in dealing with domestic disputes. Many police and prosecutors felt that for the majority of victims prosecution would not be a good solution: that the outcome, in particular, would not be worth the process.

The Thames Valley Police became aware of domestic violence incidents in the same way that they became aware of most other criminal incidents: that is, through a report by a civilian, usually the victim. They responded to all but 4 per cent of the reports by sending one or two uniformed officers, either immediately, if it was thought to be an emergency, or, in any case, very quickly. As Chapter 3 shows, the practice of 'cuffing' calls (refusing to dispatch an officer to the scene), once so prevalent, was very rare. These incidents usually, but by no means always, involved allegations of criminal offences. Regardless of who had initially called the police, they all involved 'something that ought not to be happening and about which someone had better do something *now*!' (Bittner 1974: 30.) They required the police to perform various functions—crime control, social service, and more general order maintenance.

The responding officers had to judge whether there was sufficient evidence of an offence on which to make an arrest or to base a charge, but, even if this was their assessment, they still had discretion over both these decisions. This discretion, it was found, was not exercised randomly nor was it greatly influenced by individual officer attitudes towards domestic affairs. Rather, it was structured according to evidential criteria and informal working rules established by police officers 'on the ground'. The choice of working rules, such as those relating to victim preferences or the seriousness of the offence, was guided by their working assumptions about victims, suspects, and the aetiology of domestic violence. These assumptions were influenced by the organization of policing, by, for example, the force policy, procedural law, recent training initiatives, and the sub-cultural norms and values of the police service.

It was found that clear, incontrovertible evidence of an offence often led to an arrest, not because the police pursued rigorously all cases where there was evidence of an offence, but, rather, because evidence facilitated police action when the working rules pointed towards an arrest. In other words, when the police had other reasons for wanting to arrest someone, either, for example, because the suspect had challenged their authority, or because the victim wanted him arrested, and they felt that it would be to her benefit, evidence of an offence allowed them to do this. Most decisions regarding arrest were arrived at during a process of negotiation with the disputants and any other witnesses. The control room operators, whilst influencing how quickly the officers arrived, were not found to have had any impact on their decision-making processes at the scene of disputes. Cases were, in the main, 'constructed' at the scene of the incident by the officers and disputants.

The existence of evidence of a breach of criminal law did not always lead to arrest; on the other hand, the absence of evidence did not always preclude it. Officers sometimes used their public order powers (arrests 'to prevent a further breach of the peace') to reach temporary solutions. In these circumstances arrests could be used as a coercive means of managing disputes. Most of these arrests did not result in a criminal charge because prosecution was not the intention of the arresting officers, nor, typically, of the victims, and because there was often insufficient evidence of a crime. The police used their powers as a resource to impose 'law and order', to assist the victim, and, to some extent, to issue summary punishment (see Chapters 5 and 6).

Superficial examination of the high discontinuance rate suggested that the Crown Prosecution Service was independent from the police, and that prosecutors scrutinized rigorously police decisions. However, an understanding of the working rules of both agencies showed that prosecutors made their independent discretionary decisions based on the same working rules as guided the police. They dismissed the cases where the victim had withdrawn her complaint, cases which would have been dismissed by the police had the victim withdrawn her support at an earlier stage. Both police and prosecutors' decisions regarding appropriate action were highly correlated with victims' wishes. This was partly because there was little prospect of a successful conviction in many cases where the victim would not co-operate (although this was by no means always so), and partly because of a genuine desire to respond to the apparent wishes of the victim.

Prosecutors, like the police, recognized that there were various reasons for victim non co-operation, and, in the main, spoke sympathetically about the problem of witness intimidation in these cases. However, when making their decisions about prosecution they did not seem to discriminate between cases where they thought that the witness had withdrawn because of fear, and cases where they thought that she had withdrawn for other personal or familial reasons. They were just as likely to discontinue cases where they suspected that the victim had withdrawn as a result of intimidation as they were when the victim had chosen freely to withdraw because of reconciliation with the suspect.

None of the witnesses were compelled to testify, although there were legal powers to do so in most discontinued cases. It was found that police and prosecutors shared a genuine consideration for the problems that compelling a witness to testify might visit on that witness and they were worried that attempts to coerce such victims would give out a negative message to the wider victim population (see Chapter 6). Like many of the victims interviewed they believed that victims' interests are not always best served by a prosecution, and that the criminal justice system is often an extremely clumsy tool for managing domestic violence (see Chapter 7). An examination of the sentences imposed on those suspects convicted of criminal offences lent some credence to these opinions.

What did victims want?

Only a third of the victims in the study wanted the officers to arrest the suspect and many of these did not want the police to proceed any further. Thus, arrests often did not result in a charge being laid because in many cases the victim withdrew her support for a prosecution and the officers responded to the victims' wishes. The study found that victims' willingness to co-operate with the criminal justice system, and their perceptions of the helpfulness of that system, were interrelated. Three main reasons emerged for victims not pursuing the complaint. First, some women did not want to break up the relationship or the family. Secondly, some chose to stay with their partners because they hoped that by doing so they would avoid the retaliatory violence which frequently results from attempts to leave or to support a prosecution. Thirdly, some felt that the sanctions imposed would be inappropriate or undesirable. Whatever the reason, it was found that many calls for police assistance from women who could not envisage long-term separation from their partner were likely to be requests for immediate help to halt a particular incident, rather than an attempt to get the perpetrator prosecuted (see Chapter 7).

Victims, police, and prosecutors were all aware of the inability of the criminal justice system to respond effectively and appropriately to those cases of domestic violence which were put before a court. Across these three groups there was widespread dissatisfaction with the sanctions imposed by the courts.

To summarize, much previous research has started from the premiss that victims of domestic violence who call the police seek arrest and prosecution and that withdrawal of complaints represents some kind of failure on the part of the police. It has been further argued that this would be remedied if the police, as a rule, arrested and prosecuted wherever possible. Implicit in this approach is the assumption that the criminal justice system, as it presently operates, is capable of responding effectively to the needs of victims of domestic violence. The research reported in this book challenges the validity of these assumptions.

Recent developments in the policing of domestic violence: a move from victims' wishes to victims' interests

The research conducted for this book shows that many victims do not want their partners or ex-partners to be prosecuted. That whilst they want to be able to use the police for immediate protection, and would like officers to offer them support and advice, they do not consider the present criminal justice sanctions to be worth the trauma and inconvenience of supporting a prosecution. In the early 1990s it was possible for victims to call the police for help without committing themselves to the prosecution process. Their wishes were, in most cases, paramount and their ability to withdraw their support at any time during the criminal justice process, whilst infuriating to some police officers and prosecutors, appeared to give them the control they wanted. More recently, however, there have been changes in the local, as well as the national, police response to domestic violence. These changes aim to take this control away from the victims in order to act in their interests. They relate to the adoption of pro-arrest policies and, less obviously, to the appointment of domestic violence officers. Thames Valley Police has implemented pro-arrest policies in most of its twelve territorial areas and established domestic violence officers in all.

Domestic violence officers

The 1990/60 Circular encouraged forces to set up dedicated Domestic Violence Units or to appoint officers to deal specifically with domestic violence cases. Domestic violence officers, the Circular argued, would '... perform a more active role in supporting and reassuring the victim and helping her to make reasoned decisions, and [in] co-ordinating the work of the welfare and voluntary agencies' as well as providing support for uniformed officers and ensuring that they are aware of their powers of arrest.[3]

---

[3] By 1993 just over half of the forces in England and Wales had at least one specialist unit with some responsibility for domestic violence (Home Affairs Committee 1993a; Grace 1995).

Domestic Violence Units have, since their inception, faced various criticisms: there is usually no overall co-ordination or monitoring of units (Home Affairs Committee 1993a); units are often under-resourced (Grace 1995); and tend to be marginalized from mainstream policing (Home Affairs Committee 1993a; Morley and Mullender 1994). However, despite these criticisms, victims' experiences of this type of dedicated support have been generally good. Many receive a great deal of support and help, and prefer this service to that provided by the uniformed officers (Grace 1995; Hanmer 1990). In particular, Domestic Violence Units appear to play a valuable role in linking the police with other agencies (Morley and Mullender 1994; Barron, Harwin, and Singh 1992; Hanmer 1990; Grace 1995).

However, there is some evidence that these specialist units are concentrating on their law enforcement functions rather more than their social service functions. Some studies have suggested that they are focusing on increasing the arrest and prosecution rates (Edwards 1989; Hanmer and Saunders 1991). With the recent implementation of pro-arrest policies the trend towards increasing criminalization, and towards ignoring victims' wishes in order to respond 'in their interests', might gain even more momentum.

Pro-arrest policies

An increasing number of English forces have recently adopted policies encouraging arrest. In such areas, where there is evidence of an assault, officers are now supposed to arrest regardless of the wishes of the victim. Crown prosecutors are then asked to advise and, again, in theory, prosecution decisions are taken on the basis of evidence and not the wishes of the victim.

Pro-arrest or mandatory arrest policies emerged from a belief in the individual deterrent effect of arrest.[4] An American police foundation study in 1976 established that men who seriously assaulted their wives or cohabitees, or who were responsible for their murder, were often men who were already known to the police for violence against partners in the past. This suggested that early police intervention could interrupt the escalating chain of violence which the authors found to be typical of most of these cases (Edwards 1989).

---

[4] Pro-arrest policies *encourage* police to arrest for domestic violence under certain circumstances. Mandatory arrest policies, used less frequently, *require* officers to arrest.

Various studies supported these data and yet none had identified whether one particular form of police response was more effective than another (Jolin 1983). It was this precise question that Sherman and Berk (1984) set out to answer in their experiment conducted in Minneapolis between 1981 and 1982.

The Minneapolis research suggested that arresting offenders reduced repeat victimization, and so the authors recommended a presumptive arrest policy, whereby for misdemeanour domestic violence offences 'an arrest should be made unless there are good, clear reasons why an arrest would be counterproductive' (Sherman and Berk 1984: 270). They did not, however, recommend that arrest be mandatory. This was because they were aware of methodological problems with the experiment that might have affected the validity of their findings.[5] Hence, they urged caution and delay in implementing its recommendations.

When Sherman and Berk first went public with the findings of their initial Minneapolis project they created substantial media interest which put pressure on policy makers, as well as practitioners and activists. Of course, their work was not the only variable in the impetus for change. The case of *Thurman v. City of Torrington*[6] and the *Final Report of the Attorney General's Task Force on Family Violence*, both in 1984, spurred law enforcement executives to reject the traditional police response to domestic violence cases (see Morley and Mullender 1992). Hence, continued pressure from feminist critics and campaigns for an effective legal response to domestic violence meant that many American states during the mid-1980s reassessed their laws on violence in the home and gave police officers more powers of intervention (Morley and Mullender 1992).

More recent research has, however, cast some doubt on the findings of these studies. The National Institute of Justice funded replications of the Minneapolis experiment in six other cities.[7] Arrest was found to be associated with reduced domestic violence in some cities, amongst certain (employed) people and in the short run, but associated with increased violence in other cities, amongst certain

---

[5] See Sheptycki (1993) and Buzawa and Buzawa (1990) for a discussion of these methodological problems.

[6] S95 F.Supp. 1521.

[7] In the replication studies, as in the original, there were many design weaknesses and inconsistencies, both within and between studies.

(unemployed) people in the long run (Sherman *et al.* 1991). Clearly, as acknowledged by the researchers, these subsequent experiments did not provide unambiguous support for the innovation of pre-ferred arrest, which was the conclusion of the original Minneapolis experiment (Sherman 1992). One can conclude neither that arrest-ing domestic violence perpetrators generally deters them from further abuse nor that it generally causes them to retaliate with additional, and possibly increased, violence. Despite their complex and unpredictable impact, pro-arrest policies have spread widely through North America, and, as already mentioned, there has been pressure to introduce them in the United Kingdom (Morley and Mullender 1992).

Critics have argued that without co-ordinated action from other sectors of the criminal justice system to control the perpetrator, and without adequate support and protection for women in the com-munity, arrest may fail to deter violent men. More importantly, without these measures, it may also result in further violence in the shape of reprisals from men angry at having been arrested (Davis 1988; Horley 1990a). Furthermore, fear of losing control over the decisions regarding the prosecution of violent partners might deter some victims from repeat reporting. Data from Detroit suggested that the number of calls for assistance decreased following the implementation of an aggressive arrest policy (Buzawa and Buzawa 1990). This suggests that some women who previously were regular repeat victims have stopped calling the police for assistance because they are afraid of having their control taken away from them.

The net result of both pro-arrest policies and, to a lesser extent, Domestic Violence Units, should be an increase in arrests and probably also in prosecutions. The Crown Prosecution Service, like the police, is moving away from responding *to victims' wishes* to responding *to their perceived interests.* For example, the 1992 Code for Crown Prosecutors (which was in use when the fieldwork for the study reported in this book was carried out) warned pro-secutors to consider the reliability of witnesses who have a relation-ship with the accused in assessing the evidential strength of a case. In practice, this meant that if the victim of domestic violence did not wish to proceed with a prosecution the presumption was in favour of discontinuance (based on the evidential difficulties of prosecuting without the chief witness). It explicitly referred to the 'attitude' of complainants. In 1994 the Code was revised and the cautionary note about 'unreliable' witnesses was omitted. The onus was on prosecuting cases (including domestic violence cases) where this was thought to be *in the victim's interest.*[8]

Within most of the literature to date the failure to pursue a complaint has been framed in conventional terms. But conventional terms—the police usually refer to this as a failure to support police action—conceptualize the issue from the perspective of the criminal justice system. It might be that some women do not regard prosecution as a good means of managing domestic violence. They may want their partners to be arrested but do not necessarily want prosecution as a consequence of arrest.

Taking his cues from studies which found that victimized women can be active help-seekers, Ford (1991) looked at how some victims file, but then drop, criminal charges against their partners as a 'rational power strategy' for determining the future of their relationships. Ford argued that a threat of intervention by the criminal justice system has the potential to empower victims by providing criminal sanctions as leverage to prevent further abuse. For example, women can use the threat of arrest and prosecution to bargain for arrangements satisfactory to their wishes and to deter their partners from repeated violence without having to support a continued prosecution. In this sense, Ford moved away from the accepted 'wisdom' that victim 'non co-operation' is a problem.

McGillivray (1987) also maintained that women employ a variety of strategies to gain protection by the state without ending their relationship, including calling the police and then obstructing the prosecution process, even in jurisdictions with tough police and prosecution policies. This might be because the batterer has control over the victim, but, as McGillivray conceded, it may equally be because the victim recognizes the destructive consequences of a decision to terminate the relationship. Whatever the reason, if the aim is to empower women, perhaps we should respect their immediate concerns and wishes. As Cretney and Davis have recently noted, whilst the public interest will always be in favour of prosecution of domestic violence offences, the victim's interest may be equivocal: 'One cannot assume that a "successful" outcome, that is to say conviction and sentence, is in the woman's interests' (1996: 172).

---

[8] Of course, such changes need to be considered in the light of the overriding requirement concerning 'realistic' prospects of conviction.

'No-drop' policies[9] represent the 'consensus between reformers and the state that social interests are to take precedence' over immediate wishes of the victim, not to mention her interests as *she* understands them (McGillivray 1987: 31).

Of course, pro-arrest policies do not necessarily have to be followed by 'no-drop' policies. As Chapter 5 made clear, by removing the aggressor, arrest provides the victim with immediate protection. Friedman and Shulman (1991) have argued that, because arrest guarantees immediate safety to the victim and takes control away from the offender, the police should arrest perpetrators even if the victim does not wish this and will not sign a complaint. Once arrested and held in custody for a few hours these suspects could be released without being charged. Victims in the Thames Valley study seemed to appreciate these 'resource arrests'. Indeed, some appeared to use the system as a tool to manage conjugal abuse in the same way as Ford's victims did. As mentioned above, the large number of arrests for breach of the peace provided some evidence to suggest that patrol officers actively helped victims to use police powers of arrest as a power resource.

In the light of the findings of this study, and the changes in the police and Crown Prosecution Service response, a critical debate about the role of the victim, and the influence that she can and *should* exert over the criminal justice process, is crucial.

Considering the role of the victim in the criminal justice system

Two conflicting arguments emerge from a consideration of the role of the victim in the criminal justice system. First, the line taken by many feminist writers, and now, increasingly, by the police and prosecution service, is that control of prosecution decisions should be taken away from victims in their own interests, as well as those of the criminal justice system and the wider society. The second argument is that the views of the victims themselves should be paramount, to help them maintain control of their own relationships, even if they are considered to be acting contrary to their own interests.

---

[9] 'No-drop' policies mean that the decision to charge, once taken, will not be reversed because the victim withdraws her support for prosecution.

The second approach challenges conventional criminal justice philosophy, which prescribes responding to offences on the basis of objective seriousness and evidential sufficiency. It would put the criminal law at the service of the victim in the same way that the civil law is at the service of the victim, in the form of injunctions, separation orders, and so forth, to use (or not) as she wishes. This only sounds remarkable because 'criminal' and 'civil' law are usually placed in separate boxes and rarely considered as inter-related.

Up until the mid-1980s, the police generally regarded domestic violence exclusively as a civil matter. But the civil law appeared largely ineffective in preventing the reoccurrence of violence.[10] Pro-arrest policies regard domestic violence as an exclusively criminal matter. Yet neither the civil nor criminal approach takes account of the complexity of domestic violence. Domestic violence is of socie-tal interest—society should condemn and punish violence between intimates just as it should violence between strangers. As such it requires a criminal law response. In cases of domestic violence the declaratory, symbolic, and denunciatory roles of the law are of particular relevance (see Edwards 1989). However, domestic viol-ence is also of civil interest. Any justice system should aim to ensure that violence ceases whilst relationships continue if this is what partners and their children want. The move from the 'hands off' response of the criminal justice system in the 1970s, to the 'arrest whatever the victim wants' stance adopted recently, ignores the possibility of an holistic approach to the problem which promotes both civil and criminal justice remedies where appropriate. As Edwards (1989) argues, the division of available remedies into civil and criminal law symbolically reinforces the public/private dichotomy as well as creating practical problems of access for victims. The separation confuses and sometimes frustrates victims who tend to need 'packages' of remedies, the contents of which should be tailored to the particular needs of each victim and her family.

Domestic violence should be considered as a matter for *both* civil and criminal law working in harmony with, the various other statutory and voluntary agencies. This has been recognized

---

[10] Family courts, where most applications for injunctions are heard, focus exclus-ively on individual or familial problems rather than on societal reaction to abusive behaviour. Nor do these courts help women who do not want to end the relationship.

to a limited extent: the Law Commission has recommended that the police be able to apply for injunctions on behalf of battered women; and police Domestic Violence Units have a multi-agency liaison role. Putting criminal law as much at the service of battered women as is civil law could be considered as an extension of existing arrangements, rather than an introduction of a completely new approach. This does, however, raise the question of whether there is a need for an integrated 'family justice' system in which artificial civil and criminal distinctions are eradicated.

There are apparently successful experiments that can act as partial models. For instance, in Dade County, Florida, a court, which deals only with domestic violence, hears both civil cases and criminal misdemeanour cases. It offers, for first-time offenders, pre-trial diversion (including intensive therapeutic programmes). The court can also issue injunction orders and impose bail conditions as further protection for victims. In Winnipeg, Canada, a family violence court has been in operation since 1990 (Ursel 1994), and in Minnesota a 'domestic abuse intervention programme' co-ordinates the intervention of the criminal justice system, including court-mandated counselling for batterers, with welfare services and advocacy programmes (Morley and Mullender 1992). There is no obvious reason why such intervention measures could not be experimented with in England and Wales.

To return to the question raised above: should victims of domestic violence have a choice over the prosecution of 'their' cases? The research reported in this book suggests that unless, or until, the criminal justice response to domestic violence makes serious attempts to reduce domestic violence by effective criminal and civil intervention, many women will continue to want to withdraw their support for prosecution. Unless decision-makers listen to their needs and respond accordingly, a 'no-drop' policy will be regarded unfavourably by many victims. It could be argued that a system that fails the people for whom it is meant to provide a service, should not demand their support. However, decisions regarding the future of pro-arrest and pro-charge policies should be informed by careful debate about the contradictions between individual, group, and public interests and by further empirical enquiry.

The need for further research

The research reported in this book discovered some of the reasons why some women do not want their partners or ex-partners to be prosecuted. However, there is no recent in-depth rigorous study of English women's decisions regarding arrest and prosecution: in particular; the extent to which victims' decisions are the product of police preferences; their own wishes to direct the outcome of domestic disputes; or manipulation by violent partners. In America, Friedman and Shulman (1991) have argued that the state should prosecute perpetrators of domestic violence, regardless of the victim's views, because victims are intimidated by offenders. But there is no empirical evidence to show how many victims withdraw through intimidation and how many withdraw for other reasons. It is important to discover to what extent women are currently agents of their own destiny and to what extent their decisions are the products of other agents with their own agendas. This is especially so if pro-arrest and pro-charge policies are to be pursued. Also pro-arrest practices will need to be monitored to ascertain how they affect victims' choices regarding prosecution and alternative options.

Some research on domestic violence has now taken place in areas where Domestic Violence Units operate (see, for example, Edwards 1989; Hanmer 1990; Barron, Harwin, and Singh 1992; Grace 1995), although very few studies focus on the *way* they operate. In particular, none examined the extent to which Domestic Violence Units or officers influence victims' decisions regarding arrest and prosecution, how they 'manage' hostile witnesses, or the extent to which arrest and prosecution takes place with the approval of the victim. If, as seems to be the case, Domestic Violence Units are to adopt a law enforcement goal and try to persuade victims to pursue criminal justice sanctions, it will be important to identify the impact of this on victims.

It seems that there is a need to re-think the way that the police response to domestic violence is assessed. Take the attrition rate of incidents. Critics have tended to assume that if arrests do not result in prosecutions the police have failed the victim. However, this could be a sign that the police and/or the victims used the law in order temporarily to defuse a dispute even when they had no realistic prospect of getting a prosecution. Let us suppose that Ford, writing of the American criminal justice system, is correct in arguing that victims use the criminal justice system as a power resource to achieve their own aims. This being so, mandatory arrest and prosecution policies, or even simple pro-arrest policies, would deny women the chance of managing the abuse and trying to stop the violence whilst staying in the relationship.[11]

If Ford's findings are generalizable, there are some important implications for policy. First, understanding how and why women make certain decisions with regard to prosecution of violent partners (in particular the decision to retract their statement) could perhaps alleviate the problems and frustrations of service-providers (most notably the police). These are the agents who sometimes feel that they are wasting their time with, and failing, victims who withdraw their support for what the providers feel to be the best solution. Police officers and prosecutors could benefit from a broader understanding of the assistance that can be given to victims. Second, if pro-arrest policies impact adversely on victims, we might expect them to refrain from reporting repeat victimization to the police. Only further research, though, will enable us to answer these questions.

The changes in the police response, discussed above, are based on an unquestioning belief in the benefits to be gained from a prosecution. But many police officers and prosecutors in the Thames Valley study, expressed concern that the criminal law and the prosecution system are too blunt and uncompromising to achieve a balance between society's interest in securing the prosecution of crimes, and the wishes of many victims to preserve their families and personal relationships, or to secure amelioration. What happens once a case goes to court is, of course, largely out of the hands of the police. However, the sentences imposed by magistrates and judges do have an impact on the police and prosecution response. As mentioned above, if these agents do not think that the process is worth the outcome—that the sanctions imposed by the courts neither deter offenders nor assist victims—they might be less inclined to charge suspects and persuade victims to co-operate

---

[11] This is, of course, to presume that such policies would translate directly into practice. As discussed in chap. 4, this congruence is not easily achieved. There will always be some police discretion, and whilst this is structured according to working rules, pro-arrest policies will never be implemented in all cases (see also Buzawa and Buzawa 1990; Stanko 1989). Again, empirical enquiry will ascertain the extent to which such policies have changed police practices.

with the process. This is another area for empirical enquiry. It is important to know *why* the police and prosecutors believe that the criminal justice system is a clumsy tool for dealing with domestic violence. If the sentences were more severe (more custodial sentences, for example) would they be more inclined to press for prosecutions, or would they be more keen if they perceived the sentences to be more constructive (probation programmes for domestic violence perpetrators or restorative conferences for victims and offenders, for example)?

There is a need for research to address the question of what women want from the criminal justice system. Whether, for example, they would like a 'treatment' approach which attempts to rehabilitate violent partners. It could be that if the sanctions imposed by the courts were perceived by victims to be more appropriate to their needs they would be more willing to support the prosecution of their violent partners. In other words, sentencing needs to become both useful and symbolically powerful without recourse to repression and social exclusion.

One form of criminal justice intervention aimed at tackling the problem of domestic violence is the provision of programmes, in a group setting, aimed at changing the behaviour of perpetrators of domestic violence. The theoretical basis of such groups is that men employ violence and other forms of abuse to control their families and to enforce their own wishes, and that this behaviour is learned and rooted in patriarchal traditions rather than dysfunctional relationships (Dobash *et al.* 1996).

Batterers' programmes, like pro-arrest policies, have been introduced into Britain directly from North America (Morley and Mullender 1992). Whilst such programmes are new and exploratory in Britain, self-help men's groups appear to be spreading quite rapidly,[12] usually facilitated by organizations such as 'Survivors' (Morley and Mullender 1992). The first two batterers' programmes linked to the criminal justice system in Britain were CHANGE (based in Stirling) and the Lothian Domestic Violence Probation Project (located in Edinburgh). Both are court-mandated pro-

---

[12] The proliferation of such programmes could be facilitated by the increased and imaginative uses of the probation order (under s. 8(2)(i) of the Criminal Justice Act 1991, and Sched. 1A, para. 2(1) of the Powers of the Criminal Court Act 1973). This legislation would enable a court to attach to a probation order a condition that the defendant attend a counselling course (Conway 1994).

grammes, using counselling as a sentencing option rather than as a pre-trial diversion—men are referred as a requirement of a probation order, following screening for suitability. They are based on 'pro-feminist models', and tend to utilize cognitive-behavioural techniques to challenge the assumptions of participants and to facilitate more appropriate ways of acting in relationships. They work towards eliminating violence and intimidation from the men's relationships with women.[13]

Several probation services in England and Wales have since set up such programmes (Mullender 1996) and a number of other services are planning to introduce them.[14] Programmes being established in Britain have been influenced by the pro-feminist 'Duluth' model' (so-called because it was developed in Duluth, Minnesota), which emphasizes inter-agency liaison and safety of victims.

These programmes might be thought to be particularly useful to domestic violence perpetrators because they tap into gender-specific aggressive behaviour. They challenge misogyny and confront the masculine characteristics which, if they do not cause domestic violence, certainly help to perpetuate it (Dobash and Dobash 1992). It is claimed that programmes can teach skills to enable the offender to control violent impulses and reduce violent responses (see Dutton 1995 for a full discussion of the treatment of wife abusers).

Most attempts to evaluate the effectiveness of such programmes have been criticized for being on too small a scale, too parochial, for depending solely upon perpetrators reporting their re-offending—ignoring the victim as a source of information—and for focusing only on physical violence to the exclusion of psychological harm and controlling behaviours (Brown and Williams 1996). However, evaluations of such programmes in America (Edelson 1990) and, more recently, in Britain (Dobash *et al.* 1996; Brown and Williams 1996) indicate that they have more impact on re-offending rates than alternative sentences. The thorough evaluation study undertaken by Dobash *et al.* (1996) provided encouraging results. They

[13] The pro-feminist stance sees violence as an intentional behaviour chosen by men as a tactic or resource associated with attempts to control and dominate women. By contrast, therapeutic discourses usually ignore the violence, or see it as an irrational act of emotional ventilation emerging from forces beyond the control or comprehension of violent men (for a good explanation of the differences between pro-feminist and traditional therapeutic programmes see Dobash and Dobash 1992).

[14] Results of preliminary investigations conducted by the author and Dr. Ros Burnett of the Oxford Probation Studies Unit.

studied the impact of two educational programmes on the subsequent behaviour of men who had been placed on probation for an offence of domestic violence. Changes in the behaviour of these men were measured and compared with the subsequent behaviour of men who had received other criminal justice sanctions. This showed that, according to the men's partners, a much smaller proportion of those men who had participated in the programme committed a violent act than of those who had been subject to other types of sanctions.

Critics of work with domestic violence offenders (see Horley 1990b) have argued that its efficacy is as yet unproven and that it deflects resources away from support for women. The first point is still, to some extent, valid but is not a reason for stopping programmes. What is required is rigorous evaluation of programmes which assesses not only whether such interventions work but *how* they work. In other words, research needs to examine in-depth the dynamic interactions between offenders and behaviour changing programmes, and the extent to which these are associated with desistance from, or continuation of violent, abusive, and controlling behaviours.[15] The second criticism raises a false dichotomy: should 'something be done' for victims *or* for offenders. Of course, more needs to be done for victims and this involves, amongst other things, making increased grants available to local housing authorities and increased funding of Women's Aid. Moreover, doing something for men, in the form of batterers' programmes, if successful, would ultimately *do something* for victims. It is naïve to see this as an 'either/or' issue. Furthermore, if these programmes do reduce the incidence and/or severity of domestic violence they would, in the long-term, be cost-effective.

Research should also be carried out on the potential effectiveness of restorative justice initiatives, in particular in the cautioning process (see Chapter 7 for a discussion of the police reluctance to caution domestic violence offenders). Many of the victims in the Thames Valley study wanted help to eradicate the violence without losing the relationship and breaking up the family. Others wanted to end the relationship without further violence. For both of these groups restorative cautioning might be a sensible alternative to fines or conditional discharges which offer no hope of assuagement.

---

[15] Ideas developed with Roger Hood and Ros Burnett.

Domestic violence, more than most other offences, points to a need to consider relationships damaged by crime, in particular those between the parties directly involved, but also between those parties and any children who may witness the violence or may be caught in the crossfire. Whilst this approach might be inappropriate in some cases, it may provide a useful alternative to the present criminal justice process. Of course, as with domestic violence perpetrator programmes, empirical research on the potential of such initiatives is imperative before their use becomes widespread. Indeed, as Stubbs (1997) argues, it is important to consider the process in some detail, and to examine the findings of evaluative work concerning the use of the process with juvenile offenders, before moving on to consider its potential for dealing with violence against women.

This book has shown that the police and Crown Prosecution Service response to domestic violence is not a simple matter of cultural prejudice, or of patriarchal institutions ignoring violence against women in general and 'non-influential' women in particular. It is, rather, a more complicated matter of the police adopting certain informal working rules in order to make difficult decisions where the law affords them great discretion. Previous studies have underestimated the role of the victim in these decisions and, therefore, have assumed that police and prosecutors rarely wish to prosecute cases of domestic violence. The Thames Valley study has shown that victims rarely wish to proceed and, furthermore, that their choices impact greatly on the decisions made by criminal justice agents. Further research is now needed to understand fully *why* victims of domestic violence so often withdraw their complaints.[16]

The present criminal justice response towards domestic violence is moving towards increasing criminalization. Critics of the traditional approach by the police and prosecutors now see arrest and prosecution as a panacea. They argue that the courts should respond punitively towards this group of offenders and that criminal justice agents should take the decisions away from the victims: in particular, they should not be allowed to withdraw their complaints. This is both unrealistic and at odds with developments in

[16] Such further research has been conducted by the author and Andrew Sanders. Many of the questions raised in this chapter are dealt with in Hoyle and Sanders (1998).

restorative justice elsewhere in the system. The research undertaken for this book suggests that pro-arrest and pro-charge policies could do more harm than good. It may be that the best way to police domestic violence is to respond to the wishes of the victims. To some extent, this is what the police were doing in 1993, although they had to bend the rules to do so.

There is clearly a need to address the failings of the criminal justice system as it operated during the fieldwork for this study, and to explore alternative approaches, considering, perhaps, approaches which enable the criminal justice system to respond to the varied needs of individual victims. Such an approach would return their discretionary powers to criminal justice agents. There are, of course, different opinions on the desirability of wide discretionary powers. Hawkins (1992) compares positions such as that of Kenneth Culp Davis (1969) as forwarded in his influential book *Discretionary Justice* with that of Joel Handler. Davis regarded discretion as the major source of injustice, believing that the substantial amount of unnecessary discretion in legal systems had threatened the proper application of policy. He argued for discretion to be 'structured' and 'checked' by rules in order to avoid arbitrariness. This fits with the position of many feminist critics of the police over the last two decades, and with the view on mandatory arrest and charge policies. Hawkins contrasts this position with that of Joel Handler (1986), who is more concerned with 'social justice' than narrower conceptions of legal justice. Hence his position is more in favour of discretionary powers than that of Davis. He argues that discretion allows the official to recognize the uniqueness of each situation and to respond flexibly, and with sensitivity to the particular. Hence his position fits with the argument that officers should 'tailor-make' their responses to fit the specific context of the dispute. Of course, it might be argued that this is what officers were doing in 1993—with limited effectiveness. However, whilst officers were, in the main, responding to the victims' wishes, they were not providing victims with effective alternatives to prosecution, and the police involvement with victims ended when the victim withdrew her statement. An effective follow-up service is needed if victims are to benefit from contact with the criminal justice system.

This book has shown that every domestic violence incident requires negotiation, rather than an automatic mandated response. The outcome of that negotiation should depend on many factors in addition to the seriousness of the offence. These factors must first be identified accurately by the officers who attend the incident. The police, and the criminal justice system as a whole, will only respond more effectively if they begin to adopt a more holistic approach to domestic violence: one which considers alternatives to prosecution and retributive sentences; and one which addresses the needs of victims and perpetrators alike.

Bibliography

Ackroyd, S., Harper, R., Hughes, J. A., Shapiro, D., and Soothill K. (1992). *New Technology and Practical Police Work.* Buckingham: Open University Press.

Ajzen, I. and Fishbein, M. (1980). *Understanding Attitudes and Predicting Social Behaviour.* N. J., Prentice Hall: Englewood Cliffs.

Baldwin, J. (1985). *Pre-Trial Justice.* Oxford: Basil Blackwell.

—— and Kinsey, R. (1982). *Police Powers and Politics.* London: Quartet Books.

—— and McConville, M. (1978). 'The New Home Office Figures on Pleas and Acquittals: What Sense do they Make?', *Criminal Law Review,* 196.

Banton, M. (1964). *The Policeman in the Community.* London: Tavistock.

Barron, J., Harwin, N., and Singh, T. (1992). *Report to Home Affairs Committee Inquiry into Domestic Violence.* Bristol: Women's Aid Federation England.

Baumgartner, M. P. (1992). 'The Myth of Discretion' in Hawkins, K. (ed.), *The Uses of Discretion.* Oxford: Clarendon Press.

Bayley, D. (1986). 'The Tactical Choices of Police Patrol Officers'. *Journal of Criminal Justice,* 14.

—— and Bittner, E. (1984). 'Learning the Skills of Policing', *Law and Community Problems,* 47/3.

Becker, H. (1963). *Outsiders: Studies in the Sociology of Deviance.* New York: Free Press.

Berk, S. F. and Loseke, D. R. (1980). ' "Handling" Family Violence: Situational Determinants of Police Arrest in Domestic Disturbances', *Law and Society Review,* 15/2.

Binney, V., Harkell G., and Nixon, J. (1981). *Leaving Violent Men: A Study of Refuges and Housing for Battered Women.* Women's Aid Federation England.

Bittner, E. (1967). 'The Police on Skid-Row: A Study of Peace Keeping', *American Sociological Review,* 32.

—— (1970). *The Function of the Police in Modern Societies.* Rockville MD: National Institute for Mental Health, Center for Studies of Crime and Delinquency.

—— (1974). 'Florence Nightingale in Pursuit of Willie Sutton: A Theory of the Police' in Jacob, H. (ed.), *The Potential for Reform of Criminal Justice.* Beverley Hills, CA: Sage.

—— (1975). 'Police Research and Police Work' in Viano, E. (ed.), *Criminal Justice Research*. Farnborough: Heath.

—— (1980). *The Functions of the Police in Modern Society*. Cambridge Mass.: Oelgeschlager, Gunn and Hain.

—— (1990). *Aspects of Police Work*. Boston, Mass.: Northeastern University Press.

Black, D. J. (1970). 'The Production of Crime Rates', *American Sociological Review*, 35.

—— (1971). 'The Social Organization of Arrest', *Stanford Law Review*, 23.

—— (1976). *The Behavior of Law*. New York: Academic Press.

—— (1980). *The Manners and Customs of the Police*. New York: Academic Press.

Blumer, H. (1969). 'Society as Symbolic Interactionism' in Rose, E. (ed.), *Symbolic Interactionism*. Englewood Cliffs: Prentice Hall.

Bordua, D. J. and Reiss, A. J. (1966). 'Command, Control, and Charisma: Reflections on Police Bureaucracy', *The American Journal of Sociology*, 72, July.

Bottomley, A. and Coleman, C. (1981). *Understanding Crime Rates*. Saxon House.

Bourlet, A. (1990). *Police Intervention in Marital Violence*. Milton Keynes: Open University Press.

Bowker, L. (1982). 'Police Services to Battered Women: Bad or not so Bad?', *Criminal Justice and Behaviour*, 9/4.

—— (1983). *Beating Wife Beating*. Lexington, Mass.: Lexington Books.

Brogden, M., Jefferson, T., and Walklate, S. (1988). *Introducing Policework*. London: Unwin.

Brown, D. (1997). *PACE Ten Years On: A Review of the Research*. London: HMSO.

—— and Ellis, T. (1994). *Policing Low Level Disorder*, Home Office Research Study, No. 135. London: HMSO.

Brown, I. and Williams, K. (1996). *Evaluation of the First Schedule 1A Programme for Perpetrators of Domestic Violence*. Wakefield: West Yorkshire Probation Service.

Brown, S. E. (1984). 'Police Responses to Wife Beating: Neglect of a Crime of Violence', *Journal of Criminal Justice*, 12.

Brownlee, I. D. (1990). 'Compellability and Contempt in Domestic Violence Cases', *Journal of Social Welfare Law*, 2.

Burgess, R. (1984). *In The Field*. London: Allen and Unwin.

Burnside, J. and Baker, N. (eds.), (1994). *Relational Justice: Repairing the Breach*. Winchester: Waterside Press.

Bush, T. and Hood-Williams, J. (1995). 'Domestic Violence on a London Housing Estate', *Research Bulletin*, No. 37. London: Home Office Research and Statistics Department.

Buzawa, E. and Buzawa, C. (eds.), (1990). *Domestic Violence: The Criminal Justice Response* (1st edn.). Newbury Park, CA: Sage.

—— and —— (eds.), (1993). 'The Impact of Arrest on Domestic Violence', *The Impact of Arrest on Domestic Assault, American Behavioural Scientist* (special issue). CA: Sage.

—— and —— (eds.), (1996a). *Do Arrests and Restraining Orders Work?* CA: Sage.

—— and —— (eds.), (1996b). *Domestic Violence: The Criminal Justice Response* (2nd edn.). Newbury Park, CA: Sage.

Cain, M. (1973). *Society and the Policeman's Role*. London: Routledge and Kegan Paul.

Carlson, B. E. (1977). 'Battered Women and their Assailants', *Social Work*, 22.

Carroll, J. (1994). 'The Protection of Children Exposed to Marital Violence', *Child Abuse Review*, 3/6–14.

Cavadino, M. and Dignan, J. (1997). *The Penal System: An Introduction* (2nd edn.). London: Sage.

Chambers, G. and Miller, A. (1983). *Investigating Sexual Assault*. Edinburgh: HMSO.

Chan, J. (1996). 'Changing Police Culture', *British Journal of Criminology*, 36/1, Winter.

Chatterton, M. (1981). *Report of the Royal Commission on Criminal Procedure*. London: HMSO.

—— (1983). 'Police Work and Assault Charges' in Punch, M. (ed.), *Control in the Police Organisation*. Cambridge, Mass.: MIT Press.

Choongh, S. (1997). *Policing as Social Discipline*. Oxford: Clarendon Press.

Choudry, S. (1996). *Pakistani Women's Experience of Domestic Violence in Great Britain*, Research Findings, No. 43. Home Office.

Cleveland Refuge and Aid for Women and Children (1984). *Private Violence: Public Shame*.

Conway, H. L. (1994). 'Domestic Violence: Eradication or Escape?', *New Law Journal*, 15 July.

Cooney, M. (1994). 'Evidence as Partisanship', *Law and Society Review*, 28/4.

Cretney, A. and Davis, G. (1995). *Punishing Violence*. London: Routledge.

—— and —— (1996). 'Prosecuting "Domestic" Assault', *Criminal Law Review*, March.

—— and —— (1997). 'The Significance of Compellability in the Prosecution of Domestic Assault', *British Journal of Criminology*, 37/1.

Criminal Law Revision Committee (1984). *Fifteenth Report, Sexual Offences*, Cmnd. 9213. London: HMSO.

Crisp, D. and Moxon, D. (1994). *Case Screening by The Crown Prosecution Service: How and Why Cases are Terminated*, Home Office Research Study, No. 137. London: HMSO.

Crown Prosecution Service (1992). *Code for Crown Prosecutors*. London: HMSO.

—— (1993a). *A Statement of Prosecution Policy: Domestic Violence*, CPS Policy Group.

—— (1993b). *Annual Report April 1992–March 1993*. London: HMSO.

—— (1994). *Code for Crown Prosecutors*. London: HMSO.

—— (1995). *1994 Discontinuance Survey*, CPS.

Currie, D. H. (1990). 'Battered Women and the State: From the Failure of Theory to a Theory of Failure', *The Journal of Human Justice*, 1:77–96.

Davies, P. W. (1982). 'Structured Rationales for Non-arrest: Police Stereotypes of Domestic Disturbance', *Criminal Justice Review*, 6, 2, 8–15.

Davis, K. C. (1969). *Discretionary Justice: A Preliminary Enquiry*. Baton Rouge, La.: Louisiana State University Press.

Davis, N. (1988). 'Battered Women: Implications for Social Control', *Contemporary Crisis*, 12:345–372.

Davis, P. (1983). 'Restoring the Semblance of Order: Police Strategies in the Domestic Disturbance', *Symbolic Interaction*, 6/2.

Denzin, N. (1970). *The Research Act*. Chicago: Aldine.

Dixon, D. (1992). 'Legal Regulation and Policing Practice', Social and Legal Studies, 1.

—— (1997). *Law in Policing: Legal Regulation and Police Practices*. Oxford: Clarendon Press.

——, Coleman C., and Bottomley, K. (1990). 'Consent and the Legal Regulation of Policing', *Journal of Law and Society*, 17.

Dobash, R. E. and Dobash, R. P. (1980). *Violence Against Wives*. Shepton Mallet, Somerset: Open Books.

—— and —— (1992). *Women, Violence and Social Change*. London: Routledge.

—— and —— Cavanagh, K., and Lewis, R. (1996). *Research Evaluation of Programmes for Violent Men*. Edinburgh: The Scottish Office Central Research Unit.

——, Emerson, R., Dobash, R. P., and Cavanagh, K. (1985). 'The Contact between Battered Women and Social and Medical Agencies' in Pahl, J. (ed.), *Private Violence and Public Policy*. London: Routledge.

Dolon, R., Hendricks, J., and Meagher, M. S. (1986). 'Police Practices and Attitudes toward Domestic Violence', *Journal of Police Science and Administration*, 14/3.

Doob, A. N. and Roberts, J. (1988). 'Public Punitiveness and Public Knowledge of the Facts: Some Canadian Surveys' in Walker, N., and Hough, M., (eds.), *Public Attitudes to Sentencing: Surveys from Five Countries*. Aldershot: Gower.

Dunnighan, C. and Norris, C. (1995). 'Practice, Problems and Policy: Management Issues in the Police Use of Informers', Unpublished Paper.

Dutton, D. G. (1977). 'Domestic Dispute Intervention by Police' cited in Smith, L., *Domestic Violence: An Overview of the Literature*. Home Office Research Study, No. 107, 1989.

—— (1988). *The Domestic Assault of Women: Psychological and Criminal Justice Perspectives*. Boston: Allyn and Bacon, Inc.

—— (1995). *The Domestic Assault of Women: Psychological and Criminal Justice Perspectives* (revised and expanded edition). Vancouver: UBC Press.

Dworkin, R. (1977). *Taking Rights Seriously*. London: Duckworth.

Edelson, J. L. (1990). 'Judging the Success of Interventions with Men who Batter' in Besharov, D. (ed.), *Family Violence: Research and Public Policy Issues*. Washington, DC: AEI Press.

Edwards, S. S. M. (1986). 'Police Attitudes and Dispositions in Domestic Disputes: The London Study', *Police Journal*, July.

—— (1989). *Policing 'Domestic' Violence: Women, the Law and the State*. London: Sage.

—— (1996). *Sex and Gender in the Legal Process*. Blackstone Press Ltd.

—— and Halpern, A. (1991). 'Protection for the Victim of Domestic Violence: Time for Radical Revision?', *Journal of Social Welfare and Family Law*, 2.

Eiser, J. R. (1986). *Social Psychology: Attitudes, Cognitions and Social Behaviour*. Cambridge: Cambridge University Press.

Ekblom, P. and Heal, K. (1982). *The Police Response to Calls from the Public*, Research and Planning Unit Paper No. 9. London: Home Office.

—— and —— (1985). 'Police Response to Calls from the Public', in Heal, K., Tarling, R., and Burrows, J. (eds.), *Policing Today*. London: HMSO.

Elster, J. (ed.), (1986). *Rational Choice*. Oxford: Basil Blackwell.

Ericson, R. (1981). *Making Crime*. London and Toronto: Butterworth.

—— (1982). *Reproducing Order*. Toronto: University of Toronto Press.

Evans, R. (1994). 'Cautioning: Counting the Cost of Retrenchment', *Criminal Law Review*.

—— and Ellis, R. (1997). 'Police Cautioning in the 1990s', *Home Office Research and Statistics Directorate*, Research Findings, No. 52.

Faragher, T. (1985). 'The Police Response to Violence against Women in the Home' in Pahl, J. (ed.), *Private Violence and Public Policy*. London: Routledge and Kegan Paul.

Feder, L. (1996). 'Police Handling of Domestic Calls: The Importance of Offender's Presence in the Arrest Decision', *Journal of Criminal Justice*, 24/6.

Ferraro, K. J. (1989a). 'Policing Woman Battering', *Social Problems*, 1989, 36/1, February.

—— (1989b). 'The Legal Response to Wife Battering in the United States' in Hamner, J., Radford, J., and Stanko, E. (eds.), *Women, Policing and Male Violence*. London: Routledge and Kegan Paul.

—— (1993). 'Irreconcilable Differences: Battered Women, Police and the Law' in Hilton, N. Z. (ed.), *Legal Responses to Wife Assault: Current Trends and Evaluation*. Newbury Park, CA: Sage.

Fielding, N. (1989). 'Police Culture and Police Practice' in Weatheritt, M. (ed.), *Police Research: Some Future Prospects*. Aldershot: Avebury.

—— (1994). 'Cop Canteen Culture' in Newburn, T. and Stanko, E. (eds.), *Just Boys Doing Business: Masculinity and Crime*. London: Routledge.

—— (1995). *Community Policing*. Oxford: Clarendon Press.

Fine, M. (1981). 'An Injustice by any Other Name', *Victimology*, 6.

Flynn, J. P. (1977). 'Recent Findings Relating to Wife Abuse', *Social Casework*, 58.

Ford, D. A. (1991). 'Prosecution as a Victim Power Resource: A Note on Empowering Women in Violent Conjugal Relationships', *Law and Society Review*, 25/2.

Freeman, M. D. A. (1987). *Dealing with Domestic Violence*. Bicester: CCH Editions.

Friedman, L. N. and Shulman, M. (1990). 'Domestic Violence: The Criminal Justice Response' in Lurigio, A. J., Skogan, W. G., and Davis, R. C. (eds.), *Victims of Crime: Problems, Policies and Programs*. Newbury Park, CA: Sage.

Galligan, D. J (1986). *Discretionary Powers: A Legal Study of Official Discretion*. Oxford: Clarendon Press.

Gambetta, D. (1987). *Were they Pushed or did they Jump?* Cambridge: Cambridge University Press.

Giddens, A. (1979). *Central Problems in Social Theory: Action, Structure and Contradiction in Social Analysis*. Basingstoke: Macmillan.

Goffman, E. (1959). *The Presentation of the Self in Everyday Life*. New York: Doubleday.

Goldstein, J. (1960). 'Police Discretion Not to Invoke the Criminal Process. Low Visibility Decisions in the Administration of Justice', *Yale Law Journal*, 69, March.

Grace, S. (1995). *Policing Domestic Violence in the 1990s*. Home Office Research Study, No. 139. London: HMSO.

Hall, R., James, S., and Kertesz, J. (1981). *The Rapist who Pays the Rent*. Bristol: Falling Wall Press Ltd.

Handler, J. F. (1986). *The Conditions of Discretion: Autonomy, Community, Bureaucracy*. New York: Russell Sage Foundation.

Hanmer, J. (1989). 'Women and Policing in Britain' in Hanmer, J., Radford, J., and Stanko, E. A. (eds.), *Women, Policing, and Male Violence: International Perspectives*. London: Routledge.

—— (1990). *Women, Violence and Crime Prevention: A Study of Changes in Police Policy and Practices in West Yorkshire*, Violence,

Abuse and Gender Relations Unit Research Paper, No. 1. University of Bradford.

——, Radford, J., and Stanko, E. A. (1989). 'Policing, Men's Violence: An Introduction' in Hanmer, J., Radford, J., and Stanko, E. A. (eds.), *Women, Policing and Male Violence*. London: Routledge.

—— and Saunders, S. (1984). *Well-Founded Fear: A Community Study of Violence to Women*. London: Hutchinson.

—— and —— (1987). *Women, Violence and Crime Prevention*. Aldershot: Gower.

—— and —— (1991). 'Policing Violence Against Women: Implementing Policy Changes', Report from the British Criminology Conference, 1991.

—— and Stanko, E. A. (1985). 'Stripping Away the Rhetoric of Protection: Violence to Women, Law and the State in Britain and the USA', *International Journal of the Sociology of Law*, 13.

Hart, H. L. A. (1961). *The Concept of Law*. Oxford: Oxford University Press.

Haste, C. (1992). *Rules of Desire: Sex in Britain, World War I to the Present*. London: Chatto and Windus.

Hatty, S. (1989). 'Policing and Male Violence in Australia' in Hanmer, J., Radford, J., and Stanko, E. A. (eds.), *Women, Policing and Male Violence*. London: Routledge.

Hawkins, K. (1992). 'The Use of Legal Discretion: Perspectives from Law and Social Science' in Hawkins, K. (ed.), *The Uses of Discretion*. Oxford: Clarendon Press.

Heidensohn, F. (1992). *Women in Control? The Role of Women in Law Enforcement*. Oxford: Oxford University Press.

Hilton, N. Z. (ed.), (1993). *Legal Responses to Wife Assault: Current Trends and Evaluation*. Newbury Park, CA: Sage.

Holdaway, S. (1977). 'Changes in Urban Policing', *British Journal of Sociology*, 28/2.

—— (ed.), (1979). *The British Police*. London: Edward Arnold.

—— (1983). *Inside British Police: A Force at Work*. Oxford: Basil Blackwell.

—— (1989). 'Discovering Structure. Studies of the British Police Occupational Culture' in Weatheritt, M. (ed.), *Police Research: Some Future Prospects*. Aldershot: Avebury.

Homant, R. J. and Kennedy, D. B. (1985). 'Police Perception of Spouse Abuse: A Comparison of Male and Female Officers', *Journal of Criminal Justice*, 13.

Home Affairs Committee (1993a). *Domestic Violence, Vol. I,* Report together with the Proceedings of the Committee. London: HMSO.

—— (1993b). *Domestic Violence, Vol. II,* Memoranda of Evidence, Minutes of Evidence and Appendices. London: HMSO.

Home Office (1986). *Violence Against Women*, Home Office Circular 1986/69, London: Home Office.

—— (1990a). *Domestic Violence*, Home Office Circular 1990/60. London: Home Office.

—— (1990b). *Victim's Charter*. London: HMSO.

—— (1993). *British Crime Survey 1992*, HORS 132. London: HMSO.

—— (1996). *Victim's Charter*. London: HMSO.

Horley, S. (1988). 'A Pioneering Police Plan to Help Battered Women', *Social Work Today*, March 24.

—— (1990a). 'No Haven for Battered Women', *Police Review*, 17, August.

—— (1990b). 'A Shame and a Disgrace', *Social Work Today*, 21 June.

Hough, M., Lewis, H., and Walker, N. (1988). 'Factors Associated with "Punitiveness" in England and Wales' in Walker, N. and Hough, M. (eds.), *Public Attitudes to Sentencing: Surveys from Five Countries*. Aldershot: Gower.

Hoyle, C. and Sanders, A. (1998). 'Police Response to Domestic Violence: From Victim Choice to Victim Empowerment', Unpublished Paper.

Hurley, D. J. and Jaffe, P. (1990). 'Children's Observations of Violence: Clinical Implications for Children's Mental Health Professionals', *Canadian Journal of Psychiatry*, 35.

Jaffe, P., Wilson, S. K., and Wolfe, D. A. (1990). *Children of Battered Women*. London: Sage.

Jarvie, I. C. (1972). *Concepts and Society*. London: Routledge and Kegan Paul.

Jefferson, T. and Grimshaw, R. (1984). *Controlling the Constable: Police Accountability in England and Wales*. London: Muller.

Johnson, N. (1985). *Marital Violence*. London: Routledge and Kegan Paul.

Jolin, A., (1983). Domestic Violence Legislation: An Impact Assessment, *Journal of Police Science and Administration*, 11.

Joutsen, M. (1987). *The Role of the Victim of Crime in European Criminal Justice Systems*. Helsinki United Nations Institute for Crime Prevention and Control (HUENI).

Kelling, G. L., Pate, T., Dieckman, D., and Brown, C. E. (1974). 'The Kansas City Preventive Patrol Experiment' cited in Manning, P. K. (1988), *Symbolic Communication*. Cambridge: Mass.: MIT Press.

Kelly, L. (1988). *Surviving Sexual Violence*. Cambridge: Polity Press.

Kemp, C., Norris, C., and Fielding, N. G. (1992). *Negotiating Nothing: Police Decision-making in Disputes*. Aldershot: Avebury.

La Fave, W. (1969). 'Non Invocation of the Criminal Law by Police' in Cressey, D. R. and Ward, D. (eds.), *Delinquency, Crime and Social Process*. New York: Harper and Row.

Lacey, N. (1992). 'The Jurisprudence of Discretion: Escaping the Legal Paradigm' in Hawkins, K. (ed.), *The Uses of Discretion*. Oxford: Clarendon Press.

Lea, J. and Young, J. (1984). *What is to be Done about Law and Order.* Harmondsworth, Middlesex: Penguin Books.

Lemert, E. (1967). *Human Deviance, Social Problems and Social Control.* Englewood Cliffs, NJ: Prentice Hall.

Leng, R., McConville, M., and Sanders, A. (1992). 'Researching the Discretions to Charge and Prosecute' in Downes, D. (ed.), *Unravelling Criminal Justice*. London: Macmillan.

Levens, B. R. and Dutton, D. G. (1980). *The Social Service Role of the Police: Domestic Crisis Intervention*. Ottawa: Solicitor General of Canada.

Lloyd, S., Farrell, G., and Pease, K. (1994). *Preventing Repeated Domestic Violence: A Demonstration Project on Merseyside*, Police Research Group Crime Prevention Unit Series, Paper 49.

Lunneborg, P. (1989). *Women Police Officers' Current Career Profile.* Springfield, Ill.: Charles Thomas.

McBarnet, D. (1981). *Conviction*. London: Macmillan.

—— (1983). *Conviction* (2nd edn.). London: Macmillan.

McConville, M., Hodgson, J., Bridges, L., and Pavlovic, A. (1994). *Standing Accused: The Organisation and Practices of Criminal Defence Lawyers in Britain*. Oxford: Clarendon Press.

——,Sanders A., and Leng, R. (1991). *The Case for the Prosecution*. London: Routledge.

—— and Shepherd, D. (1992). *Watching Police, Watching Communities*. London: Routledge.

McGillivray, A. (1987). 'Battered Women: Definition, Models and Prosecutorial Policy', *Canadian Journal of Family Law, 6*.

McLeod, M. (1983). 'Victim Non-Co-operation in Domestic Disputes', *Criminology, 21/3*.

Maguire, M. and Bennet, T. (1982). *Burglary in a Dwelling*. London: Heinemann.

—— and Norris, C. (1992). *The Conduct and Supervision of Criminal Investigations*, The Royal Commission on Criminal Justice, London: HMSO.

—— and Pointing, L. (eds.), (1988). *Victims of Crime: A New Deal?* Milton Keynes: Open University Press.

Mama, A. (1989). *The Hidden Struggle: Statutory and Voluntary Sector Responses to Violence against Black Women in the Home*. London: London Race and Housing Research Unit.

Manning, P. K. (1977). *Police Work*. Cambridge, Mass.: MIT Press.

——(1978). 'The Police: Mandate, Strategies and Appearances', in Manning, P. K. and Von Mannen, J. (eds.), *Policing: A View from the Street*. Santa Monica, CA: Goodyear Publishing.

——(1979). 'The Social Control of Police Work', in Holdaway, S. (ed.), *The British Police*. London: Edward Arnold.

——(1980). *Narcs' Game*. Cambridge, Mass.: MIT Press.

——(1982). 'Producing Drama: Symbolic Communication and the Police', *Symbolic Interaction*, Fall, 5.

——(1988). *Symbolic Communication*. Cambridge, Mass.: MIT Press.

——(1992). 'Screening Calls' in Buzawa, E. S. and Buzawa, C. G. (eds.), *Domestic Violence: The Changing Criminal Justice Response*. Westport, CN: Auburn House.

Marshall, T. (1991). *Victim-Offender Mediation*, Home Office Research Bulletin, No. 30.

Martin, D. (1976). *Battered Wives*. San Francisco, CA: Glide Publications.

Mathiesen, T. (1990). *Prison on Trial*. London: Sage.

Mawby, R. and Walklate, S. (1994). *Critical Victimology*. London: Sage.

Maynard, W. (1994). *Witness Intimidation Strategies for Prevention*, Police Research Group Crime Detection and Prevention Series, Paper No. 55. London: Home Office Police Department.

Mead, G. H. (1934). 'Mind, Self and Society' in Morris, C. (ed.), *Mind, Self and Society*. Chicago: University of Chicago Press.

Miers, D. (1992). 'The Responsibilities and Rights of Victims of Crime', *Modern Law Review*, 55.

Moody, S. and Toombs, J. (1982). *Prosecution in the Public Interest*. Edinburgh: Scottish Academic Press.

Mooney, J. (1994). *The Hidden Figure: Domestic Violence in North London*, Islington Police and Crime Prevention Unit.

Morgan, J. and Zedner, L. (1992). *Child Victims: Crime, Impact and Criminal Justice*, Oxford: Oxford University Press.

Morgan, J. B. (1984). 'What Do Police Officers Do?' Unpublished paper cited in Kemp, C., Norris, C., and Fielding, N. G. (1992), *Negotiating Nothing: Police Decision-making in Disputes*. Hants.: Avebury.

Morgan, R. and Newburn, T. (1997). *The Future of Policing*. Oxford: Clarendon Press.

Morley, R. and Mullender, A. (1992). 'Hype or Hope? The Importation of Pro-Arrest Policies and Batterer's Programmes from North America to Britain as Key Measures for Preventing Violence against Women in the Home', *International Journal of Law and the Family*, 6.

—— and ——(1994). *Preventing Domestic Violence to Women*, Police Research Group Crime Prevention Unit Series, Paper No. 48. London: HMSO.

Mullender, A. (1996). *Rethinking Domestic Violence: The Social Work and Probation Response*. London: Routledge.

NCH Action for Children (1995). *The Hidden Victims—Children and Domestic Violence*.

Nelken, D. (1987). 'Critical Criminal Law', *Journal of Law and Society*, 14/1.

Newburn, T. (1989). 'The Police, Victims and Victims Support', *Home Office Research Bulletin*, 26.

—— and De Peyrecave, H. (1988). 'Victims'Attitudes to Court and Compensation', Home Office Research Bulletin, 25:18–21.

Oakley, A. (1981). 'Interviewing Women: A Contradiction in Terms' in Roberts, H. (ed.), *Doing Feminist Research*. London: Routledge and Kegan Paul.

Oppenlander, N. (1982). ' "Coping or Copping Out?" Police Service Delivery in Domestic Disputes', *Criminology*, 20/3–4.

Packer H., (1968). *The Limits of the Criminal Sanction*. Stanford: Stanford University Press.

Pagelow, M. D. (1981). *Woman-Battering: Victims and their Experiences*. Beverly Hills, CA: Sage.

Pahl, J. (1982). 'Police Response to Battered Women', *Journal of Social Welfare Law*, 337–343, November.

—— (ed.), (1985). *Private Violence and Public Policy*. London: Routledge and Kegan Paul.

Parliamentary Select Committee (1975). *Report on Violence in Marriage*. First Special Report. London: HMSO.

Parnas, R. (1967). 'The Police Response to Domestic Disturbance', *Wisconsin Law Review*.

—— (1971). 'The Police Discretion and Diversion of Incidents of Intrafamily Violence', *Law and Contemporary Problems*, 36/4.

Patrick, J. (1973). *A Glasgow Gang Observed*. London: Eyre Metheun.

Pence, E. and Paymar, M. (1993). *Education Groups for Men Who Batter*. New York: Springer Publishing Company.

Piliavin, I. and Briar, S. (1964). 'Police Encounters with Juveniles', *American Sociological Review*, 70.

Popper, K. (1959). *Logic of Scientific Discovery*. London: Hutchinson.

Punch, M. (1979). *Policing the Inner City*. London: Routledge.

—— and Naylor, T. (1973). 'The Police: A Social Service', *New Society*, 24.

Quarm, D. and Schwartz, M. (1983). 'Legal Reform and the Criminal Court: The Case of Domestic Violence', *Northern Kentucky Law Review*, 10.

Radford, J. (1989). 'Women and Policing: Contradictions Old and New' in Hamner, J., Radford, J., and Stanko, E. (eds.), *Women, Policing and Male Violence*. London: Routledge and Kegan Paul.

Raven, B. H. and Rubin, J. Z. (1983). *Social Psychology* (2nd edn.). New York: John Wiley.

Reiner, R. (1978). *The Blue-Coated Worker*. Cambridge: Cambridge University Press.

—— (1985). *The Politics of the Police*. Brighton: Harvester Wheatsheaf.

—— (1992). *The Politics of the Police* (2nd edn.). Brighton: Harvester Wheatsheaf.

—— (1994). 'Policing and the Police' in Maguire, M., Morgan, R., and Reiner, R. (eds.), *The Oxford Handbook of Criminology* (1st edn.). Oxford: Oxford University Press.

Reiss, A. J., Jr. (1971). *The Police and the Public*. New Haven: Yale University Press.

Rose, D. (1996). *In the Name of the Law: The Collapse of Criminal Justice*. London: Jonathan Cape.

Royal Commission on Criminal Justice (1993). Cm. 2263. London: HMSO.

Rubenstein, J. (1973). *City Police*. New York: Farrar, Strauss and Giroux.

Sanders, A. (1986). 'The New Prosecution Arrangements: An Independent Crown Prosecution Service', *Criminal Law Review*.

—— (1988a). 'Personal Violence and Public Order: The Prosecution of "Domestic" Violence in England and Wales', *International Journal of the Sociology of Law*.

—— (1988b). 'The Limits to Diversion from Prosecution', *British Journal of Criminology*, 28/4.

——, Bridges, L., Mulvaney, A., and Crozier, G. (1989). *Advice and Assistance at Police Stations and the 24 Hour Duty Solicitor Scheme*. London: Lord Chancellor's Department.

—— and Young, R. (1994). *Criminal Justice*. London: Butterworths

—— and —— (1994). 'The Rule of Law, Due Process and Pre-Trial Criminal Justice', *Current Legal Problems*, 47/2.

Schluter, M. (1994). 'What is Relational Justice?' Burnside, J., and Baker N., (eds.), *Relational Justice: Repairing the Breach*. Winchester: Waterside Press.

Shapland, J. and Cohen, D. (1987). 'Facilities for Victims: The Role of the Police and the Courts', *Criminal Law Review*, January.

—— and Vagg, J. (1988). *Policing by the Public*. London: Routledge.

——, Willmore, J., and Duff, P. (1985). *Victims in the Criminal Justice System*. Aldershot: Gower.

Shearing, C. D. and Ericson, R. V. (1991). 'Culture as Figurative Action', *British Journal of Sociology*, 42.

Sheptycki, J. (1993). *Innovations in Policing Domestic Violence*. Aldershot: Avebury.

Sherman, L. W. (1992). 'The Influence of Criminology on Criminal Law: Evaluating Arrests for Misdemeanor Domestic Violence', *The Journal of Criminal Law and Criminology*, 83/1, Spring.

—— and Berk, R. A. (1984). 'The Specific Deterrent Effects of Arrest for Domestic Assault', *American Sociological Review*, 49.

——, Schmidt, J. D., Rogan, D., and DeRiso, C. (1991). 'Predicting Domestic Homicide: Prior Police Contact and Gun Threats' in Steinman, M. (ed.), *Woman Battering: Policy Responses*. Cincinnati: Anderson Publishing Co.

Skolnick, J. (1966). *Justice Without Trial*. New York: Wiley.

Smart, C. (1989). *Feminism and the Power of Law*. London: Routledge.

—— (1995). *Law, Crime and Sexuality: Essays in Feminism*. London: Sage.

Smith, D. A. and Klein, J. R. (1984). 'Police Control of Interpersonal Disputes', *Social Problems*, 31/4.

Smith, D. J. and Gray, J. (1983). *Police and People in London, Vol. 4, The Police in Action*. London: Policy Studies Institute.

Smith, J. C. and Hogan, B. (1992). *Criminal Law* (7th edn.). London: Butterworths.

—— and —— (1996). *Criminal Law* (8th edn.). London: Butterworths.

Smith, L. J. F. (1989). *Domestic Violence*, Home Office Research Study No. 107. London: HMSO.

Smithers, A., Hill, S., and Silvester, G. (1989). *Graduates in the Police Service*. School of Education, Manchester University.

Soothill, K., Francis, B., and Sanderson, B. (1997). 'A Cautionary Tale: The Sex Offenders Act 1997, the Police and Cautions', *Criminal Law Review*.

Southall Black Sisters (1989). 'Two Struggles: Challenging Male Violence and the Police' in Dunhill, C. (ed.), *The Boys in Blue: Women's Challenge to the Police*. London: Virago.

Southgate (1986). *Police-Public Encounters*, Home Office Research Study No. 77. London: HMSO.

Stang Dahl, T. (1986). 'Taking Women as a Starting Point: Building Women's Law', *International Journal of Sociology of Law*, 14.

Stanko, E. A. (1981). 'The Impact of Victim Assessment on Prosecutors' Screening Decisions: The Case of the New York County District Attorney's Office', *Law and Society Review*, 16.

—— (1985). *Intimate Intrusions. Women's Experience of Male Violence*, London: Routledge and Kegan Paul.

—— (1989). 'Missing the Mark? Policing Battering' in Hamner, J., Radford, J., and Stanko, E. (eds.), *Women, Policing and Male Violence*. London: Routledge and Kegan Paul.

—— (1995). 'Policing Domestic Violence', *Australian and New Zealand Journal of Criminology Special Supplementary Issue*.

Stanley, L. and Wise, S. (1983). *Breaking Out: Feminist Consciousness and Feminist Research*. London: Routledge and Kegan Paul.

Stith, S. M. (1990). 'Police Response to Domestic Violence: The Influence of Individual and Familial Factors', *Violence and Victims*, 5/1, Spring.

Strauss, M. A., Gelles, R. J., and Steinmetz, S. (1980). *Behind Closed Doors: Violence in the American Family*. New York: Anchor/Doubleday.

Stubbs, J. (1997), 'Shame, Defiance and Violence against Women: A Critical Analysis of "Communitarian" Conferencing' in Cook, S. and Bessant, J. (eds.), *Women's Encounters With Violence: Australian Experiences*. Thousand Oaks: Sage.

Temkin, J. (1995). *Rape and the Criminal Justice System*. Dartmouth.

Ursel, E. J. (1994). *Final Report, Year 2, Family Violence Court*. Criminology Research Centre, The University of Manitoba.

Victim Support (1992). *Domestic Violence: Report of a National Inter-Agency Working Party on Domestic Violence*. London: Victim Support.

Waaland, P. and Keeley, S. (1985). 'Police Decision-making in Wife Abuse: The Impact of Legal and Extralegal Factors', *Law and Human Behavior*, 9/4.

Waddington, P. A. J. (1993). *Calling the Police: The Interpretation of, and Response to, Calls for Assistance for the Public*. Aldershot: Avebury.

Walker, L. (1979). *The Battered Woman*. New York: Harper and Row.

Weber, M. (1930). *The Protestant Ethic and the Spirit of Capitalism*. London: Allen and Unwin.

—— (1949). *The Methodology of the Social Sciences*. New York: Free Press.

Whyte, W. F. (1943). *Street Corner Society*. Chicago: University of Chicago Press.

Willis, C. (1983). 'The Use, Effectiveness and Impact of Police Stop and Search Powers', Home Office Research and Planning Unit, Paper 15. London: Home Office.

Wilson, J. Q. (1968). *Varieties of Police Behaviour*. Cambridge, Mass.: Harvard University Press.

Worden, R. E. and Pollitz, A. A. (1984). 'Police Arrests in Domestic Disturbances: A Further Look', *Law and Society Review*, 18.

Young, M. (1991). *An Inside Job*. Oxford: Oxford University Press.

Index

Ackroyd, S.,
  and Harper, R., Hughes, J.A.,
    Shapiro, D. and Soothill, K., 29
Ajzen, J.
  and Fishbein, M., 80
arrest
  discretion in, 54, 55, 63–4, 65–101,
    107–44, 147, 153
  evidence of offence leading to,
    97–9, 104, 106, 107–12, 115, 113,
    131–3, 135, 136, 139, 212
  influence of alcohol on decision to, 77,
    115, 119, 133, 150
  mandatory/pro, 6, 10, 206–7, 211,
    215–7, 218, 220–5, 229
  offence seriousness leading to,
    112–14, 122, 130, 134
  risk of further violence contributing
    towards, 113, 114, 118–20, 130,
    132, 134–5
  suspect's demeanour leading to, 21,
    105, 114–18, 120, 131, 133–4,
    136–7, 140

Baldwin, J., 162
  and Kinsey, R., 15
Banton, M., 16, 66, 83
Barron, J.
  and Harwin, N. and Singh, T., 216,
    223
Bayley, D.
  and Bittner, E., 89, 105
Berk, S.F.
  and Loseke, D.R., 94, 121
Binney, V
  and Harkell, G., and Nixon, J, 3, 4,
    69, 78, 199
Bittner, E., 10, 16, 89, 98, 137, 139, 143,
    212
Black, D.J., 70, 79, 80, 118
Bordua, D.J.
  and Reiss, A.J., 139
Bottomley, A.
  and Coleman, C., 61
Bowker, L, 3, 189

breach of the peace, 97–9, 108, 116–18,
    136, 138, 148, 151 see also law as a
    resource
Brogden, M
  and Jefferson, T. and Walklate, S., 15
Brown, D., 13
  and Ellis, T., 13, 137
Brown, I.
  and Williams, K., 226
Brown, S.E., 3
Brownlee, I.D., 197
Burgess, R., 44
Bush, T.
  and Hood-Williams, J., 188, 189
Buzawa, E.
  and Buzawa, C., 10, 114, 115, 118,
    121, 217, 218, 224

Cain, M., 23, 67, 96
Carlson, B.E., 183
Carroll, J., 186
case construction, 19, 23, 36, 49, 50, 80,
    107–8, 111–12, 163–5, 176, 181,
    212
Chan, J., 12, 74, 83, 84, 85, 88
Chatterton, M., 4, 17, 69
Choongh, S., 114, 140, 141
civil law, 221–2
compellability rule, 125, 152, 158–9,
    163, 168–9, 171–5, 182, 184, 213
Cooney, M., 109
Cretney, A.
  and Davis, G., 112, 122, 154, 155,
    158, 160, 164, 165, 168, 172, 173,
    175, 178, 183, 191, 219
Crisp, D.
  and Moxon, D., 155, 163, 177
Crown Prosecution Service, 1, 8, 14,
    23–6, 28–9, 31, 38, 47, 48, 93, 99,
    113, 125, 146–81, 182–3, 203–4,
    211, 213–6, 218, 220, 224–5,
    228
  charge bargaining, 4, 104, 127, 159,
    161, 162
  evidential criteria, 156, 160, 179,
    221

Crown Prosecution Service, (*Contd.*)
  public interest criteria, 156–8, 163,
    165, 168–9, 173–4, 176–7, 179,
    180, 219
culturalism/cultural theory, 10, 12, 15,
  68, 71, 75, 207
Currie, D.H., 210
custody officers, 3, 46, 99, 146–7, 149,
  150, 152, 165, 187

Davies, P.W., 68
Davis, K.C., 229
Davis, N., 218
Davis, P., 118
Denzin, N., 26
Dixon, D., 11, 12, 13, 14, 82, 143
  and Coleman, C. and Bottomley, K.,
    140
Dobash, R.E.,
  and Dobash, R.P., 2, 3, 4, 7, 68, 69,
    83, 115, 183, 226
  and Cavanagh, K. and Lewis, R., 28,
    225, 226
Dolon, R.,
  and Hendricks, J. and Meagher, M.S.,
    115
domestic violence officers/units, 6, 89,
  215, 216, 218, 222, 223
Doob, A.N.
  and Roberts, J., 192
Dutton, D.G., 28, 51, 183, 226
Dworkin, R., 20

Edwards, S.S.M, 3–7, 9, 10, 15–17, 28,
  32, 34, 49, 51, 55, 65, 68–9, 78–9,
  110, 111, 123, 151, 155, 158, 168,
  172, 175–8, 182, 191, 205, 216,
  221, 223
  and Halpern, A., 91
Eiser, J.R., 80
Ekblom, P.
  and Heal, K., 16, 49, 52, 58, 59, 138
Elster, J., 104
Ericson, R., 11, 16, 17, 50, 55, 56, 64,
  81, 138, 143
Evans, R., 14
  and Ellis, R., 14

Faragher, 3, 7, 49, 121, 123, 201
Feder, L., 107, 110, 114, 121
Ferraro, K.J., 10, 18, 114
Fielding, N., 74, 79, 80, 83, 84, 87, 100,
  142

Fine, M., 68
Flynn, J.P., 183
Ford, D.A., 219, 220, 223, 224
Freeman, M.D.A, 5
Friedman, L.N.
  and Shulman, M., 220, 223

Galligan, D.J., 21
Gambetta, D., 104
gender
  role of, 7, 18, 69, 70, 71–4, 81, 122,
    144
Goldstein, J., 49, 67, 136
Grace, S, 6, 60, 83, 87, 215, 216, 223

Handler, J.F., 229
Hanmer, J., 5, 7, 9, 10, 188, 216, 223
  and Radford, J. and Stanko, E.A., 7,
    107
  and Saunders, S., 5, 9, 216
Hart, H.L.A., 20
Hatty, S, 7, 69
Hawkins, K., 14, 18, 21, 23, 54, 104,
  136, 143, 147, 229
Heidensohn, F., 68
Hilton, N.Z., 28
Holdaway, S., 16, 17, 23, 44, 53, 67, 68,
  80, 92, 143
Homant, R.J.
  and Kennedy, D.B., 69, 70
Home Office Circular 1990/60, 4–6,
  9, 10, 13, 50, 51, 60, 62, 63, 65,
  87, 89, 97, 103, 206, 207, 211, 215
Horley, S., 182, 218, 227
Hough, M.
  and Lewis, H. and Walker, N., 192
Hurley, D.J.
  and Jaffe, P., 186

interactionism, 8, 11, 18, 19, 23

Jaffe, P.
  and Wilson, S.K. and Wolfe, D.A.,
    186
Jarvie, I.C., 104, 105
Jefferson, T.
  and Grimshaw, R., 10, 23
Johnson, N., 17
Jolin, A., 217
Joutsen, M., 205

Kelly, 3, 27
Kemp, C.

and Norris, C. and Fielding, N.G., 7, 19, 21, 97, 103, 139, 140, 142

La Fave, W., 49
Lacey, N., 12
law
  as a resource, 17, 22–3, 97, 102, 135, 137, 140, 143, 147, 149, 150, 151, 213
Levens, B.R.
  and Dutton, D.G., 88
Lunneborg, P., 70

Maguire, M.
  and Pointing, L., 204
Mama, A., 186
Manning, P.K., 17, 51, 54, 55, 59, 60, 69
Martin, D., 69
Mathiesen, T., 210
Mawby, R.
  and Walklate, S., 205
McBarnet, D., 12, 14, 21, 23
McConville, M.
  and Sanders, A. and Leng, R., 7, 11, 19, 22, 36, 49, 82, 83, 86, 108, 111, 112, 121, 125, 142, 147, 164, 176, 177, 178, 179, 181, 206
  and Shepherd, D., 67, 68, 80, 85, 87, 90, 92, 126
McGillivray, A., 219, 220
McLeod, M., 10
Miers, D., 204
Moody, S.
  and Toombs, J., 169
Mooney, J., 183, 185, 189
Morgan, R., 138
  and Newburn, T., 16, 57, 103
Morley, R.
  and Mullender, A., 50, 93, 183, 189, 216, 217, 218, 222, 225
Mullender, A., 28, 226

negotiation, 8, 17, 19–23, 89, 103–7, 115–18, 122, 127–9, 133, 139, 142–5, 159–68, 195
Nelken, D., 210
Newburn, T., 205
no further action, 23, 32, 58, 97, 98, 108, 121, 146, 147, 148, 149, 166, 167, 168

Oakley, A., 38, 40
Oppenlander, N, 3, 17, 55

PACE (Police and Criminal Evidence Act), 5, 10, 11, 12, 13, 96, 97, 98, 99, 109, 140, 146, 147, 149, 150, 158, 165, 168, 206
Packer, H., 67
Pagelow, M.D., 3, 4
Pahl, J., 3, 7, 69, 183, 199
Parnas, R., 49, 55
Patrick, J., 45
perpetrator programmes, 32, 77, 210, 222, 225–8
Piliavin, I.
  and Briar, S., 67
police
  cautioning, 14, 15, 166–9, 207, 227
  control room, 24, 29–36, 49–58, 61–4, 93, 94, 212
  cuffing, 51, 52, 55, 111, 123, 124, 212
  culture, 9–11, 15, 17, 19, 22, 23, 44, 66–8, 70, 71, 73–6, 79–86, 88, 96, 100, 104, 106, 126, 129, 143–4, 207
  decisions regarding prosecution, 148–54, 175–81
  organisation, 17–20, 23, 32, 49–51, 53, 59, 60, 61, 64, 66, 86, 92–6, 99, 100, 102, 110, 111, 124, 125, 140, 141, 152, 160, 164, 227
  policy, 1, 2, 5–15, 18, 20–3, 50, 51, 63–5, 83–9, 95, 96, 99, 100, 102, 110, 129, 134, 138, 142, 144, 181, 206, 207, 209, 211, 212, 215, 216, 218–25, 229
  role of the, 2, 9, 13, 14, 15, 16, 17, 24, 68, 87, 104, 138–41
  training, 9, 84, 86, 87, 88, 89, 96, 99, 100, 129, 212
prosecution
  case discontinuance, 147–81, 213, 218
  evidence leading to, 114, 119, 146, 166–75
Public Order Act 1986, 96, 97
Punch, M., 23, 44, 46
  and Naylor, T., 68

Raven, B.H.
  and Rubin, J.Z., 80
Reiner, R., 15, 17, 23, 66, 67, 68, 82, 84, 143, 206
Reiss, A.J., Jr., 16, 68, 103
Rose, D., 84, 85, 95
Rubenstein, J., 23

Sanders, A., 11, 13, 19, 69, 109, 111, 112, 165, 167
  and Bridges, L., 206
  and Young, R., 11, 13, 20, 67, 146, 147, 148, 150, 160, 166, 167, 176, 206
sexual assault, 2, 4, 5, 28, 77, 87, 89, 113, 114, 158, 179, 201–3, 207
Shapland, J.
  and Cohen, D., 205
  and Vagg, J., 59
  and Willmore, J. and Duff, P., 204, 205
Shearing, C.D.
  and Ericson, R.V., 81
Sheptycki, J., 90, 91, 217
Sherman, L.W., 218
  and Berk, R.A., 217
  and Schmidt, J.D., and Rogan, D., and DeRiso, C., 218
Skolnick, J., 14, 16, 17, 66, 67, 69, 84, 103, 136, 207
Smart, C., 10, 210
Smith, D.A.
  and Klein, J.R., 90, 114, 115, 121
Smith, D.J.
  and Gray, J., 11, 16, 45, 67, 68, 69, 75, 79, 80, 136, 206
Smith, L.J.F., 4, 151, 154
Smithers, A.
  and Hill, S., and Silvester, G., 84
Soothill, K.
  and Francis, B. and Sanderson, B., 14, 207
Southgate, P., 16, 68
Stang Dahl, T., 210
Stanko, 3, 4, 7, 10, 15, 18, 68, 69, 70, 94, 107, 109, 121, 122, 123, 183, 188, 210, 224

Stith, S.M., 79
structuralism, 7, 8, 11, 23
Stubbs, J., 228

Ursel, E.J., 222

victim
  intimidation, 122, 171, 172, 173, 174, 184, 189, 191, 203, 213, 214, 223, 226
  non-reporting of offences, 183, 184, 218, 224
  role of the, 18, 24, 71, 102, 109, 110, 120–9, 133–5, 138, 141, 147, 149, 151–9, 163, 171, 214–15, 220–2

Waaland, P.
  and Keeley, S., 110, 115
Waddington, P.A.J., 53, 54, 59, 60, 80
Whyte, W.F., 45
Willis, C., 68
Women's Aid, 4, 36, 39, 182, 187, 189, 195, 200, 201, 203, 227
Worden, R.E.
  and Pollitz, A.A., 69, 94, 114
working assumptions, 15, 21, 22, 81, 82, 83, 89, 99, 100, 101, 102, 106, 109, 112, 113, 114, 116, 118, 129, 130, 144, 169, 170, 212
working rules, 11, 15, 20–23, 44, 82, 96, 98, 99, 100, 101, 102, 106, 112, 114–7, 126–7, 130, 131, 135, 136, 141–5, 147, 164, 168–70, 173–5, 176, 179, 180, 181, 206, 212, 213, 224, 228

Young, M., 68

Printed in the United Kingdom
by Lightning Source UK Ltd.
107148UKS00001B/58